CASE STUDIES IN

CULTURAL ANTHROPOLOGY

SERIES EDITORS

George and Louise Spindler

STANFORD UNIVERSITY

THE CANELA
Bonding through Kinship, Ritual, and Sex

THE CANELA
Bonding through Kinship, Ritual, and Sex

WILLIAM H. CROCKER

Smithsonian Institution

and

JEAN CROCKER

HARCOURT COLLEGE PUBLISHERS

Fort Worth Philadelphia San Diego New York Orlando Austin San Antonio
Toronto Montreal London Sydney Tokyo

Publisher	Ted Buchholz
Acquisitions Editor	Christopher Klein
Developmental Editor	Linda Wiley
Project Editor	John Haakenson
Production Manager	Cindy Young
Art Director	Burl Sloan

ISBN 0-03-073328-6

Library of Congress Catalog Card Number: 93-080359

Copyright © 1994 by Harcourt, Inc.

Address for Editorial Correspondence: Harcourt College Publishers, 301 Commerce Street, Suite 3700, Fort Worth, TX 76102

Address for Orders: Harcourt, Inc., 6277 Sea Harbor Drive, Orlando, FL 32887-6777. 1-800-782-4479, or 1-800-433-0001 (in Florida)

Printed in the United States of America

0 1 2 3 4 5 6 7 8 9   765   14 13 12 11 10 9 8 7 6 5 4 3 2

To George and Louise Spindler

for their inspiration

and friendship over the years

Foreword

ABOUT THE SERIES

These case studies in cultural anthropology are designed for students in beginning and intermediate courses in the social sciences, to bring them insights into the richness and complexity of human life as it is lived in different ways, in different places. The authors are men and women who have lived in the societies they write about and who are professionally trained as observers and interpreters of human behavior. Also, the authors are teachers; in their writing, the needs of the student reader remain foremost. It is our belief that when an understanding of ways of life very different from one's own is gained, abstractions and generalizations about the human condition become meaningful.

The scope and character of the series has changed constantly since we published the first case studies in 1960, in keeping with our intention to represent anthropology as it is. We are concerned with the ways in which human groups and communities are coping with the massive changes wrought in their physical and sociopolitical environments in recent decades. We are also concerned with the ways in which established cultures have solved life's problems. And we want to include representation of the various modes of communication and emphasis that are being formed and reformed as anthropology itself changes.

We think of this series as an instructional series, intended for use in the classroom. We, the editors, have always used case studies in our teaching, whether for beginning students or advanced graduate students. We start with case studies, whether from our own series or from elsewhere, and weave our way into theory, and then turn again to cases. For us, they are the grounding of our discipline.

ABOUT THE AUTHORS

William Crocker graduated from Yale University in 1950 and was the first of George Spindler's students to earn his M.A. in Anthropology from Stanford in 1953. He completed his Ph.D. at the University of Wisconsin at Madison in 1962, having made the first of many visits to the Canela in 1957. In 1962, he joined the Smithsonian Institution as Curator for South American Ethnology in the Department of Anthropology of the National Museum of Natural History. He continued his study of the Canela, making 11 trips to the field over the years, totalling 65 months of living with the tribe. Although Crocker has missed teaching, he appreciates the opportunity for intensive and long-term research his career at the Smithsonian has provided. He is the author of numerous articles on the Canela, and in 1990 his comprehensive monograph, *The Canela (Eastern Timbira), I: An Ethnographic Introduction* appeared as number 33 in the Smithsonian Contributions to Anthropology series. He is at work on more specialized studies of the Canela to make available to scholars and students the voluminous field data he has accumulated. In 1993, he began a last extended field stay with the Canela.

Jean Galloway Thomas married Bill in 1987 and has since collaborated informally with him as an editor. She earned her B.A. in English from Stanford in 1960 and her M.A. in English from Georgetown University in 1971. She taught literature and writing in college preparatory schools for 20 years. Jean accompanied Bill on his 1991 trip to Brazil and lived with the Canela for three weeks. For this case study, Jean used her teaching experience to orient the text for the college student. She helped organize the material and wrote some sections. Since Bill is the anthropologist, however, Jean has preserved his voice as the single narrative "I." In addition to working with Bill, Jean gives courses in contemporary fiction through the School of Continuing Education of Georgetown University.

ABOUT THIS CASE STUDY

It is impossible to do justice to this case study of the Canela in the short compass of a foreword. Bill Crocker began field research with the Canela in 1957 and has continued intermittently right up to the present. As we write this foreword (June, 1993), he is back with the Canela on a final extended research stay. He has lived with the Canela for an accumulated total of more than five years during eleven field trips. There are few anthropological field studies that surpass his in duration and intensity.

This long-term approach to the study of a culture enables Crocker not only to mount a time-stretched interpretation of culture change and adaptation, but also permits him to achieve an intimacy of interpersonal relationships with the Canela people that is often voiced as an objective of anthropological fieldwork—but rarely achieved. Bill Crocker is amongst kin, locked into an intricate pattern of terminology and reciprocal behaviors, when he is with the Canela.

Though "one of the family," he must retain perspective as an anthropologist, a viewer and interpreter of behavior into which he has been socialized. He does this, in part, by acquiring "research assistants" rather than "informants." They share knowledge and their interpretations of behavior with him. They also share responsibility for culturally correct reporting and analysis. Crocker acknowledges their input but still retains his obligation to produce alternative perspectives and interpretations flowing from his anthropological training and his position as a cultural "other" to the Canela. The result of his special, long-term relationship with the Canela is a complex, detailed description and analysis of a spectacular way of life.

Canela culture is radically divergent from European-based cultural expectations, values, and perspective, even though their common humanity is apparent. They live a joyous life of festival, ceremony and ritual that is inconceivable from the perspective of a work- and time-oriented Westerner. The Canela spend hours and days engaged in symbolic re-enactments of their cultural meanings, and parts of each day engaged in what seems like plain everyday fun—such as racing around the village perimeter carrying heavy logs on their shoulders (a great way to keep in shape, it seems).

The theme of bonding runs throughout this case study: bonding through kinship, through ritual, and through sex. The first two are to be expected, given our anthropological understanding of social life, symbolism, and the reinforcement of community through ritual and ceremony. The third, bonding through sex, is unexpected, though not unknown in tribal cultures of some parts of South America. It is not that sex is unexpected. Sexual activity and sexual restraints are everywhere, in every culture. Its regulation is what is interesting. In the United States we stimulate it with tantalizing imagery, dress, and innuendo, and then deny and punish it. This ambivalence is a major theme in European-American culture. Among the Canela, sex is a joyous expression and reinforcement of community bonding. The story of this bonding is too complex and startling to more than mention in this foreword.

Two major challenges to Western perspectives and sensibilities are sequential sex—when one woman may receive as many as twenty men—and the induction of young girls of eleven years of age, and even younger, into sexual experience involving full intromission. What is most interesting, anthropologically, is that sexual behavior that seems to involve the ultimate of licentious freedom from a Western point of view is stringently regulated by Canela custom and mores. It is just as easy to become disreputable among the Canela as it is in any Western community, but for quite different reasons. Among the Canela, one who is "stingy" with sex is scorned, for such a person does not contribute to community well-being.

The implications of this case study for understanding cultural relativism, as well as the sources of a common humanity, are of great importance for teachers and students everywhere. We are fortunate to have it available and fortunate that it is clear and thoroughly readable, despite the complexity and detail of its subject matter. For the latter, we have the Canela and Bill Crocker to thank. For the former, we have Jean Crocker to thank, who has written some portions of this book, and edited all of it.

George and Louise Spindler
Series Editors
Ethnographics, Box 38
Calistoga, CA 94515

Acknowledgments

George and Louise Spindler helped me find my life's work by inspiring me to go into anthropology, and they have been treasured friends ever since. They encouraged Jean and me in the writing of this case study, always countering our many doubts and delays with a hearty "let's get on with it." Their enthusiasm and wise counsel were indispensable.

Betty Meggers and the late Clifford Evans have supported my career at the Smithsonian in many ways, and I have benefitted immeasurably from their advice. The late Charles Wagley, who first oriented me to fieldwork in Brazil in 1956, also encouraged and advised me over the years. I have indeed been fortunate in having these distinguished mentors and faithful friends.

Gail Solomon has been my research assistant for 17 years, and it is impossible to imagine doing without her. As the archivist for all my data—field notes, photographs, films, and recordings—she retrieved and organized needed data for this case study. Her help in matters large and small has been vital. Victor Krantz of the National Museum of Natural History prepared the photographs with his usual skill and much appreciated cooperation.

The sensitivity and wise perspective of Kenneth Kensinger of Bennington College has been a valued resource. I am grateful for the Conferences on Lowland South American Indians, which Ken organizes and leads. The constructive criticism of my colleagues at the Bennington Conferences has sharpened my thinking and spurred me on. One of these Bennington friends, Katherine Adams of the Harvard Center for Population and Development Studies, read drafts of Chapters 4 and 5 and gave helpful advice.

In Brazil, Berta Ribeiro of the Museu Nacional made the 1991 and 1993 trips possible through her energetic resolution of the many technical requirements for permission to visit and do fieldwork among the Canela. Her encouragement and sponsorship have been essential. Over the years, many others in Brazil have extended to me great warmth, kindness, and practical assistance. Darcy Ribeiro helped me to obtain my original permission to conduct research among the Canela in 1957. Heloísa Alberto Torres gained the critical support and permissions during the 1960s. The late Olímpio Martins Cruz managed my financial affairs in Brazil from 1957-1963 and became a great friend and advisor. Eduardo Galvão was another mentor and advisor in the years 1957-1976. Expedito Arnaud was my representative from 1978-1979 and gave me great moral support at a time when it was much needed.

Special thanks must go to Jaldo Pereira Santos of Barra do Corda. Between 1964 and 1979, Sr. Jaldo was my representative in Barra do Corda, handling all my finances and extending limitless hospitality to me and my family. Sr. Jaldo used his prestige and ingenuity to help me solve countless difficulties. The friendship and assistance of Sr. Jaldo can never be repaid because it was so vast, generous, and open. His family's warm hospitality, his competence in handling my finances, and his clearing the way for a safe passage through the politics of the town, were so helpful over such a long period of time that his assistance must be among the greatest advantages any ethnologist has received in the field.

More recently, Júlio Alves Tavares of Barra do Corda has handled the extraordinarily difficult logistics of my 1991 and 1993 trips. Sr. Júlio managed my finances and acted as liaison with the Canela. His resourcefulness and steadfastness have made it possible to conduct my last fieldwork among the Canela. Jean, especially, remembers Sr. Júlio's alacrity in getting her excellent medical care when she fell ill in Barra do Corda before visiting the Canela in 1991. Sra. Rosamar used her great cooking skills to prepare comforting and nourishing dishes for the recovering invalid. Daughter Romenia patiently improved Jean's Portuguese and acted as her guide around the town.

Jack and Jo Popjes of the Summer Institute of Linguistics arranged for making and sending Canela informant materials during the 1980s. They have shared with me their knowledge of the Canela language. But more importantly, they have been great friends over the years.

The field research was carried out under the auspices of the Museu Paraense Emílio Goeldi and the Museu Nacional. Financial acknowledgments go principally to the Smithsonian Institution for the various years of field and office support, but, for 1964, especially to the National Science Foundation and the Wenner-Gren Foundation for Anthropological Research. Permission to carry out research among the Canela was granted before 1968 by the Serviço de Proteção aos Índios and afterward by the Fundação Nacional do Índio. For most of the trips, permissions were also obtained from the earlier Conselho Nacional de Pesquisas or the later Conselho Nacional do Desenvolvimento Científico e Tecnológico. I am deeply grateful to these cultural and governmental institutions of Brazil for authorizing my work.

Finally, I wish to pay tribute to my predecessor, Curt Nimuendajú, the great Brazilian generalist in anthropology of the first half of the 20th century. His work, *The Eastern Timbira,* originally inspired me to pick the Canela as the subject of my research and enabled me to carry out my goal of a long-range study of culture change and continuity.

Preface

The imagination of the public today is much caught up with the fate of the rain forest and its indigenous peoples. This book tells the story of a group of Brazilian Indians, far to the east of the rain forest, whose brutal encounters with the Brazilian frontier began in the middle of the 18th century and culminated in their surrender to settlers in 1814. Not until the 1830s could they live in relative peace with Brazilian society, which by then had completely surrounded their lands. The frontier had moved on, leaving the Canela to reestablish themselves, recalling and reconstructing their traditional culture as best they could.

A visitor to the Canela today comes upon a huge, circular village of perhaps 90 houses of palm-thatch construction. On the outer edge of a boulevard enclosing a cleared circle, about 1,000 Indians live in houses two or three deep, each family grouping connected to a central plaza by its own path. In this plaza, the Council of Elders may be meeting, or long lines of young women may be singing in unison before the male sing leader with his gourd rattle. At other times of day, the age groups of boys and young men may be racing with logs around the boulevard; or a group of men and women may be returning with the tractor-pulled wagon from distant gardens with piles of manioc roots.

In one of the "wealthier" houses made of mud and wattle walls instead of palm thatch, a Canela man who for years lived in a Brazilian family receives visitors. His house is surrounded by a well maintained fence of branches that keeps the pigs out, and the yard of sand is swept clean. A new appliance sits in its factory box inside one of the two rooms of his house. He returned to the Canela village after 18 years of living in Rio de Janeiro as the adopted son of a Brazilian woman. He is one of the few Canela in this century who have stayed away from the tribe for any length of time. Even those Canela who have the opportunity do not choose to leave the village permanently, preferring the Canela way of life to what they see on the outside.

The factors that have led to the survival and success—as far as cultural success can ever be measured—of the Canela people form the topic of this study. Some of these factors might be considered historical and geographical accidents and thus outside the sphere of Canela culture; they will be discussed first. Other factors lie within Canela culture itself, however, and they form the main thrust of this book. Many other nations in the same Timbira group became extinct, most of them between 1750 and 1825, and none that survived has conserved its traditional culture as completely as have the Canela. The Canela were sufficiently out of the settlers' invasion path to escape extreme cultural change. There were hills to hide in to escape the most devastating period of the late 1810s and early 1820s. Vacant lands awaited their occupation in the 1830s, lands which were of little value to the settlers. These lands had no desirable resources and were only marginally good for cattle and farming. Thus, the Canela were able to experience 100 years of relative peace from 1840 to 1940, during which time they could adjust to the settlers' backland culture and build back their own culture. In 1938, the advent of the Indian Service introduced new forces of change. The extent of Canela cultural retention, and thus the richness of their remaining culture, is unusual for a Brazilian Indian nation pacified as early as 1814.

Outstanding features of their culture worked within this framework of geography and history to bring the Canela to their position of relative prosperity and pride today. The Canela are quite conscious of their dependency upon the surrounding Brazilians, and have rationalized this position, along with the resulting practice of begging, from outsiders. But their positive morale is shown in the growth in their population, their decision to remain in one large village rather than splitting into several, and their continued resistance to emigration.

Their social cohesiveness is both the cause and the result of Canela survival. Certain kinds of bonding constitute this cohesion. Bonding through an elaborate system of kinship, bonding through rituals including daily meetings and complex festivals, and bonding through an extensive practice of extramarital sex are distinctive aspects of Canela culture. The first chapter will trace the historical narrative of pacification and resulting culture change. Then a chapter will be devoted to each of these major types of social bonding, which have served to counter the destructive forces. After a consideration of the balance between the sexes, an epilogue will bring the discussion of culture change and endurance up to 1991.

The record of Canela survival reaches back to the beginning of the 19th century and the accounts of the Portuguese Captain Francisco de Paula Ribeiro. After these historical accounts of military encounters with Canela ancestors, their story was resumed in the 1930s by Curt Nimuendajú, Brazil's foremost anthropologist of the first half of the 20th century. Nimuendajú was born a German, but became a naturalized Brazilian. His great work on the Canela, *The Eastern Timbira* (1946), inspired my choice of this tribe for my doctoral research. When I arrived in 1957 to start my study of the Canela, and over the next 34 years, I spent 65 months in 11 field stays as an adopted member of Canela families. I could draw on the experience of Indian Service agents and the memories of the Canela themselves to study culture change, my principal topic. Since the memories of the old people in 1957 reached back to the 1890s, my study of the Canela has covered over 100 years.

Contents

INTRODUCTION: A FIRST VISIT TO THE CANELA[1]

As we coasted down toward the distant landing strip, my new wife, Roma, and her three children—Tara, 11, Hugh, 9, and Philip, 8—showed the tension of awaiting their plunge into a strange culture. I told them to keep smiling no matter what happened. But I knew nothing dangerous could occur, because the Canela had learned to get along with outsiders after over 200 years of contact. Besides, I had already lived with them for 31 months and spoke their language, so I was returning to good friends and "relatives."

The thatch houses of the circular village began to take on their rectangular shape as we descended. The tiny people pouring out of the houses onto the circular boulevard grew larger, and we could see that some of them were waving to us. Other Canela began jogging down the straight pathways from each house to the round plaza in the center of the village where fireworks were being set off in our honor. From the air, the village looked like a great wheel with cogs on it: the plaza its hub, the radial pathways its spokes, the boulevard its rim, and the houses its cogs.

The single-motored missionary plane rattled to a stop at the end of the dirt runway and was soon completely surrounded by friendly Indians. They had come to see my new family and to give me a proper homecoming. Once on the ground, I groped for names and terms of address while shaking many hands. Soon my Canela "mother," Tut-khwèy (dove-woman)[2], pulled me over to the shade of a plane's wing and pushed me down to kneel on a mat she put on the ground. She put both hands on my shoulders and, kneeling beside me, her head by mine, cried out words of mourning in a loud yodeling manner. Tears and phlegm dripped onto my shoulder and knees. According to a custom now abandoned by the younger women, she was crying for the loss of a grown daughter, Tsêp-khwèy (bat-woman), as well as for my return. When my old mother had finished what she felt compelled to do, my "sister," Kô-roorok (water-fall) caught my attention and said I looked too thin, that I must have eaten very poorly while away. Her responsibility was to feed me well. Then her three adolescent daughters, my "nieces," started pelting me with sharply expressed phrases, asking me such questions as how many women I had "seen" while away—besides my wife, of course—and if I had made them "cry" with my *pùùpùp-ti,* my "big banana."

This lively uncle–niece sex joking made me feel I had fully returned and was once again at home among the Canela, just as having my first *cafezinho* and *queijo com goiabada* (cheese with guava paste) made me feel I had fully arrived in Brazil, my second country. The ribald exchange made me remember when I was learning Canela. My nieces were saying salacious words for me to repeat and hurl at Tûm-ti (experienced-very), my elderly aunt, who in turn assaulted me with equally crude expressions.

1

The Canela village of Escalvado from the air in 1970.

On another occasion, the 13-year-old Kô-nkrêê (streams-three)[3], my late niece, "insulted" her great-uncle, Kaarà-?khre (deer's-hole/nest), as he appeared naked in the family doorway—naked according to custom—with "your penis is screw-turned like a large yam's root, and its naked head is rotten and so is purple like a sweet potato." Highly amused, he retorted, "your vagina is so big from use that it needs the grinding of a penis as large as a manioc pestle with a rutting goat's energy." These privileged verbal endearments, and other forms of sex joking, kept life amusing and vivid during my years of fieldwork, as they do for the Canela every day.

When my nieces were finished with their fun, my number one informant and helper, the younger[4] Rãrãk (thunder), approached me with a serious demeanor. After a long handshake and courteous questions about each other's wives, he pointed out that my wife and three children were waiting under the plane's other wing, getting hot and impatient. They had asked for water and were pointing to themselves and to the houses, indicating they wished to be there for protection against the heat. Recalled to my family responsibilities, I asked Paul, the missionary[5] pilot, to unlock the vacant missionary house, where we would spend a few days until we could establish our own quarters in the house of whichever Canela family was willing to adopt Roma and her children. Then I would live with Roma in her adoptive house and visit the house of my own "kin."

After lunch we settled into our hammocks for naps, but I was sleepless with the excitement of my return. Adding to my sleeplessness was the disturbing news received the preceding day in Belém at the mouth of the Amazon 400 miles away to the northwest (Map 2).

During the afternoon in Belém, the national Indian Service[6] official had inspected my Brasília-issued authorization to work with Indians. He had given me the standard

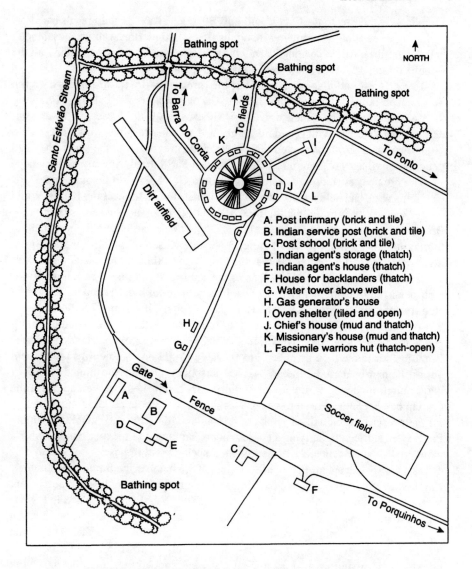

Bathing spot

Bathing spot

Bathing spot

NORTH

Santo Estévão Stream

To Barra Do Corda

To fields

To Ponto

Dirt airfield

K

I

J

L

A. Post infirmary (brick and tile)
B. Indian service post (brick and tile)
C. Post school (brick and tile)
D. Indian agent's storage (thatch)
E. Indian agent's house (thatch)
F. House for backlanders (thatch)
G. Water tower above well
H. Gas generator's house
I. Oven shelter (tiled and open)
J. Chief's house (mud and thatch)
K. Missionary's house (mud and thatch)
L. Facsimile warriors hut (thatch-open)

H

G

Gate

Fence

A

B

D

E

C

Soccer field

F

Bathing spot

To Porquinhos

Map 1. Escalvado village and Indian Service post buildings, 1975.

warning that I must not be a financial burden on the tribe and that I must not try to teach them anything or to change them. Then he had told me about the epidemic of measles among the Canela and the neighboring Apanyekra (Piranha) Indians, who speak the same language. Of the 397 Canela, only three children were lost. The Service's vaccination program, administered in the village by the Service's personnel from the town of Barra do Corda 50 miles to the north, had been effective. The Canela's Service agent at the post by the tribe, Sr. Sebastião Pereira, had helped immensely, he said. In contrast, among the 227 far less accessible and still unvaccinated

Piranha, a sister tribe to the Canela and only 30 miles away, 31 individuals had died, including three adults. During my insomnia, I kept wondering who was lost among "my" two tribes. After spending 29 months with the Canela and two months with the Piranha during the 1950s and 1960s, I knew most tribal members.

The official had also spoken about the three new post buildings which the Service had built 500 yards from the new Canela village of Escalvado during my three-year absence. The Canela move their village every 5 to 15 years, so I was wondering what their new village would be like and whether families would occupy the same traditional positions around the village circle in relation to the sun as they had done in the villages of Ponto, Baixão Preto, and Sardinha during my earlier visits.

The previous evening in Belém, Dr. Eduardo Galvão, anthropologist, and Dona Clara, his wife, had held a gathering of local professionals to meet my family. While others were partying, Galvão had carried out his roles as the representative of Brazil's National Council for Research (CNPq), which had issued my research authorization, and as the official of Belém's Goeldi Museum, which was sponsoring my project. He had informed me that the Canela and Piranha Indians, and also their sister tribe the Krahó some 150 miles to the southwest, had become renowned for their persistent "begging" in the state capitals throughout most of Brazil. They traveled free of charge in groups of 4 to 12 to these capitals, including Recife, Salvador, Rio de Janeiro, São Paulo, Brasília, and Belém. Once there, they tried to obtain goods for their people, such as shotguns, cloth, beads, axes, and machetes. Often the Brazilian Air Force flew them back to Barra do Corda on routine trips to get them out of the hair of regional Indian Service personnel. Galvão questioned whether I had enough money with me to carry out my research, because he had heard the Canela had become so used to city prices that they were demanding much money for their services even in their village. I had assured him, uneasily, that I thought my funds were sufficient, but lying sleepless in my hammock in the missionary house, I wondered what new financial pressures the Canela would impose.

My family had spent that night in Belém at the base of the Summer Institute of Linguistics (SIL) missionaries, packing and weighing our supplies and equipment for the early morning's flight to the Canela village of Escalvado. Jack and Jo Popjes, linguistic missionaries with the Canela, had put us up in their house and had given me much current news from the tribe. Chief Rop-khà (jaguar's-coat) was still on the wagon, and Thunder had joined him—great examples for the whole tribe. Kàà-kookhyê (plaza-splitter) had taken I-kurê's (I'm-angry's) virginity, thus marrying her, but his family had paid a shotgun, an axe, and two machetes to get him out of the marriage. So, poor I'm Angry was "on the street"—available to all comers. The new Indian Service post at Escalvado had a new gasoline generator which lighted the post building, the infirmary, and the school house. In the village, the plaza had three bulbs for dancing and the chief's house had one bulb given to him by the Service to enhance his prestige. However, Chief Jaguar's Coat was not impressed. He had said his people could not eat light bulbs.

I gave up trying to nap and listened to the familiar village sounds of women pounding rice in wooden mortars, children crying until quieted with a breast, and chickens clucking near the wall of the missionary house. Roma and the children slept on, weary from the trip. I was glad, as plenty of culture shock awaited them.

Canela relay log race. The runner will turn and shift the log to the shoulder of a teammate.

At about four in the afternoon, the familiar sounds of Canela log racing drifted over the mud walls and through the palm-thatched roof of the missionary house as I was climbing out of my hammock and putting on my sneakers. I rushed over to Roma and the children, urging them to get up and get ready to go out and face the Canela world. The log race would be a joyous introduction.

Out in the boulevard, we stood watching a crowd of Canela approaching along the sandy road from Barra do Corda. There must have been at least 80 men out there. Two logs were riding smoothly above a sea of brown and red shining bodies, the farther log slowly moving up to a position abreast of the leading one. I knew that these tree trunk sections sometimes weighed over 275 pounds. Among the racers, Pàn-hi (macaw's bone) was chanting to urge his leading team on, and Chief Jaguar's Coat was shouting at his team to try harder to carry their log past the other team's log and get it to the village boulevard first. The sound of several horns repeatedly blasting away, each on its one tone, rose over the general shouting of the runners and onlookers. As they came closer, we could see that about every 25 yards a runner with a log on his left shoulder turned to pass the log onto the left shoulder of a following racer. Young women ran alongside the mass of jogging men, offering certain men, whom I knew to be their lovers, water from small gourd bottles.

As the teams approached the boulevard, the excitement and cheering intensified, and crowds of onlookers swirled around the mass of runners, making way for their inexorable advance. "They don't even know we're here," shouted Roma in my ear as I was trying to look over the mass of bodies to see which log was dropped first. But the outcome really didn't matter, because the Canela were racing for the fun of the sport. The children commented on the redness of the racers' bodies, which I explained was urucu paint put on them by their wives and sisters. The sound of the horns was also notable, so I explained that they were ordinary cows' horns, smoothed by stones or metal files, with a wooden mouthpiece added and tightly fitted.

With the race over, the crowd dispersed into the houses and the racers went down to the several swimming holes to bathe. As we watched from the shade of a house, we could see old men walking slowly down the radial pathways from their houses to the plaza in the pleasant warmth of the late afternoon. When they were seated in the center, the village crier sang from the edge of their circle in my direction, instructing me to appear before the assembled Council of Elders. Then my naming uncle, Krôô-tô (boar-sticky) appeared and said he would escort me to the Council of Elders, as usual, but reminded me that I needed a present to give them. So we went back to the missionary house, where Sticky Boar courteously motioned my family to sit on racing logs placed against its front wall, while I went inside to unpack a machete. Although Uncle Sticky Boar could speak to my wife and children only in backland Portuguese, his gentle manner was reassuring. I explained that he was the one of my three diary writers whose writings were often poetic.

Sticky Boar walked just ahead of me up the radial pathway toward the plaza, carrying a ceremonial lance and chanting loudly. I knew he was playing the role of a returning warrior, declaring what he had done and seen while away. The elder, Tep-yêt (fish-hanging), met Sticky Boar just before the entrance to the plaza, stopping his progress. Then Sticky Boar thrust the point of his ceremonial lance into the ground and, pounding his foot strongly in the sand, screeched at Hanging Fish in the loudest possible voice. Thereupon, all movement and talking in the plaza ceased. Everyone focused on the returned hero, who was swearing he would always defend his tribe with his life when the tribe was attacked. Roma must be wondering, I thought, about the supposed gentleness of this poet. After Sticky Boar was through expressing his fealty, Hanging Fish stepped toward me, so I gave him the machete. As my naming uncle, Sticky Boar was performing this traditional act in my place. It was really I who was the returning "warrior," but my screeching ability was not up to the role. Nevertheless, through this act I had just been accepted for presentation to the elders, and they would now interrogate me about my exploits among other "tribes."

Seated in the plaza facing me, Chief Jaguar's Coat asked how things were in the land of my relatives and if my country was at peace with Russia. Of course, he asked about my former wife and said I would have to reckon with her Canela family. Then he asked what I had brought the tribe. Did I have money to buy cattle for the festival? I knew he had to press me when before the Council, but that later, matters could be settled quietly in his house.

Nevertheless, I worried about Galvão's warning in Belém on the Canela's growing awareness of city prices, and I knew of their traditional pride and reluctance to be taken advantage of. Next, one of the youths listening on the edge of the circle of elders, Krôô-pey (pig-good), 32, asked whether it was true that my relatives had been walking on the moon. He said he had heard this while in São Paulo and had seen it in a movie there. I answered that this was true and that Americans had built fireworks so powerful and big that they had shot one to the moon with three Americans inside. The Americans had landed on the moon and even walked around on its face. This story angered the old shaman I?hô-tsen (its-leaves likes), who chided me for not having remembered what he had taught me years ago: that Sun and Moon were both male persons and that they had walked in the savannahs on the face of the earth before the Canela and the *civilizado* had been made. Rather than draw further fire from the elders, I admitted Likes Leaves was right and that what I had said about my relatives was merely a bad rumor which had amused me.

After the council meeting, I walked down the radial pathway to my wife and children to find them talking haltingly in Portuguese with Sr. Sebastião, the Service post's new agent. He was pointing out various features of the village, such as the well for drinking water the missionaries had drilled and the new barbed wire fence around the village they had provided to keep out the Service cattle and the Canela hogs. He also pointed to the new outhouses behind most Canela houses that the Service official in Barra do Corda had required. He said that while the fence keeps the village largely clean of animal droppings, and the Canela like this, they seldom use the outhouses because they find the savannahs cleaner and less smelly. Sr. Sebastião, an educated native of Barra do Corda, had come to invite us to dinner at the post, so I thanked him in my most courteous Portuguese and said we would be delighted to enjoy his company and to meet his wife there.

My family returned to the missionary house, where I suggested they dress more warmly for the evening. In such grassy savannahs—composed of low, single-standing trees and bushes—situated 900 feet above sea level near the equator, the temperature descends into the low 60s in the July evenings. I said we would walk around the village boulevard counterclockwise from the missionary house to my "sister's" house, where she had invited us to appear after the Council meeting. Then, we would go out of the village 500 yards down to the Service's post house for dinner and return to the village by way of the house of the wife of Chief Jaguar's Coat. There we had to formally report in and pay our respects to the chief, since he was responsible for all outsiders spending a night in his village. But this appearance amounted merely to a friendly visit in our case, because Chief Jaguar's Coat and I had known each other for so many years. We also were related to each other as Informal Friends who, in Canela tradition, always joke when they meet. Finally, we would return to the missionary house to unpack and sleep.

Walking along the boulevard with my American family, one Canela woman after another shouted out to me, scolding, that I had left Yàt-khre (sweet-potato's wisdom), her "sister," my American ex-wife. One woman said that she would pull my ears and yank my hair out when she could catch me away from my new *civilizada* wife. She asked, was my new wife so much better than her "sister" that I had had to switch? I knew that she meant better at sex, so I decided to have fun with her, answering that my new wife was much better at sex than Sweet Potato had been, and I added a few juicy descriptive details which had become easy for me to say in Canela but which were embarrassingly impossible for me to say in English, especially in mixed company. I was glad my wife and step-children couldn't understand a word. The women calling were classificatory wives, since they were my former American wife's Canela sisters or cousins. Sisters-in-law and their female parallel cousins of any degree are the other joking relationship for a man besides his aunts (father's sisters) and nieces (sisters' daughters).

My prime Canela sister, Waterfall, sat in front of the house in the boulevard with her sisters, her female parallel cousins, and almost all of their unmarried children. Several men sat by their wives or in back. Our father had died the year after I first arrived. This formidable array of people made up most of my extended matrilateral Canela kin. Waterfall, 45, was the one who had volunteered to adopt me on my second day among the Canela in 1957. She was the manager of this extended household, and her husband, Macaw's Bone, merely cooperated.

Waterfall stood and welcomed us in a gentle and dignified tone, which was reassuring to my American family. First, she pointed to the young babies and children who had been born in my absence, mentioning their names. Then I presented my new wife and her three children. Waterfall, speaking to my wife and children as if they could understand, slowly and carefully introduced her sisters, their children, and their husbands. I whispered to Roma and her children to remain standing and to bear with the recital patiently.

Finally, Waterfall, with a graceful gesture of her hand, invited us to sit down on three mats laid out for us. Tara and Hugh abruptly dashed for the first mat, Philip took the second one, while Roma and I ambled over to the third. Almost immediately I noticed sounds of amusement, along with exchanged smiles, and guessed what was provoking the fun-loving Canela. Tara and Hugh, though opposite-sex siblings, were sitting next to each other on the same mat, an incestuous act for the Canela. Only opposite-sex people having sex can do this. How well I remembered classificatory wives tempting me in fun to sit with them and eat on the same mat, and once when I had mustered enough courage to do so playfully, the woman had dashed away to the amusement of everyone present. So, I asked Hugh if he was married to Tara. When he answered with a wondering no, I warned that the Canela must think he was married to her because they were sitting on the same mat. Hugh jumped up so quickly that the crowd roared with laughter, and the ice of formality was broken. Waterfall and her sisters came forward and shook hands with my American family and took them around separately to shake hands with the rest of my Canela kin. The child-to-child contact was especially touching.

I told Waterfall that our kin's presents were waiting for them and that I would give them out individually some dark night (to avoid the jealousy of others) once my new wife and children were settled in a Canela family. Then we said good night and started walking out of the village toward the Service post. The lights of the post buildings at the end of a wide, well-kept road showed us the way in the dark. On the right we found the store of Yōō-khên (buttocks-scraped), the son of Chief Jaguar's Coat, who had spent two years in a convent in Barra do Corda learning to read and write and another year in the army in São Luis. Next came the hut housing the gasoline generator, which produced electricity to pump water from the post's well into a pressure tower. Electricity was also used to run the lighting system and the post's radio for communication with the Service personnel in Barra do Corda and São Luis. On the left was a large straw house built in the style of the interior backlands, which served to house backland merchants spending the night in the area. The Service prohibits outsiders, except anthropologists and missionaries, from spending nights in the village for fear such casual visits would lead to cohabitation and consequent adulteration of Indian genes. While the Canela disapprove of such contacts with outsiders, a few Canela women made some money in this manner during the late 1950s.

Sr. Sebastião met us at the gate of the post's wire fence enclosure and led us past the post building of whitewashed brick with a red-tiled roof to his own house of mud and wattle with a palm-straw roof situated on the path leading to the stream. His wife, Dona Fátima, greeted us and introduced a small child and a baby. I remembered her growing up around the Service post in the Canela village at Sardinha in the mid-1960s, and here she was—the wife of a young Service agent instead of the daughter of an old one. Sr. Sebastião seated us at a long table, with himself at the head, and passed us separate bowls of chicken, beef, and pork stews from which to serve ourselves. We ate off enameled metal plates. His family's generosity honored us greatly. "But where is Dona Fátima seated?" Roma asked me in English when Sr. Sebastião had gone to arrange something. I returned that in the backlands, the women do not eat with the men, though city women are treated as men.

On the way back to the village, I described for Roma and the children some of the cultural differences between Barra do Corda and the backlands. International magazines and urban clothing and styles were found in Barra do Corda; in the backlands, no such magazines and styles could be found. In the town one heard the popular songs of Brazilian and American cities, though American songs had Portuguese words dubbed in. Backland songs were more like American country music. In the 1950s, styles had been quite different. I had attended festive occasions in the backland communities of farmers and ranchers, at which violins and fifes were played as the principal instruments and traveling musicians had told stories about counts and duchesses. By 1960 these old instruments were replaced by small accordions, and the minstrels with their tales about the nobility of Brazil and Portugal had disappeared. Still, the cultural differences between urban America and Barra do Corda were less than those between Barra do Corda and the backlands.

Some of the poorer backlanders lived in conditions no better than the Indians, in houses of mud and thatch with packed earth floors. The better-off ranchers lived more substantially, but because the land was marginal for cattle, most ranches and herds were small. But no matter how poor, the backlanders considered themselves vastly superior in culture to the Indians.

Once in the village, we approached the large mud-and-wattle house of the wife of Chief Jaguar's Coat, which was set back from the circle of houses for prominence. His wife, Põõhù-ʔkhwèy (corn-woman), 50, beckoned us to enter and be seated on square hide-covered stools and offered us coffee and tinned cookies. We accepted to please her but hoped to drink as little as possible considering the hour.

Jaguar's Coat asked me if "our wife," meaning Roma, and "our children"— Tara, Hugh, and Philip—would consent to have haircuts in the tribal style. For a moment I was taken aback, because when he had said "our wife" on previous trips, he had meant his wife who was also my "wife." (Canela has a first-person inclusive pronoun which includes two people.) I had the right to his wife because we had gone through a ceremony that made us Informal Friends. In earlier times, Informal Friends shared their wives sexually. Though Jaguar's Coat was now referring to Roma as his and my wife, I knew he would not take advantage of his people's ancient practice. The custom had almost died out and Roma was an outsider. So answering for Roma and the children, I agreed to the tribal haircuts, which would leave them with horseshoe-shaped pathways around the crowns of their heads, from forehead to the occiputs.

Leader with gourd rattle leads the sing-dance line of women.

I asked him if he thought Corn Woman's mother and father would like to adopt and take in our wife and our children. I explained how caring old Katsêê-khwèy (star-woman) and Kô-ham (water-standing) would be for our wife and children. Moreover, he and I wouldn't have to change terms of address for our wives, because if Roma were Corn Woman's "sister," these two women would be doubly "our wives," both as sisters-in-law and as wives of Informal Friends. The idea amused him, so he talked to our wife about it (this time meaning Corn Woman), and she went over to her mother's house to see if they would like the arrangement.

Jaguar's Coat asked me if our wife (meaning Roma) and I would like to get married Canela style. I realized that going through such a ceremony would mean I would have to pay for an all-day festival during which all the tribe would eat at my expense. This was typical Canela: Get what is possible from the outsider, but do it kindly and courteously. Rather than say no—nothing should be direct with the Canela—I suggested that we talk about it later.

Suddenly Corn Woman grabbed my ear from behind, twisting my neck, and almost yanked me off the stool. "Don't you ever 'look at' other women than Roma," she scolded, "or I will pull your whole ear off." Now I knew, painfully, that Roma and her children had just been adopted and accepted into Star Woman's family line and that I would soon be living in an extension to her house with my American family. ("Look at" in Canela is the euphemism for having sex.)

We said goodnight and strolled toward the plaza where enthusiastic dancing was going on. About 40 women had formed a line across most of the lower side of the plaza and were all facing uphill toward a man who was singing vigorously and marking the rhythm with a gourd rattle. This activity was informal social dancing, not a ceremonial or sacred performance. Social dances used to take place three times a day, most days of the year, but now occur less frequently. Sing-dancing was a principal form of recreation to keep the young people occupied and happy.

Passing behind the dance line, where mothers with babies and children were sitting in the sand, we wandered slowly down the radial pathway of the missionary house, noticing the activities of the village. Two files of men were progressing around the boulevard in opposite directions, singing low and dancing undemonstratively. Most middle-aged and older people were in their houses; only younger people were still moving around outside.

In the missionary house, my wife and children took to their hammocks quickly, exhausted from a long and unusual day. But I still had work to do. Events and observations had to be recorded. So I took out my small, hand-held, Sony recorder and began to describe on my daily journal cassette what I thought had been important, starting with the beginning of the air trip from Belém.

In the plaza the dancing was over, but a group of young women and men were still singing in the circular street in front of the houses. They walked slowly and chanted in long-held chords in a minor key. These were the Canela late evening songs. The soulful, relaxing, slow-changing chants of this hour always seemed appropriate to the end of the day.

I looked over at Tara, Hugh, and Philip. Fast asleep in their hammocks, they were already adapting to their new world. The calm strains of music moved farther away and then closer as the singers strolled around the circular village street. The sound soon lulled me to sleep also.

NOTES

1. This "first visit" to the Canela is a composite of trips made in 1969, 1970, 1974, and 1975, with 1970 being the base year.

2. Personal names used in this book are real Canela names. However, to protect the privacy of individuals, the names have been switched. If qualified researchers need to follow the activities of certain Canela from one of my publications to others, they can write me for the key to personal names.

3. When I translate names and expressions from Canela to English, I use the same word order in the translation as in the original Canela expression. I also keep the same number of word units in the translation as in the Canela by using spaces, hyphens, and dashes appropriately. While this procedure may reverse the word order or make less sense in English, it helps the reader identify the meaning of each Canela term.

4. Canela males pass their names on to nephews, so, in this case, the nephew is called the *younger* Thunder, and his uncle is called the *older* Thunder.

5. Summer Institute of Linguistics missionaries, also known as Wycliffe Bible Translators, worked among the Canela from 1968 through 1990, when they left, having translated the entire New Testament and some Old Testament "stories" into Canela.

6. For simplicity I use the expression "Indian Service" for the federal service that takes care of the Indians of Brazil. Between 1910 and 1968, the Serviço de Proteção aos Índios performed this service, while from 1968 to the present time the Fundação Nacional do Índio has performed it.

1/The Historical Context

PACIFICATION AND ADAPTION

The geographical location of the Canela and their relatively early pacification eventually proved to be positive factors in their survival. Early surrender to the Brazilians and location on lands which the settlers did not want meant that the Canela won a century of relative peace in which to accommodate themselves to the Brazilian society, which surrounded them on all sides once the frontier moved on to the west. In this chapter we will trace the history of the Canela through their pacification and up to the time they established a relatively stable existence in their present lands.

Timbira nations: The Canela's ancestors   Before we begin our historical narrative, we need to establish just who are the Canela of today. Around 1750, peoples like the Canela lived in relatively self-sufficient and isolated villages of 1,000 to 2,000 in population, comprising "nations" of 1,000 to 5,000, between the Parnaíba and Tocantins rivers (Map 2) or not far beyond. Although no one knows exactly how many nations of the Canela type existed, due to the scarcity of historical chronicles of the period, there were probably between 50 and 75. Brazilian settlers called these nations the Timbira, but the Indians called themselves the Mẽhĩĩ. By 1820 the Brazilian pioneer front had moved completely through the region of these peoples, from east to west, having decimated most of them. By 1860 Brazilian quasi-military bands had totally pacified[7] all these peoples. At that time they numbered about 20 nations, but by now only seven survive as significant groups.[8] Today the groups called "nations" by their descendants are the units we call "tribes."[9] The people of some of these nations live in several villages, but the Canela occupy only one village, which has grown from probably less than 100 during the 1820s to passing 1,000 in 1993.

The Timbira nation-tribes speak a language called Gê, which is found only in Brazil and is very distantly related to Carib.[10] Today, the tribes which speak this language are divided into the Southern Gê (Kaingang and Xokleng), the Central Gê (Shavante and Sherente), and the Northern Gê (principally Kayapó and Timbira). The Canela understand the Kayapó language only well enough to catch occasional meaning from a Kayapó debate in the plaza. They cannot understand Shavante or Kaingang at all, though linguists point out that these peoples' variations of words like fish (tep), rain (ta), meat (hĩĩ), and mother (nàà) come from the same roots.[11]

Before pacification, Timbira nations who were enemies fought each other seasonally, thus keeping down their numbers. Friendly Timbira nations formed alliances and traded.[12] These allies could not rely on each other at the time of enemy

13

attacks, however, because raids were too sudden and because the nations lived too far apart to come to one another's aid in time.

The Timbira nations lived almost entirely in the "closed" savannahs, grass lands with widely spaced low trees and shrubs, and their way of life was well adapted to this environment.[13] Their military organization allowed them to move swiftly at a moment's notice. They relied mostly on hunting and gathering, but they carried out some agriculture in the forests along the streams by cutting out the brush, using stone axes and traditional slash-and-burn methods. The savannahs were too sandy to

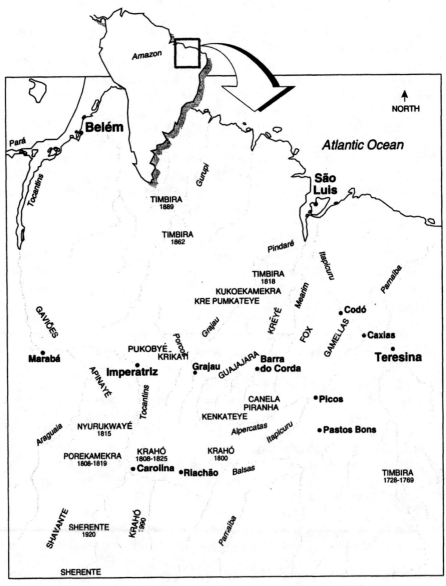

Map 2—The Timbira and their neighbors, past and present.

be cultivated. The Timbira were semi-nomadic, moving their villages every several years to locations that were better for foraging and limited agriculture. They had gourds instead of ceramic pots, which were too heavy and breakable to travel with easily, and their cane arrows had only sharpened points, not arrowheads. Thus they have left no potsherds and projectile points to aid archeological studies.

Just north of Barra do Corda and Grajau, the "closed" savannahs end and the forests begin. In these dry forests[14] lived a type of Native American people who spoke a totally different language, Tupi. The Tupian Guajajara practiced more extensive agriculture, lived in smaller, relatively immobile communities, and were far less athletic and warlike. The current Guajajara even look different from the Canela, being shorter, stockier, and far more Asian. Timbira tribes traded occasionally with Tupian tribes, but rarely deigned to fight them. Instead of the seasonal skirmishes between the same hostile Timbira tribes each year, the warfare between Timbira and Tupian tribes was rare but drastic.

The Canela currently believe they are descended from at least five different Timbira nations. They still celebrate this belief in their summer-long festival, called the Facsimile Warriors (Pep-kahàk: warriors—as-if-they-were). In one act of this festival, male descendants of the principal nation, the Mõl-tũm-re (going-along, enduring people), sit in the center of the plaza. The Mõl-tũm-re are Nimuendajú's[15] Ramkokamekra. The men of the nations which joined the Ramkokamekra (a name forgotten today) sit at the edges of the plaza in the geographical directions from which they are believed to have come. These are the descendants of the Mud (Karẽ-?katêyê), Boar (Krôô-re-khãm-mẽ-?khra-re), Piranha (Apanyekra), and Fox (Tsoo-khãm-mẽ-?khra) peoples. The Canela have no name for the totality of the remnants of former nations which make up their current tribe. Consequently, they accept "Canela," which was applied to them[16] by local Brazilian authorities early in the last century, as their tribal name.

Nobody claims to know the origin of the word Canela as it is used in this name. Nimuendajú suggests that it comes from the earlier name of a hill, Serra da Canella (hill of the cinnamon [trees]), located in the greater Canela region, but in Piranha lands. Nimuendajú points out[17] that the early chronicler of the Canela, Ribeiro, used the expression "Canellas finaś" (shinbones fine: calves thin) to describe them, but that Ribeiro himself did not know the origin of this expression. My guess is that Brazilian authorities of the times, who were more used to the Guajajara, contrasted the squat, short-legged Guajajara with the far taller and thinner Canela by referring to their longer and thinner calves. While *canela* means either cinnamon or the calf/shinbone of a person's leg in local Portuguese, "calf" as the original name makes more sense than "cinnamon" to me, given the context of the obvious Guajajara–Canela contrast in body type.

Pioneers decimate the Timbira nations   To gain an impression of the ancestors of the Canela before pacification, we can turn to the accounts of Captain Ribeiro,[18] the commander of a Brazilian military post maintained at the confluence of the Alpercatas and Itapicuru rivers and called Principe Regente. A road had been pushed from Caxias around 1760 to maintain this post and protect settlement farms and cattle ranches along the two rivers.[19] Within several years this post had to be abandoned due to the ferocity and effectiveness of Indian attacks. Over 50 years later, Ribeiro wrote of Indian bravery in these attacks:

In 1807 we . . . observed the audacity of a Forest [Fox] Timbira . . . , who dashed from some ambush into the midst of over a hundred of our people employed with sundry tasks at the founding [reconstruction] of the Arroyal do Principe Regente; he killed one man, attacked several others and dexterously withdrew before he could be made to suffer any injury. . . . Man to man, there seem to be few [of our] men able to vie with them in point of bravery. Even the women are not inferior in robustness and we have seen one such brought in as a captive who tried to escape by dragging along her guard under her arm and would have succeeded if he had not received aid. She was of goodly stature and so well built that our soldiers dubbed her "the big sorrel mare."[20]

The valor of the Canela is dramatized in a Canela war story collected by Nimuendajú about a young man, who, after achieving the status of warrior *(hààprãr)*, was sent by his mother to retrieve the bones of her brother and to avenge his death at the hands of Brazilian settlers:

She gave him [her son] an exact description of the site, which was at the foot of a big tree, in the center of a little wooded island by the headwaters of a certain brook. The youth set out alone and found the bones at the spot indicated. He collected them, packed them up, and carried them to a mountain halfway from his home. There he laid them down, as well as his provender and everything he was able to spare, then he once more went back to the settlement, carrying only his weapons. Here he lay in ambush not far from the houses, near a road with many footprints. He waited for a long time, then two men with rifles came past, whom he followed. After a while one of them lingered behind to ease himself, and the youth utilized this opportunity to lay him low with a club. The companion heard the noise, turned back, and cocked the trigger when he caught sight of the Indian, but before he could shoot, the young man had killed him too. Then he picked up the rifles and fled, for the inmates of the houses had taken cognizance of the incident and immediately gave pursuit. He ran all day, but his pursuers would not give up, so that at last his strength was exhausted. With a final exertion he climbed the mountain where he had left his uncle's bones. He was unable to move farther and prepared to fight. From his height he saw his pursuers arriving at the foot of the cliff, but they were even more fatigued than himself, hence unable to ascend the mountain. Accordingly, after a rest they turned back. The warrior recovered the bag with the remains, also his baggage, and returned to his village, where he put down the two rifles in the plaza before the chiefs and elders. The trigger of one of them was still cocked, for at that time these Indians did not yet understand how to release it.[21]

The Europeans of the time found that the Canela ancestors fit their Romantic notions of the noble savage. Ribeiro identifies the Apinayé, cultural cousins of Canela ancestors, as being particularly handsome.[22] Hemming[23] translates Ribeiro and two other authors as follows:

The Apinagé, in common with other Timbira tribes, were and still are strikingly handsome. Many travelers were impressed by their slim, graceful bodies, pale colour, and the perfect figures and beautiful faces of their women. Johann Pohl found these good looks enchanting. "They are particularly distinguished from descendants of whites by their firm, turgid breasts." He [Pohl] wanted to take away one girl and her mother. "This young Indian girl was graced with the most distinctive beauty . . . which would have aroused attention in Europe."[24] Some years later, the magistrate Vicente Ferreira Gomes visited the Apinagé and was romantically charmed by them. "The ease with which these people generally greet strangers, the goodness with which they treat visitors, their simplicity, ingenuousness, that same state in which the Creator placed them on earth—all this produced a feeling of love, friendship, compassion and interest. . . . One observes nature in all its simplicity: one sees no adornments concealing natural defects, nor artifice or caprice hiding beauty. . . . These people are by nature peaceful, laborious and hospitable. . . . They live in perfect tranquility and harmony, obeying their chiefs. And yet they all live completely naked!"

Ribeiro's accounts are of skirmishes and warfare which took place while the Timbira tribes were being displaced. Brazilian settlement of the region came mostly from the state of Bahia in the southeast, but also from São Luis in the north, the capital of the state of Maranhão. These two advances of settlers came together between Caxias and Pastos Bons (Map 2). The pastoral front from the southeast was composed of cattle ranchers with cowhands to support them, who were often gunmen enforcing the head rancher's power. The agricultural front from the north consisted of farming families, coming up the Itapicuru River.[25] These loosely organized peoples settled the area during the last decade of the 18th century and the first decade of the 19th century. They completed a thinly settled band of occupation across the flattest part of the area by 1810, from Pastos Bons through Riachão to Carolina, following the Parnaíba and Balsas rivers all the way to the Tocantins River. Their population pressure pushed one Timbira tribe of three to five thousand people, the Krahó, completely from their ancestral position, just southwest of the Canela, all the way to the Tocantins and then south along the river. The pioneer thrust pushed Timbira tribes such as the Fox, Mud, Boar, Canela, Piranha, Pukobyé, and Krîkatí into the northern parts of their ancestral territories and into the protection of hills and forests, diminishing the lands they controlled by 70 percent to 90 percent.

In the typical pattern of settlement, family farmers or cattle ranchers moved west to find and occupy new lands. Indians, objecting to such intrusions into their ancestral lands, attacked randomly, stole cattle, and killed individual settlers, but seldom wiped out whole settlements. Settlers with such losses called on the populations of the more established communities to the east to organize posses to kill or capture as many Indians as possible. These posses *(bandeiras)*[26] took months to assemble and were seldom well organized. Thus the pacification of the Timbira Indians took half a century. Smallpox, which spread to all the Timbira nations during 1816 and 1817, was the great agent of the Indian demise, as it usually was throughout the western hemisphere.

When the settlers' communities were weak, their leaders signed treaties of peace with the most threatening Indian nations, but when these communities became stronger, or had a military post in their vicinity to assure their safety, they forgot the peace treaties and killed Indians when they could. When punitive expeditions failed, they sometimes turned instead to the destruction of already peaceful Indians. They even enticed Indians out of protected areas with promises of fair treatment in order to kill or enslave them. An important motive for fighting Indians was to capture them and sell them into slavery in the coastal cities of São Luis or Belém. The treacherous nature of promises offered by the settlers became well known among all the Indian nations of the region during the decade of the 1810s and poisoned relations between the two groups.

The treachery of the settlers is amply illustrated in their actions against the Pukobyé and the Canela. Nimuendajú writes that the Pukobyé were the most warlike of the Timbira nations. In contrast to the Canela, who were more exposed in open country and closer to both of the settlers' invasion routes, the Pukobyé were farther west and north of the settlers' line of march across southern Maranhão to the Tocantins. Thus the Pukobyé could escape into the forests to the north of their lands. The Pukobyé, together with the Krĩkatí just to their east, were so strong that they defeated all attempts of the *bandeiras* to subdue them. Hemming interprets from Captain Ribeiro's memoirs that in 1815 a settlers' reprisal posse/*bandeira* of men from Pastos Bons and Carolina was ignominiously repelled by the Pukobyé. As the posse shamefully retreated through the plains, they imprisoned instead of the Pukobyé some docile Timbira Indians, the Porekamekra. Two months earlier, Captain Ribeiro had watched the Porekamekra perform a formal ceremony of alliance with the Brazilians on the banks of the Tocantins. Nevertheless, when the Porekamekra heard that the *bandeira* was returning from its defeat by the Pukobyé, they fearfully hid their women and children in the woods.

Some Krahó Timbira Indians were with the *bandeira*, helping this group of settlers militarily. The Krahó were ordered to call out to the hidden Porekamekra in their language, asking them to come out of hiding. The Krahó were told to say that the settlers wanted only "peace and friendship and to fill them with good fortune," which meant many gifts, as they had already given the Krahó themselves. Consequently, 364 Porekamekra came out to experience the good faith of the *bandeira* only to find they had been tricked. Hemming's translation of Ribeiro is as follows:

> Imagine to their horror, grief and belated regret when [the Porekamekra] found themselves seized and robbed by the Krahó, their maidens deflowered, and their sons dragged off to be distributed among our men. Some Indians were revoltingly killed on the plain so that their better-looking wives could be raped—and this with the full consent of [our officers] who could have prevented it! I saw these enter this town on 27 July 1815, as sad and downcast as can be imagined at the miserable state to which they were reduced by that horrible treachery—for these were people who had voluntarily sought to become subjects of our august Sovereign. At four o'clock that afternoon, 130 of them were branded with hot metal on their right wrists, just like slaves bought for trade goods on the coast of Africa. The brand was a large O. Naturally, the youngest were destined for sale in the usual manner: they were taken to Pará [Belém] a few days later in two boats by João Apolinario. The older and unsalable were condemned to work in private service in the town. I saw that parents could only [bear to] gaze at their children for a moment, when they contemplated the slavery to which their credulity had reduced them. But the tenderness with which they observed them at that moment was so intense that I have retained a very vivid memory of it. I can never easily forget this affair.[27]

Slavery was against the law of the times, but in 1808 a royal law had been enacted allowing the capture and enslavement of the Botocudo Indians, because they ate human flesh. The Timbira were held to be like the Botocudo, so they could be enslaved also.

The Indian nations seldom cooperated among themselves, so the settlers never faced an effectively united Indian front. Timbira Indian nations of this period still fought each other, with the consequence that the losers sometimes became so weak that they surrendered voluntarily to military posts of the settlers for protection from more attacks from their Indian enemies. The Fox people defeated the Canela so badly in 1814 that the Canela surrendered the same year to the Brazilian *bandeira* based at Pastos Bons, for safety. They agreed in a treaty that they would never fight settlers again, but that they would help the Brazilians fight other Indian groups. This treaty constituted the actual pacification of the Canela. The Krahó had already made such a treaty with the settlers; we have just seen how they helped the settlers enslave an already peaceful Timbira nation. Early in 1815, the Canela helped the settlers raid a group of Fox people then at Burityzinho.

Although pacification of the Canela—their surrender and treaty with the Brazilians—had been achieved, relations between the Canela and the settlers were far from peaceful. Later in 1815, settlers lured the Canela to Caxias, ostensibly to participate in additional raids against the Fox people, but really to infect the Canela with smallpox, which had broken out in the town.[28] The Canela were left to shift for themselves around this community instead of being organized by its authorities, who were to have taken care of their economic needs. Left on their own, the hungry Canela broke into small groups and inflicted almost more damage on the settlers through theft than they had earlier through warfare. Subsequently, men who had stolen cattle and women who had pulled up manioc and other vegetables from the settlers' fields were flogged. Women were put in chains without consideration for the needs of their nursing babies. When Chief Tẽmpê and other male Canela remonstrated, the chief was flogged and several others were killed. They resolved to escape regardless of the treaty and marched off to the southwest toward the northernmost part of their homelands just south of Barra do Corda, between the Porcos and Ourives streams. A settler's posse caught up with them 50 miles from Caxias and shot down a number of them, while smallpox was killing many more.

From that time on, the Canela have remained in this northwestern part of their ancestral lands, which formerly had extended south beyond the middle Alpercatas to the Itapicuru and east to Picos (Map 2). The Canela remained hidden in an inconspicuous valley of the Alpercatas hills for some time, completely away from settlers' communities (Map 3).

Tales about becoming aware of peace   Old Canela men in the late 1950s told a pitiful tale about the years when their ancestors hid from the settlers. Individual Canela had to sneak daily from the valley in the Alpercatas hills to fetch water from a spring. Eventually they were seen from a distance by settlers, who reported the presence of dangerous wild savages to the military. One day, the story goes, an army major with troops sent from São Luis to tame the Indians approached the area of the hidden valley, and a group of Canela scouts fired on them with shotguns from a hill.[29]

Forewarned by their scouts, the Canela armed themselves and left the village to set up a defensive position. One young warrior, however, whom the elders were considering as a potential chief, said he was tired of spending his life hiding in a mountain valley. He said they should give themselves up and that he would act as the go-between with the soldiers. Thus the young Hĩĩ-khrô (flesh's-tail) descended alone and unarmed to the troops' encampment. The soldiers prepared to fire, but their commandant ordered them to wait. Flesh's Tail, approaching, said, "Do not kill me," but they could communicate only through hand gestures. They shook hands and embraced.

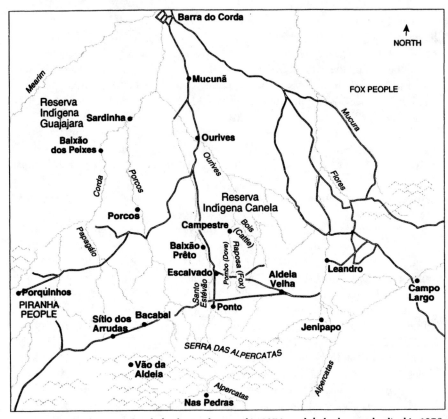

Map 3—The Canela region. Canela lands were demarcated in 1971, and the borders were legalized in 1978.

The commandant asked where the Canela were, and Flesh's Tail pointed to the hills. Since they believed him, they offered him a meal and named him Mesquite. The commandant showed Mesquite the presents brought for his people—machetes, axes, cloth, dried meat—and requested that Mesquite summon his people to come out of the valley, saying that his soldiers would not harm them. Mesquite went back to his people, where their chief, Tĕmpê, assembled them. After Mesquite had spoken, Chief Tĕmpê supported him and said, "Let's deliver ourselves; they will not kill us."

I vividly remember Antônio Diogo Mĩ́-khrô (alligator's-tail),[30] surely in his early 80s in 1958, emphasizing with his weak voice the fear with which his grandparents descended onto the unprotected savannahs. They were afraid of being massacred or put in chains and sent away into slavery. However, by this time the attitude toward wild Indians was changing, since they were no longer a threat in this area. They were given the presents, and 10 cattle were killed for them to eat.

It was hard for me to realize in the late 1950s that it was Alligator's Tail's grandparents, not his great-grandparents, who had walked down from the hills to the dangers of the savannahs, fearing the fate of other Indian peoples. Alligator's Tail heard many such stories from his grandparents, who had experienced these dangers.

Another Canela story told by old Alligator's Tail places his people south of the Alpercatas River in their former lands (Map 3), already occupied by families of cattle ranchers. This is where the Canela may have gone after they left the protection of their hidden valley. The place was called Nas Pedras. Ranchers' men often visited the Canela village there for trading and obtaining women for pieces of cloth. One rancher asked Chief Pompeu Tẽmpê if he could take away a young Canela woman he had seen and liked. Tẽmpê allowed this, and the rancher gave a quarter of a cow for her. Many adolescent women were delivered to settlers to appease their desires, and little boys and girls were given to ranchers' families to be raised and educated as house servants. Tẽmpê lost much respect among his people because of such dealings, but these were successful ways of placating an overpowering rancher and getting along with the settlers in general.

After some time, a very beautiful and spirited young Canela woman who had been sold to a rancher ran away and returned to her people, followed by her owner. Because of the rough treatment she had suffered, her father became very angry at Chief Tẽmpê. Her father declared, "They will take her away again only after they have killed me." This refusal to give a rancher what he had paid for was the cause of a skirmish with the settlers some days later. The Canela Arèykooko threw a bow at the settler Barnabé, who fended it off. Barnabé sliced Arèykooko with his machete so that his guts fell out onto the ground and he soon died. The Canela Manuel Gomes Pep-tsen (war-likes) confronted Barnabé, who begged not to be killed, offering his machete, but another Canela killed Barnabé.

For fear of retaliation after this incident, the Canela left Nas Pedras and fled north across the Alpercatas River and the Alpercatas range of hills to the Papagáio area (Map 3), just west of their present lands.

Another story of Alligator's Tail, probably of the late 1820s or early 1830s, tells of a rancher in the present Porcos area who had earlier taken a young Canela girl as mistress. She had learned Portuguese well in this role.[31] Later, when she was a grown woman, her father visited her. Through him, she was able to help negotiate an agreement between the Canela and the Brazilian authorities of the region. The Canela were to settle near the unoccupied headwaters of the Santo Estévão Stream. There they built a small circular village in the savannahs according to their tradition. While the Canela have moved their village to various other locations on the different streams of the region, the Santo Estévão Stream has become their principal location.

Old Alligator's Tail took me in 1959 to see the remains of one of his ancestral villages near the headwaters of the Santo Estévão Stream. There we could identify the remains of a circular plaza by the slightly different shade and texture of the grasses growing in its sandier soil. Next we saw, leading out from the plaza in every direction, distinctly lower radial pathways, formed by many feet kicking out sand over the years. These arrow-straight depressions along the ground led our eyes across the distinctly colored circular boulevard to each house site, where we found post holes at appropriate intervals. Alligator's Tail said this was one of the villages of Luis Domingos Kaw-khre (white-clay hole), the Canela's first backlander-oriented chief, who led them during the 1830s and 1840s. White Clay cooperated fully with the so called *civilizados* (backland and urban settlers) of the region. He had been raised from boyhood and educated by a rancher's family in the Nas Pedras area, so he could read and write Portuguese.

Once the Canela had been assigned lands along the Santo Estêvão Stream (a small part of their ancestral territory), and once they had accepted such a limitation, they faced an entirely new world. They had become recognized as a social entity in the world of the backland *civilizados,* though placed on the bottom rung of the social ladder as *índios* or *caboclos.* Backland merchants visited them periodically for trading, and Canela families were accepted in the traders' settlements and family houses.

A myth is created to justify inferior status   Here we should pause in our historical narrative to consider the myth which enabled the Canela to preserve some dignity in spite of their low social position. In 1845 the Emperor of Brazil, Dom Pedro II, issued a far-reaching decree[32] protecting Indians and establishing the national relationship between Brazilians and Indians. One order that the Canela attribute to the decree was that all Brazilians were to send Indians in captivity back to their tribes out of respect for their ways of life. The Canela believe the decree also forbade Brazilian miscegenation with Indian women, which had been taking place extensively. Remnants of the Timbira nations, feeling that the emperor had concern for Indians, identified him with their culture hero, Awkhêê (no translation). According to what may be the Canela's most important myth of the 19th and 20th centuries, Awkhêê (Dom Pedro II) summoned the Indian and the backlander/*civilizado* to appear before him in his palace in Rio de Janeiro (now the National Museum). The following is a version of this myth spoken by the Canela Hanging Fish, the son of Alligator's Tail, which I taped in 1975 and later published[33]:

> Two by two the Indians and Christians [backlanders/*civilizados*] were called to gather together. And when the Indian saw the shotgun—the Devil . . . —fully loaded, he thought that the shotgun was hostile and threatening. "It has its mouth open. It has a mouth. I'm afraid."
>
> Awkhêê ordered the Christian to pick up the shotgun and fire it to show the Indian. The Christian picked up the shotgun and fired, and the Indian fell to the ground. He felt his back and the pain spread all over his body. The lead balls had not hit him; it was just the blast from the explosion which hurt him. The magical powers of the shotgun had penetrated the Indian's body. The stupid Indian had felt pain without having been shot. The Christian had shot without aiming and the Indian had fallen to the ground in pain.
>
> When the Indian had recovered from the pain, he said: "We don't need this shotgun. It is wild; it has powers that we don't need." So Awkhêê ordered the Christian to pick up the bow and arrow, but the Christian did not know how to shoot the arrow from the bow. Awkhêê ordered the Indian to pick up the bow and arrow and shoot it. The Indian did so and shot off the arrow, which traveled through the air noiselessly. The Indian liked the bow and the arrow and spoke of receiving them. It was exactly this that Awkhêê did not like, and he became really angry with the Indian. Right then and there he ordered the Christian to take the shotgun and the Indian to take the bow and arrow. . . .
>
> [Awkhêê] spoke in the Indian language. "It is because of this that you are going away and will roam aimlessly through the world. You will travel around in the forests (dry brush) scratching and tearing your bodies, and doing little of significance. You will live any which way, any way you can, traveling throughout this world. Leave now! I'm very angry with you. . . .
>
> The great-grandfathers came walking here in the forests, doing pointless things, just like animals, traveling without direction. It seems it was at this time that the Indians came here, eating rotten wood. . . .

This was the story that the old men always told there in the middle of the plaza. . . . I think the story goes like this and I never heard it told differently. Others told it the way I just finished telling it. So, it is only like this, the story of Awkhêê.

The myth goes on to say that the backlander, since he had won the more prestigious shotgun, would become wealthy, but in return, he would have to give the Indian *everything* the Indian would ever want and need. This myth justifies for the Indian his dependency on the *civilizado,* and it legitimizes the Indian's begging. The Canela's insistence on his right to be taken care of became "traditional" and institutionalized through the myth.

In 1958 I carried out a study of Canela attitudes about specific backlanders of the Canela region. I asked if a certain man of a backland community was good or bad, and why. The Canela individual invariably connected a backlander's "goodness" with how much the backlander had given him or her and "badness" with the lack of such personal giving. A Canela's assessment of a backlander had nothing to do with how much the backlander could afford to give. The worst backlanders were those who were poor and kept their stock of supplies for the year to themselves. Rice harvested in May had to be stored and consumed slowly, lasting until the following May, or else it had to be bought at a high price that the poor backlander could not afford. Thus a backlander who was reserving rice for his family's consumption during the entire year was seen by the Canela as stingy. The good backlander gave the Canela rice whenever requested, but the backlander who refused to give, when rice was actually in his storage room, was thought to be evil and without compassion.

The myth of Awkhêê (or of Dom Pedro II) justified to the Canela their existence in an inferior social position, dependent on the *civilizados*. The Canela believed their culture hero had assigned them to this position. Moreover, according to the myth, the *civilizado* owed the *índio* (the Canela) any items that the Canela needed. Thus, no Canela lost face when begging; this was their traditional right, since leaving the emperor's palace in Rio. This belief was held firmly until the mid-1960s, when it began to erode. Though unexpressed, the belief is still an underlying assumption of many Canela today, even though they have become somewhat embarrassed by it. The analyst of Canela culture and behavior must not underestimate the importance of this myth, which has enabled the Canela to maintain relatively high morale and self-esteem since the mid-1800s.

In 1960, Mãã-tsè (ostrich-bitter), 32, demanded that I give him a machete. Almost all grown Canela males wanted machetes, but to provide one for each would have broken my budget. I had assigned two machetes to large households and one to small households in trade for artifacts. The Canela Council of Elders had agreed to this rationing, accepting that I could not buy a machete to trade with every adult male, and that they were best spread around to every house in the whole tribe. I tried to explain to Bitter Ostrich that his household had already received two machetes through trade and that I could not trade a third. Bitter Ostrich, knowing that I had not yet distributed all the machetes, insisted on trading for one. Simple need was his total justification for being adamant. Of course, I had to give in to keep the peace, a prime Canela priority. I could not afford to be considered evil. By the mid-1970s, the Canela had changed and I had no trading problems of this sort. Most of them even had come to understand why poor backlanders saved rice over the period of a year, and some of them were trying to be "stingy" with their own families' stores of rice.

Learning their place among the civilizados   Let us resume our historical narrative with the death of Chief White Clay in the 1850s. From his death bed he had appointed Zé Cadete Pal-khre (foot's-hole) to succeed him, though this individual was known to be bad natured. Chief Foot's Wound was summoned by the Brazilians, along with Chief Bernardo of the Fox people, to punish the non–Timbira-speaking Gamella Indians 100 kilometers to the east (Map 2), called the Ha?khà-?po (lips-broad) by the Canela, because they put discs in their lower lips. They had killed a settler who unfortunately had entered one of their villages. Twenty Canela and 10 Fox People proceeded east through the dry forest thickets under the command of the army's Captain Soi and his troops. Two Canela, Kõk (iguana) and I?twèn-tsen (fat-loves), knew the direct route through the forests, but when they nevertheless became lost, the captain "used a machine that pointed the correct direction" to find the way, according to the story of old Alligator's Tail. The punitive expedition surprised the Gamella, and after killing a number of them, withdrew swiftly. Captain Soi used only fierce Canela warriors in his attack, not wanting to risk his own troops.

During the 1850s, while Foot's Wound was chief, the prominent Arruda ranching family migrated from the east into the Canela area. The Arrudas took over the geographically high land of the area, known today as the Sítio (Map 3), which has the most fertile soils of the area. Foot's Wound ordered his men to catch some of the cattle of the new arrivals. He feared nothing, not being sufficiently aware yet of the Canela's new position in the backland society. Chief White Clay had been quite aware of the Canela's new position of necessary dependency and subservience, because of his childhood on the backland ranch near Nas Pedras.

When the Arrudas' gunmen arrived in force in the Canela village to complain about the cattle rustling, Foot's Wound simply said, "Yes, we killed the cattle and ate them." The Arrudas sent word to the government in Barra do Corda that Foot's Wound was fierce and uncontrollable. When government troops arrived, they found only two Canela in the village. Later, Foot's Wound obeyed orders and went willingly with five Canela to Barra do Corda, where they were all put in jail. Foot's Wound sang loudly in jail all the time, disturbing the community. One night the jail keeper, annoyed by the singing, let the prisoners out. The five Canela companions escaped, but Foot's Wound refused to go, though he did leave later when he wanted to.

Some time later, Foot's Wound went to São Luis, the state capital 250 miles to the north, with his brother-in-law, who died there. Foot's Wound was arrested and thrown in jail first in São Luis and then in Alcântara, the old town across the bay from São Luis. The authorities confined him because of his notoriety for cattle rustling and because of his general antisocial behavior, including getting drunk and singing obnoxiously. He returned to the Canela with one eye lost to an infection and with a venereal disease. He soon died among his people.

By the end of the 1870s, the Canela were surrounded on all sides, whether by backlanders or by urban Brazilians. Barra do Corda, 50 miles to the north of the newly assigned Canela area on the Santo Estévão, had been settled by 1835, and in 1854 the settlement had officially become a town (*vila*). During the late 1850s, ranchers had moved into the former Canela region around the Sítio dos Arrudas, 20 miles southwest of the Canela's new central area, and in the 1870s farmers moved into the region of Leandro, 25 miles to the east of this area. For a half century farmers and ranchers had already lined both sides of the Alpercatas River, which ran 15 miles south of the new Canela base on the Santo Estévão at its nearest point.

The Canela have controlled up to the present time the central area between these communities established by the settlers during the last century. This control has given the Canela about 500 square miles of closed savannahs and streams lined by jungles, called gallery forests, in which to hunt, fish, and plant small farms. This amount of land was insufficient for the Canela to support themselves by gathering fruits, roots, and seeds in their aboriginal manner. Consequently, they had to turn for their maintenance to slash-and-burn agriculture, which had sustained less than 25 percent of their former way of life. Since nothing could be planted in the sandy savannahs and since the gallery forest soils could support only one crop a year, they had to cut new fields out of the stream-lining forests each year. Eventually, the new fields would be so far from the village that it made sense to move the village to the fields. For this reason they moved their village up and down the Santo Estévão and to the other streams in their area, returning to the same place about 20 years later, when the gallery forests had grown tall enough to provide sufficiently fertile soils.

Since the settlers had to live on sizable streams, they could not move closer to the Canela than the distances mentioned. This gave the Canela considerable space in which to live in relative peace and develop a new post-pacification way of life. While one or two settlers' families may have lived within five miles of the Canela village, varying with the decade, the nearest backland communities were never closer than 15 miles.

We know little about the 1860s and early 1870s. The Canela were governed by chiefs Roberto and Gororop, about whom I was not given stories, possibly because these chiefs were not dramatic leaders. Presumably, the Canela were becoming more accepting of their social environment. We know more about the mid-1880s and 1890s, because old Canela in the late 1950s had passed through their late adolescence during those years. I found, while working up Canela history, that individuals remembered their late adolescence better than any other time of their lives. Thus, to cover the 1920s during the late 1950s, I needed Canela research assistants around 45 to 55 years old; or to cover the 1890s, I needed research assistants from 75 to 85, of which there were half a dozen, among whom Alligator's Tail was the most verbal.

One Sunday, Alligator's Tail took me from the current Baixão Preto village to two of the old village sites of the 1880s and 1890s in the area know as Escalvado (a?-khrã-?khà-?tèy: its head's surface hard: Hard Ground area). This happens to be the site of the present Canela village. As we poked around and identified the remains of each house site around the two village circles, memories flooded back to Alligator's Tail. Unfortunately, 1959 was before the days of portable "D" or "C" battery-run tape recorders, so I had to rely on my speedwriting, which was insufficient for the old man's fluency. My relationship as his named-nephews' named-nephew (see Chapter 2) surely helped rapport and encouraged the flow of his words. My greatest surprise was that the Canela of the 1890s maintained mutually respectful relations with backlanders and urban Brazilians. The Canela had become conscious of their place in their new world, and they were cooperating fully.

As with the co-chiefs Roberto and Gororop, the Canela were lead by two chiefs toward the end of the 19th century. The senior of the two chiefs, Colonel Tomasinho, made clay pipes and mended backlanders' cauldrons and shotguns for a price. He even had a make-shift forge in which he soldered silver coins onto iron implements to repair them for Canela and backlander customers. We found fragments of old pipes in the remains of his mud-and-wattle house, a type which was quite advanced for the Canela even in the 1970s when palm straw was still easier to use.

The junior chief, Major Delfino Kô-?kaypo (no translation), had a business relationship with a firm in São Luis, which he visited several times to deliver and sell home-grown cotton (katsàt). The Canela had their own aboriginal variety. Major Delfino transported his cotton on commercial launches and boats down the Mearim River to São Luis, an undertaking which required a certain degree of sophistication in the Brazilian business world. Major Delfino made enough money this way to buy and maintain between 20 to 30 head of cattle. He kept this herd for over three decades while the Canela lived in six different village locations between 1880 and 1914. Reliable information about Major Delfino's small but significant herd of cattle surprised me, because I knew that the hungry Canela of the late 1950s could not raise cattle at all. They ate a calf before it could grow up to reproduce. This information about Major Delfino's era suggested that the times were more affluent, or that game of the region was more plentiful, or that chiefs maintained higher discipline.

Olímpio Fialho, the historian-geographer of Barra do Corda and São Luis, confirmed that the turn-of-the-century Canela were prosperous, as did André of Lagoa, an old backlander of the Canela region. Both of these men, whom I interviewed in 1959, were adolescents around the turn of the century. In his house in São Luis, Fialho and his wife (an Arruda descendant) assured me that Major Delfino's Canela produced surpluses of manioc flour, which they sold in Barra do Corda: "It was yellow and of very fine quality." André of Lagoa told me that the size of Delfino's herd of cattle, 30, was due largely to growth rather than many purchases. Information from the oldest Canela with whom I worked in 1960, Justino Khà-?po (body-broad), 83, supported the fact that Major Delfino maintained his herd over a period of 30 years. Broad Body said that Major Delfino left his herd with his backland compadre (co-godfather), Virgulino, in Rancharia, 20 miles to the southeast of the Canela village, and that when Major Delfino died in about 1914, Virgulino kept whatever cattle were left.

When Awkhêê, the Emperor Dom Pedro II, died in 1889 and the Republic was founded, the authorities declared that Indians no longer had free passage and protection when they traveled throughout Brazil. When they heard of the loss of these rights which had been granted to Indians by the emperor, Colonel Tomasinho and Major Delfino went to São Luis to reclaim them. They were received well and showered with gifts: "shotguns, machetes, axes, cloth spoons and all things," and the Republican government gave them permission and protection to travel in all parts of Brazil.

Major Delfino, in contrast to Chief Foot's Wound, was honored a number of times in São Luis during the 1890s and the next decade, where the authorities made him an army major and gave him a uniform and sword to wear. According to Olímpio Fialho, when Major Delfino came to Barra do Corda with his wife, they were both appropriately dressed and well behaved in social situations. The Canela were becoming more aware of their social surroundings; they were accepting them and adapting to them.

The Fox people join the Canela   The Fox people joined the Canela in 1900, leaving their ancestral Timbira village, Mucura, 30 miles to the northeast, because their numbers had become too reduced to maintain their independence from Brazilian settlers encroaching on their lands. The Mud and Boar nations had undoubtedly joined the Ramkokamekra, the ancestors of the Canela, for similar reasons, but the current Canela have forgotten when the migrations occurred. I suggest that these two national mergings occurred soon after the pacification of the Ramkokamekra-Canela in 1814; if any later, they would be remembered. The Fox people were the Timbira nation that had decimated the Ramkokamekra-Canela's ancestors in 1814, forcing their surrender for survival to the regional Brazilian garrison. It is ironic that the Canela of the late 1950s claimed they had always been at peace with the Fox people, even when both nations had been "wild Indians."

A descendant of the Fox nation, Ka?hi, told me in the late 1950s, when he was 60, that he was carried in his mother's arms from the old Fox village to the Canela one. He said that his people and the Canela already had installed ceremonial chiefs (*tàmhàk*) in each other's tribes so that communicating with the Canela was relatively easy. In fact, the two tribes were already allies. In contrast, before pacification, members of enemy Timbira nations, such as the Ramkokamekra and the Piranha people, shot each other's warriors on sight, unless they were approaching each other's nation in a small group in a traditional manner that indicated peaceful intent.

My special group of very old Canela research assistants told me in 1975, while we were working on the remembered history of the Canela, that to help bring about the joining of the Fox and the Canela peoples, a Fox group of elders took the initiative and visited the Canela in 1900. During this visit they reinstalled their Canela ceremonial-protection chief, adorning his body with red urucu and white falcon down in the center of the plaza. Then each Fox individual placed presents on the mat on which their Canela ceremonial-protection chief was standing to honor him and his people and to express their individual commitments to peace. A few months later, a group of Canela visited the Fox village and reinstalled their ceremonial-protection chief among the Fox people. Still later, a Fox group visited the Canela and proposed moving to join them in the old Timbira way. They wanted to know if the Canela elders would accept the Fox people into the Canela group of formerly independent tribes as respected equals, as was the Timbira custom. The Canela elders, after consulting their extended families and after several weeks of debate during the late afternoon council meetings, decided positively. They needed more Indians of their Timbira kind to protect them against the mounting Brazilian incursions. Subsequently, representatives of the elders of both peoples, sitting together in the Canela plaza, planned how they would put on the ceremony for the joining of tribes in the correct traditional manner. They tried to recall how it had been done much earlier, and surely with many minds helping one another remember earlier events of this sort, such as the merging of the Mud and Boar peoples, they largely succeeded.

During the agreed-upon season, probably in June when new farms have to be started, the Fox nation, comprised of 30 to 60 members, marched in single file to the region of the Canela village which consisted of 150 to 250 individuals. The Fox warriors left their arms with their women about 500 yards short of the Canela village, and, entering it, walked down a radial pathway performing the Tired Deer (*poo-tùkrĩn:* deer tired) act. The Fox warriors acted as if they were exhausted, shuffling their feet, breathing heavily, and hanging their heads as they walked slowly in single file to the center of the plaza. The men were representing tired deer, disillusioned by their exasperating experiences far away, returning to their preferred home pasture land. The Fox warriors, having completely surrendered, were entering what they hoped would be their home tribe forever. As a part of the ceremony of unification, the Fox people formed a circular camp of beehive-shaped palm frond shelters for their extended families about 500 yards from the Canela village in the Canela's Escalvado region.

After setting up their shelters, the Fox people built an especially large shelter for the family of their best female singer. This woman was one of the two to four women in the tribe who had been awarded a highly prized cotton sash of honor (*hahĩ*) for her outstanding ability to sing and for her faithful attendance and helpful attitude at the daily group singing events over a number of years. In this special shelter, her family built a platform bed on which she was to receive almost all the Canela warriors sexually, one after the other, as they filed to and through the Fox camp. These men left presents in her mother's shelter after they had satisfied themselves. Similarly, the Fox warriors filed to the Canela village and had sex sequentially with the Canela woman who wore the cotton sash and who was offered for this purpose, and left presents in her mother's house.

The remnants of the Fox nation had set up their overnight camp as if they were going to make a surprise attack on the Canela village at dawn, but as prearranged, the warriors exchanged sexual favors instead. Participation in sex reduced the potentially aggressive orientation of the warriors on each side so that cooperation and friendship became more likely.

One of the most characteristic Canela bonding mechanisms is sequential sex carried out by certain traditional groups of men with the full cooperation of two to six women. In an act of the Facsimile Warriors' festival, men who are ceremonially high (Wet Heads) and men who are ceremonially low (Dry Heads) walk back and forth in the plaza in parallel files, but in opposite directions, not looking at each other. This ceremonial avoidance indicates the two groups' symbolic opposition. If individuals in these two files were to do 90 degree military turns to face each other, as they do in some other ceremonies, the act of facing each other would assure the symbolic cooperation and peace between the two opposing groups. However, this does not happen in this ceremonial case, and their "hostility" is continued into the next day. Then in the afternoon, the Wet Heads take some of the wives of the Dry Heads out to a farm's hut to have sex with them, while the Dry Heads have sex with some of the wives of the Wet Heads in a house in the village. This sexual exchange ends the symbolic opposition between the two groups. However, since only women without children are expected to cooperate in such situations, the men are likely to outnumber the women by at least 10 to 1. The necessary result is the reception by the woman of one man after another, or sequential sex. The cultural institution of sequential sex will be discussed in Chapter 4.

It is a general female role among the Canela to stop male excesses in a number of traditional situations. Sometimes in the course of daily events, the two relay log racing teams challenge and rechallenge each other to an additional race so many times that the racers become exhausted, but cannot stop rechallenging the other team. Then one of the two ceremonial girls of the tribe (a young Wè?tè) walks over to the men with a bowl of food. The moment the men see her coming with her bowl, they stop their racing activities, and the losers are relieved of their need to challenge once more to save face.

In the Ghosts' summer-long ceremonial, when members of the male initiates' two foot-racing teams sprint from the village out into the savannah, they might keep racing on indefinitely, it is said, each side determined to win. However, to stop the excessive enthusiasm of these young initiates, the two young ceremonial girls associated with these initiates' groups as classificatory wives suddenly appear standing stark naked in the middle of the racing path. This view of exposed female genitalia stops the racers in their tracks.

Consequently, it should not be surprising that remnants of Timbira nations, when merging, carried out the "marriage" of their tribes by their warriors having sex with an especially honored woman of the other nation.

Canela warriors put down a Guajajara Indian uprising   In 1901 the authorities in Barra do Corda summoned the Canela to help put down an uprising among the Guajajara Indians against the Capuchin Convent at Alto Alegre, just west of Barra do Corda. The Guajajara had killed about 200 *civilizados,* including a dozen nuns and monks, and the local Brazilian military could not subdue them. When about 40 Canela warriors under Major Delfino arrived blasting away on their cow horns and shouting threats, terror struck the Guajajara, who surrendered swiftly to the traditionally feared and hated Canela, backed by Brazilian forces. The Canela had remained true to the promise made by their ancestors in 1814 not to fight any more against Brazilians, but to fight only other Indian tribes if summoned by Brazilian authorities to do so.

Executing a witch begins social disorganization   In 1903 the Ramkokamekra-Canela killed a Fox-Canela who was accused of witchcraft by the Ramkokamekra elders in the absence of the Fox elders. This placed Colonel Tomasinho, a Ramkokamekra, against Major Delfino, a Ramkokamekra with Fox kin, and caused a tribal schism which lasted 10 years. In the account of this event which I collected during the late 1950s, a Ramkokamekra woman who had refused to grant her sexual favors to the alleged Fox witch, Francelino Kaawùy, subsequently became ill and died. The Ramkokamekra thought Kaawùy had taken his revenge through witchcraft, so they tried and executed him.

Three young Ramkokamekra volunteers caught Kaawùy by surprise from behind as he was log racing with his team. Just as he was turning to pass the log from his shoulder to his teammate's shoulder, they hit him on the head with heavy clubs. This occurred near the Ponto village where I first visited the Canela in 1957. Canela research assistants proudly showed me the spot of the execution. Timbira tradition was to cut out the eyes of a witch who had been convicted and executed by a tribal council to deprive his ghost of sight. If a ghost could see, he could kill again. Then they made cross-shaped gashes in the executed witch's palms to immobilize them. Interment followed without further ceremony.[34] When news of the "murder" reached Barra do Corda, militia were sent to Escalvado to capture the Canela executioners, who surrendered willingly. They were tried in Barra do Corda, but after a number of months in jail were set free. The Canela complained that if they could not kill their own convicted witches, their world would come to a sorry end through witches' continuous murders.

Major Delfino moved with his Fox-Canela followers three streams to the east to the Cattle Stream, while Colonel Tomasinho moved one watercourse to the east to the Dove Stream (Map 3). After a few years, Major Delfino proposed a ritual he hoped would reunite the tribe. Each part of the tribe would install a ceremonial chief in the other part, so the two parts would come together to celebrate the installation and stay together. Unfortunately, memories of the execution were too strong, so this procedure did not succeed. The male line descendants of these two honorary chieftainships still exist today, and their reinstallation takes place every time the Canela put on the Facsimile Warriors' festival.

In this Facsimile Warriors' pageant, which is still performed, the Falcon society male members, 40 to 50 strong, march from the plaza to mock attack the platoon of Facsimile Warriors stationed on the outer edge of the boulevard. Both sides sing the rousing war song, the Apikrawkraw-re. The Formal Friends of the membership of both sides form the two front lines facing each other, the "enemy," holding clubs horizontally. The din and drama is truly momentous, as the two sides march slowly into position opposite each other. Just at the last moment, however, as the front lines are about to make contact with their clubs, father-to-son descendants of the two honorary chieftains insert themselves in the gap. They do not have clubs; the high honor of their ceremonial rank is sufficient to oblige the two sides not to fight. Nevertheless, several of each chieftains' Formal Friends insert themselves in the gap and face the two enemy ranks with clubs, keeping them apart. The opposing "hostile" ranks respect the inserted presence of the two honorary chiefs with their Formal Friends, but they sing louder than ever, stamping their feet rhythmically, raising a cloud of dust. Finally, the singing stops, the festival act ends, and the crowd disperses. The ferocity of this festival act is convincing evidence of the Canelas' former bellicosity. But it also shows the high value the Canela place on maintaining internal peace.

Ranchers massacre the Kenkateye-Canela   The tribal schism which started in 1903 continued until well after the death of Colonel Tomasinho in about 1911. In 1913 a drastic event caused the scattering and reuniting of both parts of the tribe under Major Delfino. The story from Olímpio Fialho, from old Canela research assistants, and from Nimuendajú is that cattlemen from the ranch of the Sítio dos Arrudas wandered into the Chinello village of the Kenkateye-Canela, population 150, ostensibly to "help celebrate a Kenkateye wedding." The Kenkateye were the furthest southwest of the three tribes known to backlanders by the Canela name.

When the approximately 50 cowboys from the Sítio arrived in the Chinello village, they were playing an accordion and leading a mule carrying a barrel of *cachaça* (home-distilled rum) and other equipment. After the gunmen got most of the Kenkateye drunk, they pulled out the other equipment from the mule pack—chains for tying the adult Kenkateye males to each other. These *pistoleiros* chained them and then deliberately shot about 50 Kenkateye men, while the women, children, and old men ran away to the Piranha tribe, the Apanyekra-Canela 15 miles to the northeast, or to the Krahó Timbira Indians 150 miles to the southwest. The Kenkateye had stolen too many cattle for their presence to be tolerated. The ranchers were determined to reinstate their dominance. Nimuendajú writes[35]:

> The Indian inspector of Maranhão had the murderers put on trial, but the jury of Barra do Corda unanimously acquitted them, and even today the residents proudly point out the members of the Arruda's troop who began the massacre.

When news of the massacre arrived at the two Canela villages, the Canela scattered and hid among the local stream-lining thickets for protection, thinking their turn for death would come soon. However, when the time for danger had passed and with Colonel Tomasinho no longer alive as an obstacle to unifying the tribe, Major Delfino brought the Canela together from the Cattle and Dove streams to form a new village on the Fox Stream. They spent about eight years in peace there before returning to their principal stream, the Santo Estévão, in about 1921. Major Delfino died in the village on the Fox Stream, and Faustino, the older Rop-khà (jaguar's-coat), took over the chieftainship in his place.

Without warfare, discipline starts breaking down   By the 1910s, the Canela were four generations away from fighting the settlers. Chief Tẽmpê fought them consistently, but chiefs White Clay, Foot's Wound, Roberto, and Delfino did not. Canela socialization and intergenerational authority was based on military discipline. When there was no enemy to fight, the discipline had to seem unnecessary to the young, so they began to challenge or disobey it. Such discipline did not make sense any more. In the next section we will discuss the deculturation resulting from these changes and from other outside forces coming into play throughout the 20th century.

CULTURE CHANGE IN THE 20TH CENTURY

As warfare and displacement gave way to a more settled existence for the Canela, other forces from the outside threatened their way of life. Influences from the Indian Service, the backland and urban cultures of Brazil, and visiting anthropologists and missionaries challenged their beliefs. Alternating periods of sufficiency and starvation, confidence and demoralization, buffeted the Canela. A messianic movement and temporary exile brought hopes and subsequent disillusionment. This section will deal with these events and pressures to show how tenacious Canela culture must have been to survive.

Weakening of discipline and loss of elders' authority   During the 17th century, Timbira tribes fought one another annually, and during the 18th century, as we have seen, they fought successive waves of settlers. The older generations of Canela enforced the discipline necessary to train the youth for military prowess. As the incidence of warfare diminished in the 19th and early 20th centuries, however, the youth did not see the urgency of the discipline and the elders lost much of their power to enforce it.

Loss of the community-marriage ceremony

The failure of the Canela to enact a marriage-by-the-community ceremony in 1913 and in 1923[36] was an indication that the authority of the elders was waning. This great occasion, which was supposed to take place about every 10 years, was the last of a series of ceremonies required to graduate a class of militarily trained young men between the ages of about 17 and 27. According to tradition, the age class members sat in their plaza location, waiting to be summoned one by one. When called, each graduate-to-be was led along the boulevard at the head of a long file of elders, his arms held on either side by two of their representatives, probably the youth's maternal uncles or grandfathers. Another elder, marching at the end of the file, sang a song that was special for the occasion. Each youth was led in this manner into the house where his wife or contracted-but-virginal bride lay on a mat waiting for him. Once in the house, the young man was ordered by his uncle or grandfather to lie down facing his bride. They were instructed to put their arms under each other's heads and to interlock their legs, holding each other closely. While in this embrace, each was asked if he or she cherished the other. After receiving positive answers, the couple's uncles admonished them to treat each other well, to avoid jealousy of each other's lovers, to raise many children, and to stay together at least until the last child was grown. The people of the whole village, who had been standing outside their houses, had seen the "uncles" escort their "nephews" into the houses of each young man's in-laws. They were thus all witnesses to the marriage bonds, ties that would be hard to break.

The process of marriage had begun when a girl gave her virginity to an unattached man, a man not attached to children "biologically" his own. The Canela say *ra-mã mẽ hikhwa* (already they lie-down-together) and *são casados* (they-are-married). The marriage-by-the-tribe ceremony was another important step in solidifying

An age class marches along the boulevard.

and finalizing a marriage. Before this stage of the marriage-solidification process, the young husband was not supposed to spend time in his wife's house except during the middle of the night. Then he sneaked quietly into her house in the dark and climbed swiftly up the notched pole ladder onto her platform bed under the rafters to spend part of the night with her, unseen by her relatives. The likelihood of pregnancy was reduced by the infrequency of the visits and the lack of privacy.

An advanced pregnancy was considered inconsistent with the model state to be exhibited at the time of the marriage-by-the-community ceremony. Couples in such a condition, since they were setting an untraditional example, were excluded from the occasion. With a baby coming soon, the couple did not need the reinforcement of the age class marriage ceremony to keep them together—the ceremony's principal purpose. A surviving baby solidified the marriage. After the ceremony, but without a baby, age class members would reinforce one another's marriages, bringing intransigent members back to their wives, as I saw occur in 1960.[37]

Each age class has a political leader, who marches at the end of the age class file (*mẽ-?kapõn-katê:* them-sweep-master: the leader who sweeps/strokes them [into cooperation]), and a ceremonial leader, who marches at the head of the file. The ceremonial leader, the *mam-khyê-?ti* (from-the-lead-position, pulling-them-along, greatly), was supposed to set the example for the age class of youths which marched behind him. The ceremonial leader of the class of 1923, however, had gotten his wife too obviously pregnant before the age class marital ceremony could be celebrated. Because these two individuals were no longer the model leaders of their age class, their marriage could not be sanctified and reinforced by the act of group marriage.

According to custom, the ceremonial leader of an age class does everything first, and his class members follow him. If the ceremonial leader with his great psychic, future-seeing powers could not go first in some activity of his group, it was considered inauspicious for the activity to take place at all. Thus the group marriage ceremony of 1923 was not held, and the Canela never attempted to put it on again. The ceremony was lost for good, a loss which was part of a widening gap between the generations.[38]

Loss of youths having sex with opposite-sex elders

Restrictions on diet and sex were part of the traditional training of youths. Just after reaching puberty, the time of first sex, a youth began serious discipline under the direction of a principal uncle, who chose to take on this responsibility. The youth had to avoid sex as much as possible and to have it mostly with older women when he did have it—women who were near or past menopause. In this way he would gain the strength of these older females and avoid the weakness and "pollutions" of the girls and younger women. This style of life continued for several years for young men, after which they could have sex with available women in their 20s, but not openly and frequently with the very young girls, even their young wives.

The members of a Canela age class during the year of their graduation are called the *pep-yê* (warrior-plural: warriors). As part of their military training, the youths are interned in cells for about three months, where they are supposed to grow strong by avoiding "pollutions" from consuming meat juices and contacting sexual fluids.

They eat large quantities of unpolluted special foods. At an advanced stage of the training, each warrior-in-training's "uncle" calls his "nephew" out of his cell, so the growth of the youth's body can be seen by the elders. In a loud scolding tone, the uncle demands to know if the youth is already strong enough to go out and kill the enemy, if they should appear in the savannahs outside the village. Since the traditional answer at this point in the series of ceremonies is no, the youth is re-interned. At the very end of the Warriors' festival, after the marriage-by-the-community ceremony has taken place, the youths are pronounced graduated and their age class is given a special name. They have become the warrior age class for the next 10 years, until the class behind them succeeds to their position.

Young women were also subject to some restrictions and discipline. Although women did not engage in combat, they had to be as mobile as the men in case of flight and strong enough to carry loads. After their first menstruation, girls underwent similar dietary restrictions and were required by their maternal uncles and their paternal aunts to have sex almost exclusively with men in their 40s to 60s to gain their physical and moral strength. Sex with younger men was believed to weaken young girls.

Thus we see that husbands were supposed largely to stay away from their young brides and have sex mostly with older women in special trysts outside the village or with women their age in the plaza at night. Young brides were supposed to have sex only rarely, and when they did, mostly with much older men. These customs tended to delay conception. The average age of first conception in 1970 was 15.75 years. This figure may seem surprisingly high since girls first had sex before menstruation, at ages 11 to 13, with men they liked who were about 10 years older and thereby became "married" to them. They had first sex so consistently *before* they menstruated that it was believed that the loss of virginity *caused* menstruation. The average age of first conception in earlier times was even older than 15.75 years. However, when young husbands were beginning to defy members of the older generation and starting to spend whole nights with their young wives, as sometimes was occurring during the 1910s, the young women began getting pregnant at an earlier age.

The younger Standing Water, the late Chief Standing Water's nephew, was a member of my research assistant council in 1960, 1964, and 1966, as was his wife's mother, Pyê-?khàl (earth-striped), in 1964 at age 70. Striped Earth was clear about how she had had sex mostly with much older men when she was an early to mid-teenager (from about 1906 to 1910) and about how her maternal uncles and paternal aunts prevented her from having much sex during this period. Standing Water was also clear about how he had gotten his wife, Star Woman, pregnant too early, and about how he had visited her house openly even during the daytime, long before her first childbirth. He had known he was leading his age class astray, away from ancient practices. Nevertheless, he and his wife had wanted each other too much, he explained, for them to be apart during the daytime. Moreover, the elders did little to enforce the tradition for the prenatal separation of spouses, since they were afraid they would not be obeyed. It is clear that adolescents had sex principally with older persons only because of the coercion of the older generations. When their authority began to weaken, this practice diminished. The young preferred to have sex with younger people.

One morning in 1960, I had an unusually revealing research assistant council meeting. My council consisted of four articulate men, who were the current leaders of four successive age classes: Standing Water (age 59), the older Thunder (50), Jaguar's Coat (39), and the younger Thunder (28). Standing Water (his age class's ceremonial leader), whose age class was interned roughly between 1913 and 1923, said:

> that he and his age class mates still had sexual relations mainly with older women and seldom with girls their own age during their two to three postpuberty years, and that sex with young girls had to be largely hidden from their . . . [maternal grandfathers and uncles] . . . for fear of drastic hazing and shaming in the plaza. For [the older Thunder, the political leader] of the age class being formed between 1923 and 1933 . . . , sex with older women was still the practice but relations with young girls were easier because the . . . [elders] caused less trouble. In contrast, the age class of [Chief Jaguar's Coat, their ceremonial leader], 1934 to 1940, only occasionally had sexual relations with the older women, and the age class of the younger [Thunder, their political leader], 1941 to 1951, *never* had sex with older women. [The younger Thunder] . . . said it just was not done anymore out of respect for their age.[39]

Loss of the hazing-shaming ceremony of youths

The hazing and shaming referred to above describes an act that frequently took place in the late afternoon in the plaza, when the men of the younger age classes danced in front of the wide row of singing women. The act's purpose was to instill respect/fear (*hũũpa tsà:* it-fear thing) in young men by shaming them directly before the female dance row and before most members of the tribe assembled around the edges of the plaza to enjoy the social sing-dancing as the sun was setting. If a young man was known to be having sex with young girls, eating polluted foods, or being generally uncooperative with the elders, an older man, who had the temperament of a fierce warrior, summoned the youth to appear before him in the following manner.[40]

The warrior, surprising the people, entered the plaza during a late afternoon's social sing-dancing, turning it into a ceremonial occasion. He brandished a weapon (most likely a shotgun), screeched vociferously at the supposed enemy, and declared he would be the first to go out to defend his people against the attackers should they approach the village. At the appearance of the warrior, the sing-dancing stopped abruptly and all conversation ceased. Silence descended upon the people, as they prepared to witness the drastic punishment of an uncooperative youth.

One of the warrior's close male associates swiftly took the weapon from him, because no one was allowed to approach the center of the plaza—a sacred place of mediation and enjoyment—with a weapon. Somewhat more subdued, the warrior proceeded to face the center of the female line of possibly 50 women spread in a single row across the lower part of the plaza. Then, shouting in harsh, threatening terms, the warrior, acting out the role of the unfortunate young man's principal uncle with its traditional disciplinary authority, challenged the youth to emerge from his age class's troop and come before the female line. Once the youth was standing respectfully before his "uncle," this warrior ordered his "nephew" to turn around to face the women and to prepare to suffer, but not flinch or utter a sound, if he was indeed a man. In earlier times, he was placed in front of the young girl he had had sex with so that she also was shamed.

An uncle disciplines his nephew before the female dance line.

The warrior might have stamped on the youth's insteps, yanked him off the ground by his sideburns, and given him a blistering lecture, describing his shameful infractions for all the women to hear. Before about 1915, research assistants said, the warrior might have scraped the youth's legs with rodents' teeth until they bled, whipped a sharp-toothed blade of grass through an armpit to draw blood, forced quantities of pepper into his mouth, and—worst of all by far—drawn back his foreskin for the assembled men and women to see the glans of his penis. Girls who had violated the norms of sexual and dietary restraint were shamed in this ceremony by having their leaf aprons torn off and their genitalia exposed.

In a world of almost complete nudity for both sexes, standards of modesty still existed. Before about 1910, when Canela women began to wear wraparound skirts, naked women kept their knees together at all times, so their labia minora could never be seen. Such exposure would be the greatest embarrassment and social disgrace. Everyone would talk about the details of what they had seen—mockingly and derisively—and about the carelessness of the offender, which was seen as social disrespect. Similarly for men, only their wives or long-term "other wives" might fleetingly see a glans without creating extreme embarrassment in both parties. Even husbands or "other husbands" were not to see the vulva wide open or their eyes would develop boils.

To this day, a man should never see the glans penis of another man. Men pull back their foreskins to wash the glans under the water of a stream in a way that must not attract attention. If a man or woman is careless, malicious gossip could spread throughout the community. Then a little niece of 8 years could remind her uncle in a customary joking context that so-and-so had seen his glans and that it was green, purple, or some other embarrassing color or distorted shape, and he would have to laugh with her. Nephews might tease their aunts if their genitalia had been seen exposed, naming the viewer.

The shaming ceremony in the plaza effectively enforced the authority of the elders over the youths. Its practice began to wane by 1915, and it had to be abandoned completely after 1940. The reason for the complete loss of this ceremony was quite simple. Indian Service agents and their families came to watch the afternoon sing-dances, but because they could not tolerate the "barbarities" sometimes inflicted on youths on these occasions, their presence discouraged the practice.

Impact of outsiders on the Canela in the 1930s and 1940s   The first Indian Service agent to live with his family by a Canela village was Castello Branco, who arrived in 1938. Because of his fierce nature and his willingness to use guns, he convinced several backland families to move entirely off the Canela lands, which was a great service to the Canela. However, Castello Branco did not become involved in Canela life, as did his successor, Olímpio Martins Cruz, who arrived with his family in 1940.

Loss of childless women sleeping with men in the plaza

Another important traditional practice was lost suddenly, around 1940, because of Indian Service presence. After their postpubertal period of seclusion and restrictive practices, mid-to-late adolescent women without children slept in the plaza, enjoying sex—often sequential sex—with the men of the opposite age class moiety[41] from their husbands'. A woman's husband would be on one edge of the 50-yard wide plaza and she on the other edge, thereby avoiding sexual jealousies. However, the Service personnel of the early 1940s emerged frequently from the post building in the early morning to roam around the village, observing extramarital relationships and casting shame on the "culprits" the next day. The Canela do not want to offend individuals they like and have to deal with, such as these Service personnel, so women without children simply stopped sleeping in the plaza.

Nimuendajú reinforces Canela's belief in themselves

The presence of another individual in the tribe, the anthropologist Curt Nimuendajú, had major consequences for the Canela. Nimuendajú studied the Canela during six summers between 1929 and 1936, and his magnum opus on them, *The Eastern Timbira,* was published in English in 1946.[42] Nimuendajú's influence was generally positive; he helped the Canela to feel proud of their traditions and to believe that what they were doing was right. Nimuendajú especially supported their festivals, ceremonies, and life cycle rites. He learned about their extensive extramarital practices but left the Canela with the impression that he disapproved, thus reinforcing their stereotype of Brazilians as necessarily disapproving of extramarital sex. His presence led to their concealing such practices from outsiders even more completely than before his visits.

Nimuendajú encouraged the Canela to put a monetary value on their festivals and material artifacts. They began to expect to receive a number of head of cattle for performing a festival or a high price for an artifact. The travels of Canela chiefs to large Brazilian coastal state capitals, where they sold their artifacts for high prices and were honored with expensive presents, also taught the Canela to expect and demand prices from urban visitors that were far out of line with local market values.

At the time of his final departure in 1936, Nimuendajú recommended that the Indian Service employ his principal Canela helper and horse and mule train packer, the older Thunder. The Service did so in 1938 and began a trend of employing individual Canela as fully salaried Indian Service employees. By 1957 six Canela males were employed in this way, including the two principal chiefs, Jaguar's Coat and the older Thunder. Indian Service control of the Canela was thus increased, and monetary values became greatly exaggerated in Canela thinking and expectations.

Nimuendajú's most important recommendation to the Indian Service was that the Canela not be allowed to maintain lasting schisms, like the one which sundered the tribe between 1903 and 1913. A tribal schism between his last two visits in 1935 and 1936 taught Nimuendajú how damaging they were for Canela morale and for economic self-sufficiency. The Canela scattered from the village on the Santo Estévão that they occupied in 1935 when smallpox broke out there and killed the principal chief, the older Standing Water. His successors divided the tribe, taking part to the Cattle Stream and part to the Dove Stream (Map 3). Nimuendajú, through his great prestige, succeeded in summoning them to put on a Fish festival in a new village on the Fox Stream, halfway between the two other streams, thus reuniting the Canela. Later, in 1939, they moved back to the Ponto area on the Santo Estévão.

If the Canela are not together in one community to discuss and solve problems in the plaza meetings of the elders every morning and evening, problems fester. Vicious rumors fly back and forth between the two villages. I experienced this in 1957, when a farm community in the Baixão Preto area was recognized as a new village. This schism was really part of the procedure of succession to the tribal chieftainship. The last old-style chief, Doroteo Hàk-too-kot (falcon-chick-green), had died in 1951 in the Ponto village, and several potential leaders were quietly striving to take his place. In 1957, the Indian Service sent a new Indian agent to the Baixão Preto farm huts and appointed the older Thunder as the new chief of the village there. Thus, I had young Chief Jaguar's Coat, Green Falcon Chick's successor, in the Ponto village and the new Chief Thunder in the new Baixão Preto village to reckon with, both of whom were my Informal Friends. This relationship allowed me to joke with and get along with both chiefs. From my neutral position I could see how reputations were ruined in both villages by politically and personally motivated rumors.

Further shocks to Canela culture in the 1950s   The year 1956 was another landmark for Canela change, due again to an Indian Service action, this time on the national rather than on the local scene, and to the economic growth in Brazil in general, which was expanding from the great coastal cities into the interior.

Indian Service turns from paternalism to self-reliance

Anthropologists at the top federal level of the Indian Service in Rio de Janeiro changed its policy from what they called "paternalism" to "self-reliance." From 1956 onward, Indians were supposed to raise foods for themselves instead of receiving handouts each year. From 1940 to 1956, the Canela were given considerable quantities of cloth, shotguns, shot, gunpowder, lead, salt, and even staples such as manioc flour and rice by the Indian Service. After 1956, Indians were still to receive medicines free, but were to buy other supplies with the proceeds from selling their crops. Unfortunately, the Canela had become so dependent since 1947 that they were not sufficiently motivated and organized to produce enough crops to last the year. Because of their loss of control over the age classes, the chiefs could not dispatch them to work in the fields, as they had formerly. Instead of organized self-support and individual hard work, the Canela had come to rely on the help of the Indian Service, especially during the lean months of their agricultural cycle: October, November, and December. By January, some new crops could be harvested, but the principal crops matured in April and May. During my two stays in 1957 through 1960, I heard a number of complaints against the Indian Service about how the *civilizado* was no longer living up to the promise of Awkhêê, who had guaranteed the *índio* full support in return for the use of the shotgun.

A successor to the Emperor Dom Pedro II (Awkhêê) as culture hero to the Canela was Marshal Cândido Rondon, the founder in 1910 of the Indian Service. He received a Nobel peace prize for his work among the Brazilian Indians. Rondon's death in 1958 left the Canela without a culture hero in the national capital of those days, Rio de Janeiro, to look after their interests. Groups of Canela males had been accustomed to traveling free to Rio de Janeiro, visiting their protector Marshal Rondon, receiving countless presents such as cloth and shotguns, and returning on a Brazilian Air Force plane to Barra do Corda.

A new bridge gives trucked commerce access to the area

The year 1956 was a landmark in regional change for an additional reason. This was the year the first substantial bridge was built over the Alpercatas River to the southeast, so trucks could enter Barra do Corda from the earlier-developed Brazilian Northeast (Map 2). Previously, only mule trains, small boats coming up the Mearim River from São Luis in the north, or small airplanes reached Barra do Corda. Before 1956, differences in material culture between the backlanders of the Canela region and the Canela themselves were not overly conspicuous. After 1956, however, and especially by 1960 with the opening of Brasília as the new national capital, the gap in material culture between the Canela and the *civilizado* began widening rapidly. When I arrived in Barra do Corda for the first time in June 1957, inhabitants proudly pointed out their new heavy furniture and gas-run refrigerators and stoves, all transported by truck from the Northeast. By 1959 these items were arriving in the backland communities of the Canela area.

Canela turn to believing the *civilizado* way is better

The Canela of Nimuendajú's time still believed in themselves and their cultural values. Nimuendajú fostered this belief, even talking to the Canela against the backlander to reinforce the Canela faith in their own traditions. Nimuendajú reports[43] that 20 Guajajara Indians of both sexes came to visit the Canela in 1930, hoping to make friends with them. When the Guajajara men could not take off their clothes to dance and race in the daily festivities, and could not go swimming naked, the Canela realized how completely different the Guajajara were. The Canela during the 1930s were still confident in their belief in male nudity, especially in the sacred center of their plaza during a formal meeting of the elders. During the late 1950s, I often saw old members of the Council of Elders remove, out of respect, the square of cloth hanging from their belt to cover their genitals just as they were stepping into the plaza.

During the late 1950s, however, the Canela were beginning to lose confidence in their way of life. For the first time, fathers cut trucks and airplanes out of the pulp of buriti palm frond stalks as toys for their sons. Mothers bought plastic dolls in Barra do Corda for their daughters instead of providing the traditional dolls of buriti stalks with tucum string girdles and breasts of beeswax. By 1959 the Canela started to dance in the couples-embraced manner of backlanders, and by 1960 Canela men were buying shirts, long pants, and shoes, and women were buying blouses, skirts, and sandals to dance properly in the backland style.

When I arrived in 1957, Canela spoke of the backland life as stingy, mean, and unenjoyable; but by 1960 I saw that backland culture had become fashionable and Canela traditions were felt to be inferior. This fundamental change had been going on inexorably for five decades: From 1910 to 1940, the elders were losing their authority to control the adolescents. In the late 1940s, general demoralization was depriving people of energy to plant sufficient crops. In the mid-1950s, the Indian

Service "reneged" on Awkhêê's promise of special status, and in the late 1950s new proof of the *civilizado's* overwhelming material superiority kept arriving in Barra do Corda and the Canela backlands. In 1957 backlanders danced to the music of a fife and violin; by 1960 they required city-made accordions for their *festas.* By 1960 the Canela, who watched these *festas,* had become more conscious of the Brazilian world, and they were accepting and liking it.

The messianic movement of 1963   In 1962, for the first time since 1947, the Canela produced a crop surplus. In 1947 Olímpio Cruz, the much-loved Indian Service agent, left the Ponto village post for higher duty in Barra do Corda and eventually São Luis. The forceful Olímpio Cruz had, in effect, taken over the leadership of the Canela himself, and for seven years he had led the Canela age classes in extensive work on the family farms, producing crop surpluses. The problems resulting from such effective outside help surfaced when he left, because neither the succeeding Service agents nor the Canela chiefs, Green Falcon Chick and Ku?khrã-tsà (honey-bee thing), had enough force of character and leadership ability to make the Canela produce sufficient crops.

Maria Castello, the prophetess, sits in the middle of the front row of a group of women.

Solution to life through extensive agriculture and work

The surplus in 1962 occurred essentially because the younger Thunder, 30, had absorbed, adopted, and accepted much of the *civilizado* approach to life as well as the self-reliance for Indians recently promoted by the federal Indian Service. In 1958 he had even called a newborn nephew Kupẽ-ʔkhĩn (*civilizados*-likes). The younger Thunder, my principal research assistant and helper, understood that to restore high morale to his people he had to help them become agriculturally self-sufficient again. This meant exhorting and leading them into producing larger family farms, as the old-time chiefs had done, or into producing a great collective community farm—a new approach. For this latter purpose, the younger Thunder developed a novel relationship with the head rancher, Messias, in the ranching community of Leandro, 30 miles to the east. Canela will not work on a collective farm that is away from their family farms unless they are fed during the noon rest period. Thunder solved this problem by getting Messias to advance him beef on credit to eat during the lunch periods of these farm working days. Later, Messias took half the harvest in payment for the advanced cattle. This procedure worked so well in 1962 that the Canela began to enjoy the luxuries of good living again and began to want even more. In the classic pattern of rising expectations creating ever greater frustration, however, the stage was being set for a drastic expression of the Canela's deeper discontent.

Solution to life through mythic transformations, prophecy

In late January of 1963, a woman around 40 called Maria Castello Khêê-khwèy (no translation) had what seems to have been a psychic experience. She was working in her family field during the heat of the noonday sun when the fetus in her womb began to communicate with her. Apparently, the kicking of the fetus was "understood" by Maria. The dialogue went like this in an account taped from Maria in the backyard of Olímpio Cruz's house in Barra do Corda in June 1964:

FETUS: *Mother, it is hot. I want to go home.*

MARIA: *What is that?*

FETUS: *Mother, this is me, your daughter. It is hot; I want to go home.*

MARIA: *Who are you?*

FETUS: *I am your daughter, Kràà-khwèy (dry-woman), and it is too hot out here in the field. I want to go home, where it is cool.*

MARIA: *Wait, while I finish weeding this line of manioc.*

DRY WOMAN: *Mother, we must go soon, because father has just killed the small kind of armadillo and a cutia [a large rodent], so we must be ready with a pot of hot water to cook the meat.*

MARIA: *Let's go home.*

When they had arrived home and had boiling water ready, Maria's husband, I-khè (my-stench), arrived, indeed, with the small kind of armadillo and a cutia. It was because the fetus had predicted accurately that Maria began to believe her fetus was someone very special who must be obeyed. Several nights later, Dry Woman appeared to Maria from outside the womb as a girl of 10 dressed in the Canela style. Now fully convinced of Dry Woman's reality, Maria went to her uncle with the news, and the uncle presented her case to the elders in the plaza. Dry Woman's prediction was that the culture hero Awkhêê was going to come again on the 15th of May to join her, his sister, in saving their people, the Canela. On May the 15th, Awkhêê was to put an end to the current world dominated by the *civilizado* and bring in a new world governed by the Canela. The *índio* would be living in the cities, driving the trucks, and flying the airplanes, while the *civilizado* would be living in the forests, hunting game with the bow and arrow. Awkhêê's original contract of the mid-1800s would be reversed because the *civilizado* had not kept up his end of the bargain; he was no longer supporting the *índio,* giving him everything he needed.

With the elders convinced also, Maria began to take control of the leadership of the tribe, gradually displacing the elders and the chiefs but always acting on instructions from Dry Woman. Maria's first move was to join the various farm communities and villages of the tribe, which by 1963 numbered four. She had made her predictions before the elders of the village called Aldeia Velha, so she moved with these people to the Campestre village, where she won the people over in two days. There she danced with all the males present, including male babies, in the backland embraced manner, signaling the pro-*civilizado* nature of her movement. She also started appointing individuals to membership in her group of special followers, her "employees."

Prophetess defiles the chief's daughter to assume full power

The political chiefs of the tribe were in the way of Maria's total assumption of power. Maria effectively challenged and eliminated the power of the first tribal chief, Jaguar's Coat, who was in Campestre, in a novel way. She ordered her new male "employees" to carry around Jaguar's Coat's oldest daughter, Pep-khwèy (war-woman), standing on their shoulders. This appeared to be an honor at first, as it was in several festivals. However, Maria eventually ordered the men carrying Woman Warrior to put her feet on the shoulders of two different males, to pull off her wraparound cloth, and to spread her legs so that all those close by could see her inner genitalia—the greatest embarrassment for a Canela woman. Dry Woman had ordered this, Maria said.

This display of power crushed any resistance to Maria's assumption of leadership. If Maria could insult the first chief's daughter, and thereby her father too, in such an extreme way, she could be expected to do almost anything to further her purposes and those of Dry Woman. Everyone had to fear her. Moreover, Woman Warrior was a woman of ceremonial high honor, an ex-girl associate of the Warriors' festival's male graduating age class of her adolescence. Thus, Maria was demonstrating that she did not respect or accept the Canela ceremonial hierarchy any more than she did the political hierarchy. She had killed two birds with one stone: male political power and female power held through high ceremonial honors. Since Canela women had no social structure on which to base their leadership of the tribe, she had to create a new power base. This base was her small group of carefully selected employees, who followed out the commands of Dry Woman by inflicting sexual embarrassments and other punishments on uncooperative individuals of both sexes.

After two days in Campestre, Maria marched with its inhabitants and those of Aldeia Velha to the village of Baixão Preto, where they held the first all-night dance in the backland/*civilizado* style. The following day Maria, with most of the women, walked from Baixão Preto to the principal Canela village of Ponto. In one version of the story, her employees shielded Maria from the sun with palm fronds while she rested and sucked oranges in several places along the way. In another version, Maria walked on a trail of palm fronds as she entered the village. Once in Ponto, she sat on a stool in the center of the plaza, the men's spot, waiting for the two men's teams racing with heavy logs.

Maria's prophecy: The Canela will live in the cities

After the men arrived and before Maria dismissed them to go to their houses, they had to listen to her talk on the prophecy of Dry Woman: Awkhêê would come down from the sky on May 15 to change their world around to be like that of the *civilizado*. However, for this to occur, she said, they would have to dance all night long every night, to please Awkhêê, to assure that he would come. The people also had to give her their possessions to pay for the feasting. If they gave her 10 cruzeiros, they would automatically receive 10,000 cruzeiros on May 15. If they wore a palm straw band on their wrist all the time, a wristwatch would appear there. They were to dance in the Canela style on week days, but in the embraced style of the *civilizado* on weekend nights. If they absented themselves from these dances, or appeared not to enjoy them, Awkhêê would be displeased and might not come down to save them.

The compulsory nightly dancing started in Ponto in March, and people began giving her their possessions so she and her employees could provide food to keep the cult going. Maria's employees punished young Canela if they did not dance every night. Nevertheless, members of the oldest generations, the strong shamans, and the two older displaced chiefs, Jaguar's Coat and the older Thunder, exempted themselves without incurring punishment. Some of them left to live elsewhere, especially in Baixão Preto.

Maria required her employees, and those who were her faithful followers, to file by her house each morning to stoop and kiss her belly as she sat on a stool just outside her door. In this way her followers were paying homage to Dry Woman in her womb, and Maria could tell who was loyal. Canela research assistants spoke of kissing her (*beijando ela*) in Portuguese, but sniffing her (*amẽ ku?pã*) in Canela, which confused me until I realized that there was no word for "kiss" in Canela. Canela lovers do not kiss, but they sniff each others' face, neck, and shoulders, avoiding lips because of unpleasant breath.

Maria commandeered the large palm thatch house of the father of a ceremonial Wè?tè girl and installed her family and her employees in it. It had a thatch-covered but open-sided dance floor, a room for her employees off the raised pounded-clay dancing place, and a room along a corridor for her two lieutenants. Then, further along the internal corridor, they constructed a private room for Maria, a luxury unheard of among the Canela, and an additional room for her parents and daughters. Maria summoned from Barra do Corda the young son of Chief Jaguar's Coat, Likes Food, who was studying in the convent there. He was to be her new husband. My Stench, with whom she had no children, was summarily dismissed. Thus, Maria and Likes Food presided over an establishment the size of which the Canela had never seen in any of their villages. Presents poured in from families who hoped to gain high posts in the new world, and these presents paid for ample feasts.

Indian Service personnel complained later to me that to gain entrance to the inner sanctum of Maria they had to pass through an inspection line of her employees, then of her lieutenants, and finally of Likes Food, her new husband. Service employees said Maria and Likes Food had set themselves up like a king and queen. Maria took on as her employees only prestigious individuals of the age class in their 20s and early 30s. The younger Thunder was not one of her two lieutenants at the start, but later became her principal officer.

At first Maria forbade stealing the cattle of ranchers, an old Canela custom, but later a strong male leader, Macaw's Bone, prevailed upon her to send youths after cattle to keep the dancers fed. A powerful shaman, the older Deer's Nest, told the Canela that when Maria allowed youths to hunt cattle, God in Dry Woman departed and the Devil entered the body of the fetus.

On May 13, two days earlier than predicted, Maria's child was stillborn, a deformed male instead of a female. The entire community was in shock and mourning. Maria almost died because the afterbirth was slow in detaching. The dead baby was buried behind the house of its mother, according to custom, but Maria experienced powerful dreams that night which caused her to require a special burial for the baby. In the morning the baby was disinterred and transported from hand to hand from behind Maria's house almost to the central plaza by a long file of followers. They were waiting their turn to pass on the special entity who, Maria pronounced, was going to return if everybody behaved in the right way. "The little baby" (*o bebêzinho*) was said to be very light and transparent, as if all the moisture of its body had evaporated—a mystery.

In the grass to the left of the path from Maria's house to the plaza, Maria's followers swiftly erected a small mausoleum of tied sticks and molded clay bricks, about three by four feet and five feet high. They placed the corpse on a platform inside this structure, which had a window for the followers to look in to see the small shrouded figure. Maria required her followers to pay homage in this way every morning for a number of days. I visited the remains of this structure in 1970, having walked from the new Escalvado village to the abandoned Ponto village of the messianic movement, to find it mostly melted down by the rain. Later, the Canela referred to the old Ponto village as the place of Maria's deceit (*Khêê-khwèy ?hêy tsà: Maria's mistake place*).

After the stillbirth, the younger Thunder helped Maria reformulate her prophecy: that Awkhêê would come down from the skies with Dry Woman later, when the Canela had danced enough and were sufficiently obedient. This time, wisely, no date was set. Many older Canela began to doubt Maria and Dry Woman at this time and left Ponto for the other villages.

Sex-oriented punishments used to maintain control

Maria had to order her employees to administer punishments more frequently than before the stillbirth because even youths were beginning to doubt her authority and the source of her power, Dry Woman and Awkhêê. Uncooperative individuals of either sex were made to sit naked for about half an hour on the uprighted cross-section of a buriti palm log, which has natural spikes capable of piercing the skin and drawing blood if the sitter changes position carelessly. Uncooperative young men or women were tied naked to a post on the dance floor, while the young of the opposite sex were ordered to pass by and yank out pubic hair. Uncooperative young women sometimes were ordered into a side room and onto a platform bed, where several unrelated young men could have sex with them in turn. If women resisted they were carried in and tied down to the bed. Extremely uncooperative young men were ordered down onto the sand off to the side of the plaza dance line at night, where they were obliged to have sex with several young women in turn. The women sat on top of the men—a totally uncustomary position for the Canela. A painfully shameful punishment for either sex was to be ordered to commit incest with distant kin or Formal Friends. Maria had effectively distorted customary sexual practices of the extramarital sex system and turned them into punishments. Likewise, marriage to distant kin or Formal Friends was customarily possible when the participants renamed their relationship. That custom could become punishment is one of the strangest reversals and conundrums of the messianic movement. These customs in their earlier forms are discussed in detail in following chapters.

Ranchers attack the Canela to stop cattle theft

Once the messianic prediction was reoriented and accepted, the cult dancing and cattle rustling continued until July 7, 1963. On this day, the leaders of a backland town, 30 miles to the east of Ponto village, employed a professional thug and 10 men from a neighboring município to come and lead the attack against the cattle-stealing Canela.

The ranchers' men burned Campestre to the ground, killed one Canela male, Khen-khũm (hill's mist), and wounded another, Aytsê (decorated-one). Faced with this attack, the younger Thunder took firm control of his people in the Aldeia Velha community. Thunder sent two runners, Burnt Path and Tsêp-khà (bat's-breast), to Barra do Corda to inform the Indian Service personnel about the disaster. Thunder also posted sentinels around Aldeia Velha to provide warning against the next attack. Then Thunder led a young male group to collect cane for arrows in the hills. They had turned over their guns to Maria for favors in the predicted new world order, which she had sold for food to help keep the daily dancing going.

The Canela were ready when the follow-up attack by 200 backland men came on July 10. Sentinels warned of the imminent arrival of the enemy, so the younger Thunder ordered the women, children, and old people to abandon Aldeia Velha and to hurry across the adjacent São Vicente Stream and through its jungles. These savannah stream thickets are impassable except through machete-cut tunnels and foot bridges over swamps. As most of the Canela streamed through the narrow passage, a dozen males kept the ranchers' men at bay. They used arrows primarily, but Hàkrît's (falcon's-sight's) famed two-barreled shotgun I had given him as my brother was said to have been effective, as was a pistol stolen from the gunmen during the July 7th skirmish.

The defense was completely successful, saving about 150 lives. Nevertheless, a dozen Canela males led by the fierce older Tààmi, 48, dashed from the thickets' shelter in the early afternoon's heat, hoping to surprise and kill *civilizados*. The ranchers and farmers, who were resting and hiding behind remains of the burned straw houses of the village, rallied and shot down three Canela, who were dodging bullets in the open as if they were arrows. The warriors had not intended to defeat the ranchers' men, but just to kill a few and bring back a hat or gun as proof, according to ancient tradition.

Thus older Tààmi (*to hààmi:* do-it bury) and two others his age, Khen-tùk (hills-dark) and the older Krôô-pey (pig-good), were killed unnecessarily. Their actions were reckless but completely within character for Canela warriors. The fifth Canela killed was a feeble 80-year-old man, Yàt-roy (potato-dodger), who was returning to Ponto village with a younger friend. They knew nothing about the earlier attack on Campestre and so did not run on seeing horsemen coming from backland communities to the west. Potato Dodger was gunned down where he stood, but his companion managed to evade bullets and get away. The Canela toll was five killed and six wounded. The ranchers lost one man later to an arrow wound which became infected.

Indian Service heroism saves the Canela people

The Indian Service personnel of Barra do Corda rose to the occasion. The head of the local service, Sr. Pedro Lemos, got the mayor of Barra do Corda to accompany him in a jeep with three Service employees, Virgílio Galvão, Bento Viera, and a Canela, the younger Bury It, driven by the professional driver, "Mocinho." They arrived too late to avert the July 10 attack on Aldeia Velha, but soon enough to save the Canela from the third attack. When they stopped at the ranchers' military post on the dirt road between Leandro and Aldeia Velha, the ranchers tried to pull Bury It from the jeep to his certain death, but the Service personnel and the mayor prevented it. The ranchers had to let the jeep pass through their lines out of respect for the mayor of their município (township), Sr. Edison Falcão da Costa Gomes. Once released, they drove the jeep over the closed savannah grasses 15 miles to Ponto village, where the Canela were hiding in the thickets along the Santo Estévão Stream.

The mayor, Sr. Lemos, and the driver dropped off the others at the village and returned to Barra do Corda by the roundabout way of Leandro. Few Canela were in the village, so the Service employees had to round them up before they could lead them north out of their lands to the safety of Barra do Corda and its relative good will toward the Indians. A forced march was in order, because the Service personnel had overheard that the ranchers planned to cut off the Canela escape at the halfway point to Barra do Corda, at the small community of Ourives (Map 3). From there the ranchers would move south, spreading out and moving up the several Canela streams simultaneously, flushing Canela out of the thickets and shooting them down like game. The leaders were greedy for the Canela lands and some of the followers wanted the Canela women. To many of them, the *índio* was not entitled to his land because he did not produce marketable surplus foods as did the *civilizado*.

The younger Bury It, one of the tribe's best sing-dance masters, sang loudly as they walked northward downstream, ordering the Canela to come out of the thickets to join in the march to Barra do Corda and safety. He was especially motivated to lead with his singing, as his naming-uncle had just been killed by the ranchers. The Canela passed Ourives during the middle of the second night, with the federal Indian Service employees Virgílio and Bento walking in their midst. The backland *civilizado* could kill the *índio, o bicho do mato* (the beast of the forest), but the *civilizado* could not fire at the Canela in the dark, knowing that he might be killing Virgílio and Bento.

In the morning, trucks sent by the mayor met the Canela three-quarters of the way to Barra do Corda at the end of the dirt road. The Canela spent that night being fed and cared for near the city and the next day were transported by truck to the Sardinha Indian Service post on the Guajajara Indians' reservation. Unfortunately, Sardinha was deep in the dry forests. (These forests extend 75 miles to the northwest toward the Amazon River basin, where they become wet tropical forests.) Accustomed to the closed savannahs, the Canela could not adapt sufficiently well to the new environment.

A former Indian Service employee stated in 1991 that without the mayor's presence, the ranchers would not have let the jeep pass through their lines. He also stated that without the presence of Virgílio Galvão and Bento Viera among the Canela, while they were walking past Ourives in the dark of the night, the *civilizados* there would have killed many *índios*. Thus the Canela owe their continued existence to this compassionate mayor as well as to the courageous Indian Service personnel.[44]

Exile to the forests of Sardinha   By coincidental timing, I arrived with my wife in Sardinha three days after the Canela were relocated there. I have often wondered what I would have done if I had arrived among the Canela in their savannahs during, instead of after, their messianic movement. Would Maria have seen me as a threat to her movement and organized the Canela against me? Would I have foreseen the ranchers' attack and warned the Canela and the Indian Service personnel against it? If I had arrived just after July 7, what would I have done during the attack of July 10?

As it was, I arrived in Sardinha before the Canela had built any huts for protection against the climate. No rain falls there during July, so their efforts were aimed at providing protection against the noontime sun and against the cool early mornings. Much to my surprise, the Canela had already cut a round plaza out of the forest near the post buildings, and they had arranged their families around this plaza according to the customary order. Thus it was easy to find any of the families by remembering the order around the plaza back at Ponto village, where I had lived for 24 months during the late 1950s.

Maria was there in Sardinha, and some of the women had already attacked her physically, blaming her for the loss of their husbands and claiming that the story of

Dry Woman was a lie. Some men held off these angry women, probably saving Maria from considerable harm. Maria was thoroughly discredited in Canela eyes for having claimed that Awkhêê would divert the bullets if the ranchers attacked.

Information about the messianic movement was soon given to me by Canela friends I had worked with since 1957. One of the most exciting moments in my life of field research was when I began to realize, as bits of the puzzle fell together, that the Canela had experienced a full-blown messianic movement. I had studied such movements, but to find one in the field was remarkable. It was extraordinary luck for me that I happened to be on the spot so soon after the collapse of the movement. I would be able to obtain unusually fresh information on its activities from experienced Canela research assistants. Since I knew them already, they would tell me the truth instead of concealing matters from me, as they would do for a newcomer. Thus I was able to know what I should do when several critical situations occurred.

Crocker, the academic, became an activist

The first situation was when the accordionist of the cult dancing, Tsaa-hù (root's-seed), came to me one evening for encouragement to put on a *civilizado*-style dance. I saw quickly that my usual role as an observer and student of culture had to be put aside; lives were at stake. These dances had to be stopped for the good of the Canela. For the first time, I reported immediately what I had learned to the Indian

Canela in exile in the dry forests of Sardinha in 1963.

Service agent in Sardinha, who prevented the evening dance. We could not let the cult movement start again and incur the wrath of the settlers.

The second situation was when the Service personnel wanted to put all the blame for the movement on the younger Thunder. He was to appear in Barra do Corda to account for his behavior. They did not know about Maria's far more basic instigation of the movement. After a long talk into the night, I persuaded the Service agent, Sr. Antônio Nascimento, to send Maria into Barra do Corda instead, where she was kept for a number of months for her own safety and to be sure she would not start predicting again.

The third situation evolved out of my learning that the ranchers wanted the younger Thunder's life. I advised Thunder not to leave the Sardinha reservation and convinced him of the dangers he could face if he visited the local backland communities, where he had been intending to sell artifacts for food. He agreed to stay on the reservation and to send others in his place. I also wrote letters to the leading ranchers involved in the attack, whom I had met in the late 1950s, to explain that the Canela had experienced a religious cult movement, which was now completely discredited and unlikely to occur again. I also made it clear that the younger Thunder had not caused the movement, but that a Canela woman had been the leader, a woman now being held indefinitely in Barra do Corda.

I had been taught in the early to mid-1950s that anthropologists do not intervene. Their role was that of observer and student. Contributing their own actions would muddy the cultural waters: They would be studying the results of their own activities instead of the indigenous culture. Thus I felt ambivalent about the actions I had taken but convinced myself they were necessary to save Canela lives. Within the decade, however, anthropology would become so activist that anthropologists would feel morally obligated to help "their" people.

Adaptations of a savannah people to forest living

The five years in Sardinha appeared to be a disaster for the Canela. They were so demoralized that many of them preferred to do nothing rather than hunt and put in farm plots. The soils were harder, the thickets denser, and the trees larger, so putting in a farm took much more work. That the products of such a farm could be significantly greater, because of the richer soils, was a point that escaped most of the Canela. The benefits were too far away in time. Hunting appeared to be more difficult, but it really just required different procedures. Instead of tracking and running down game, hunting in the dry forests required knowledge of the game's habits and waiting for it to pass by. In any case, hunting and farming were seldom carried out successfully and the Canela were starving most of the time during 1963 and 1964, relying on handouts from the Indian Service. Many children died of diseases, especially dysentery, and many older people died at a younger age, often of tuberculosis. Extramarital sex became scarce because weakened women demanded meat before they would be generous. Canela men had to wear shorts for the first time in history, because the ubiquitous Guajajara women had strong sensitivities against male nudity. Nevertheless, the greatest Canela complaint was an aesthetic one: They missed the beautiful open vistas of the savannah countryside. To the Canela, the dark dry forests were gloomy and uninspiring. They languished for their homelands.

On the positive side, the young age class in its late 20s to mid-30s, led by the younger Thunder, learned how to till the soil and hunt in the dry forests and therefore produced ample surpluses by 1966 and 1967. They did not want to return to the poor savannah soils in 1968 and suffer the consequences. Moreover, the proximity of Barra do Corda only 15 miles away by road from Sardinha interested many of the younger Canela because they found there ready markets for some of their customary artifacts. The Canela were acquiring a new way of making money, fabricating artifacts by the hundreds: baskets, mats, whisk brooms, and so on, and even decorated bows and arrows for tourists.

Some of these sales could be made right in the Canela village at Sardinha, because Barra do Corda residents and tourists came to see how the Indians lived. The tourists from other cities were more respectful of the Canela than were the backlanders and Barra do Corda citizens, so the Canela began to develop a new sense of their special worth. Tourists were often good for their morale, strange as this might seem.

By mid-1966, word came from the Indian Service in Brasília that the Canela could return to their homelands in small groups. Some families did, and by late 1968 the entire remaining community was required to return. The Canela returned to their savannah homelands as quite a different people from the ones I had known during the late 1950s. The most obvious difference was that no men went naked any more, unless they were old and inside their own houses. (Women continued to go topless in the village and in the backlands.)

The deeper difference between the late 1950s and the late 1960s, however, lay in the contrast between the messianic solution to the future and the agricultural solution. The latter was attempted and successfully demonstrated by the men of the second youngest graduated age class during the dry forest stay. The messianic solution relied on traditional myths and on faith in the transformations found in these myths. Since Awkhêê had changed himself into a jaguar, anaconda, falling leaf, gnat, and cinder in earlier times, and since he had created the world of horses, mules, chickens, pigs, and cattle ranches of the *civilizado,* surely he could come again and change the Canela world once more, switching the roles of the *civilizado* and the *índio.*

The alternative demonstrated by the younger Thunder in 1962 through his advanced credit relationship with Messias of Leandro, and through the agricultural successes of his age class in Sardinha, was a solution based more on the backland way of life than the Canela one, at least economically. Thus the profound difference between the Canela when I first knew them and in the late 1960s lay in their reliance on backland economics instead of on their traditional myths. The Canela had changed from believing they were culturally and morally better than the *civilizados* to believing that the urban *civilizados* were culturally superior to the Canela. But even though they now relied on backland agriculture more extensively, they still looked down on the backlanders' character and morals.

Outside influences from the 1970s onward   During the stay in Sardinha, low morale and hunger caused some temporary emigration from the community. The knowledge of the outside world which the returning emigrants brought back constituted an important influence during the 1970s. In the lean months of 1963 and 1964 (September through December), about 40 young men left to seek their fortunes elsewhere. These youths were mostly between 14 and 18 years of age, though one was in his late 20s. Only five of these youths stayed away permanently. Three from the same Canela family married in Recife and dropped all contacts with their people; their family does not know exactly where they are. One Canela was killed while traveling near Imperatriz and another was killed in Brasília. He had been working at a gasoline station.

Emigrants return bringing urban knowledge

The other emigrants all eventually returned, bringing influences from urban Brazil. One of the emigrants, Khrã-?tèy (headed-hard), acquired Protestant supporters in São Paulo, who sponsored him as a kind of missionary to the Canela. Hard Headed returned periodically during the 1970s to the Escalvado village, claiming that he would found a Protestant church there and that the Indian Service would empower him to take over the leadership of the Canela. Behaving in the customary manner, Hard Headed arrived with many presents for his family and others of significance. He then acted against custom by expecting to live off his family for many months. He showed off his city goods: clothing, Seiko watch, radio, tape recorder, and so on, and often got drunk. He boasted of the superiority of city ways.

Chief Jaguar Coat's son, Likes Food, spent two years studying in a convent in Barra do Corda, two years in another convent near Montes Altos 70 miles to the west, and one year in the military in São Luis. Likes Food returned during the 1970s speaking and writing excellent Portuguese. In 1979 his house had more urban items in it than any other, and in 1991 he built a house on the road leading out of the village to the west. He hoped to start a row of Canela houses along each side of the road in the backland style, but by 1991 only one other family had joined him.

Bat's Breast spent three years away from the tribe during the mid- to late 1960s. Bat's Breast worked in hotels as a cook's helper in Fortaleza and São Luis. He likes to help visitors establish themselves in Escalvado and is willing to be a temporary servant to them. His knowledge of urban living and Portuguese enables him to be of considerable help in this way.

Kuukhên (cutia: rodent) lived in The House of the Indian in Rio de Janeiro for more than a year and spent additional time away from his people. Quite urbanized, Cutia returned during the 1970s and is now the political leader of the age class in its 30s to 40s. He is the fourth political power in the tribe and surely will become a village leader some day. I suspect his group may eventually find some way to defy the elders in order to leave and found a more modern community of their own, some place on the Canela reservation. They would be open to suggestions for modern economic solutions.

All of the above young men (no women lived away from the community) and others like them brought back urban notions which have changed their values. While they still trust their traditional curers for certain purposes, they believe in modern medicines. While they still live out their ancient festivals, they nevertheless enjoy embraced, paired dancing. While they still like log racing, the young also play soccer very competitively. While some like to hear stories of their ancestors, they experience deep feelings at a Catholic service which they have adopted from the backlanders for use on Good Friday.

Another kind of external influence during the 1970s was the increasingly strong presence of the Indian Service. The first brick-and-cement, red-tiled house was built as the Service post in 1970. It has a large central room for meetings as well as several guest rooms. By 1974 a school house was built, by 1978 an infirmary, and by 1991 an Indian agent's house, all of the same substantial construction. By 1975 the post had a gas-run generator for electric lights and a radio station. The construction of these expensive buildings and services was convincing evidence to the Canela that the Service was committed to their support.

Indian Service's strong support

Sr. Sebastião Pereira, an excellent Indian agent, was assigned to the post in 1970. He won the confidence of the Canela by going to their houses daily with a basket of medicines rather than requiring them to come to him, as had been the practice. Sebastião soon conquered childhood dysentery and by 1975 he had eradicated tuberculosis. He trained a soccer team which soon had an undefeated season in the backlands. Sebastião went to the evening council meetings regularly and learned to understand the language well, though he did not try to speak it. He became one of the most highly respected Indian agents, along with Olímpio Cruz of 1940–47 and Virgílio Galvão, who walked with the Canela through the deathtrap of the backland *civilizados* at Ourives in 1963. As Olímpio Cruz had in the 1940s, Sebastião took over the leadership of the tribe, though he relinquished some of this power during the 1980s. Sebastião's efforts and force of character contributed immensely to the stability and growth of the Canela during the 1970s. Alcoholism was almost eliminated, by 1975 the post had an excellent trained nurse, and by 1978 a good schoolteacher. Between 1971 and 1978, the lands of the Canela were demarcated and became an official government reservation.

Effects of missionary presence

Another significant external influence of the 1970s was the presence of the missionary couple, Jack and Jo Popjes of the Summer Institute of Linguistics, or Wycliffe Bible Translators. They arrived in 1968, built a residence on the village circle in 1969, and were adopted by Canela families. I was not aware during the 1970s that they ever preached their beliefs to the Canela. According to their organization's rules, they were not supposed to do so until they had been there many years and could communicate adequately in the Canela language. From what Jack has told me, the Canela elders invited him to talk about Christianity in the plaza on Sundays during the 1980s. The Wycliffe missionaries believe that the word of God is better communicated to a people through a well-translated Bible than through preaching. Jack and Jo probably communicated their Christian beliefs through their personal behavior among the Canela over the course of 22 years. The Popjeses finished their translation of the Bible into Canela and published it in 1990. They had fulfilled their mission, and, after putting on a large festival to celebrate, they left the Canela for good, though they may visit every second year as friends.

It is very hard to estimate the effects on the Canela of the Popjeses' 22-year presence. To do so would require a number of months of residence and research among the Canela, which I hope to have in 1993. My three weeks among the Canela in 1991 were insufficient to be sure about anything of this sort. Whenever I asked a question that had something to do with the effects of the work of Jack and Jo, I received meaningless responses or denials. Whether or not my Canela research assistants were being defensive was unclear. I can say that there were no obvious transformations which could be attributed to the presence of Jack and Jo other than that individuals were occasionally reading the Bible in Canela. Nevertheless, there surely have been some subtle and significant cultural changes as a result of their presence and teaching. The Popjeses involved 60–100 Indians in learning how to read and write in Canela, thus significantly advancing the literacy of the tribe.

Effects of anthropologist's presence

When asked about the greatest influence my presence may have had on the Canela, I respond that an anthropologist cannot responsibly make such an assessment of his own work. But when individuals push me to give it a try, I remember the diaries that I had Canela individuals writing and taping for me between 1964 and 1979. In 1964 I paid three writers for their daily manuscripts, and in 1979 there were 12 individuals involved in writing and recording on tapes. Some wrote exclusively in Portuguese or Canela; others wrote in Canela one day and translated what they had written the next day. Some spoke community and personal news onto tape in Canela several times a month.

In 1964 only six Canela could write well enough in Portuguese to send simple messages. They had learned these limited skills from an Indian Service teacher, remembered simply as Dona Nazaré, between 1944 and 1948. She had learned enough Canela to teach in the language. Service teachers from 1948 to 1978—there was an intermittent flow of them—taught only in Portuguese and did not produce a single student who could write well.

I took three of Dona Nazaré's Canela writers and interested them in writing diaries for me, a procedure which these three continued until October 1979, except for a month off a year. Two of the three eventually became involved in translating, as did three other writers who entered my service in later years. My belief is that the almost continuous writing of diaries—especially the translating—trained the writers' minds, teaching them to analyze in a new way.

Hunter-gatherers involved in incipient agriculture like the Canela analyze and interpret tracks in the sand effectively. However, their customs may not enable them to analyze quantitative and qualitative concepts used in trade and social relations with their surrounding national societies. The Canela were faced with complex quantitative calculations and fine qualitative distinctions in their contacts with backlanders and urban Brazilians that they could not handle. However, after writing and translating diaries for years, a skill which requires making fine distinctions when trying to match Canela concepts with Brazilian ones, these diarists learned to think more along Western lines and to understand and handle their relationships with outsiders better. For instance, in the aboriginal Canela counting system, words exist

A Canela research assistant and translator works at his diary.

only for "one" (*pùtsêt*), "two" (*píyakhrut*), and "three." Their word for "three" really means "more than two" or "many" (*ncré*). For "four" and "five," Canela say *te quat* and *te cinc,* using the Portuguese terms for "four" (*quatro*) and "five" (*cinco*).

Thus, when I think of my most significant contribution to the Canela scene, my mind turns to my diarists and their contributions to Canela life. Such contributions are hard to assess, but whomever the Canela elders turn to as their first chief over the years would presumably be the person who could best manage their internal political and external social relations. Between 1981 and 1991, the Canela put in 10 new chiefs. All but two, Kô-rã (water's-flower) and the younger Deer's Nest, had been diarists for me.

Effects of Indian Service's activist

Between 1977 and 1980, the Indian Service placed a powerful activist, José Porfírio Carvalho, in the agency in Barra do Corda. His purpose was to make Indians aware of their unique value and their potential role on the national scene. He established a pan-Indian newspaper in Barra do Corda through which Indians of different tribes could communicate with one another.

This forceful and dominating Indianist lectured the Canela on the great worth of their culture and urged them to send delegates to national conferences. Since the Canela had a custom already, dating from the mid-1800s, of traveling to the great cities of Brazil, this Indianist's program of "bringing consciousness" (*conscientização*) to the Canela may not have been as extraordinary for them as for many forest-bound Indian communities in the Amazon basin. Nevertheless, this Indianist's work surely contributed to Canela self-esteem and encouraged Canela chiefs to travel to great Brazilian cities, such as São Luis, Belém, and Brasília, the seats of power over Indian well-being.

The Canela were joining the pan-Indian political activism that was developing in Brazil in the 1980s. The Canela were not as active as the Kayapó, who in 1988 protested and defeated the building of a dam on the middle Xingu River which would have flooded their lands. Nor were they as active as the Guajajara who, in November of 1992, took Brazilian hostages to protest a settlement on their lands. The Canela, in contrast, have engaged in more peaceful political activity. When Jean and I were staying in São Luis on our way out of Maranhão after our visit to the Canela in 1991, we thought we had said our farewells. But we heard a knock on our hotel room door and opened it to find the chief, Burnt Path, standing there. He had come to São Luis to participate in a conference. In fact, the Canela usually knew our whereabouts whether we were in São Luis or Barra do Corda. Whenever we ate in the outdoor restaurant of our hotel in Barra do Corda, Canela visiting the town would approach us with various requests. Their intelligence system was very effective.

The changing Canela view of themselves—a summary   Canela consciousness and awareness of their value and position in the national Brazilian society have changed remarkably since the time of pacification in 1814. At first, the Canela hid in a valley from their conquerors, whom the Canela saw as being likely to shoot them down on sight or sell them into slavery. Then the Canela mixed with the settlers as dependents in the Nas Pedras ranching community. The Canela saw themselves as being totally subject to settlers for their very survival. Thus they gave up their women and children to appease the whims of individual backlanders. Nevertheless, by the 1840s they had survived to gain their own lands on the Santo Estévão Stream, and the emperor of Brazil had issued a decree of amnesty and respect for Indians in general. The surviving Timbira tribes, including the Canela, made this decree over into a myth which made them a special people, protected by the Emperor, their own culture hero Awkhêê. While the *civilizado* was to protect and totally support the *índio*, the *índio* owed the *civilizado* the recognition of the latter's complete superiority. The idea that Canela inferiority and the outsiders' superiority were decreed rather than deserved left the Canela with their self-respect. They had fashioned a myth which was their social contract, the definition of their geographically settled but socially dependent, post-pacification world. The myth of Awkhêê must have taken shape by 1870 at the latest to have served its purpose so effectively.

The first chief of the settled era around 1835, Chief White Clay, accepted the Canela's new position in the backland world, probably because he had been brought up by backlanders in Nas Pedras. In contrast, their second chief, Foot's Wound, in the 1860s and 1870s, challenged the Brazilian authorities, probably because he and the Canela had not yet fully accepted the requirements of their new position. Chiefs Tomasinho and Delfino, from the 1880s to the 1910s, appear to have accepted the

Canela's new social contract fully, worked within it, and achieved considerable respect from the Brazilian backland and urban communities. The 1890s were a cultural high point and time of relative affluence for the Canela.

With the execution of a witch in 1903, which resulted in a community schism for 10 years, they began to experience annual economic deficiencies, partly because they were living on streams whose soils were far less fertile than those of the Santo Estévão. In addition, social disorganization, best understood through the concept of the "age gap," was beginning to set in. Youths were well aware by the 1910s that their traditional military training had no point, because there was no enemy to fight any more. Their great-grandfathers were prepared as warriors, but the new social contract of Awkhêê had stabilized their world, a world without warfare. Thus youths began to visit the houses of their wives before childbirth and stopped having sex only with older people during the several years after puberty. Youths started challenging the elders, who became hesitant about issuing orders only to have them disobeyed. Consequently, the group marriage ceremony was lost in the 1910s and 1920s, but the Canela social system stumbled onward, largely due to the momentum of the old ways, until the 1940s. Nimuendajú studied the Canela in the 1930s, their last decade of "traditionalism," before an onslaught of outside influences commenced. Thus the Canela had 100 years of relative peace and stability, from 1840 to 1940, during which they adapted fully to the world of their culture hero's social contract.

In 1940 the Indian Service agent Olímpio Cruz was a hero to the Canela, continuing Awkhêê's tradition of *civilizado* support with his generosity. But the very strength of his leadership deprived the tribal leaders of their ability to take over after he left the Canela in 1947. Sr. Olímpio's moral orientation prevented the continuation of the Canela's traditional hazing act, so the elders lost any remnants of power over the youths other than mild persuasion and ceremonial awards. For the same reason, women without children no longer slept in the plaza at night. By the 1950s, with their economic deficiencies resulting in endemic hunger from September through December, the Canela became seriously demoralized. Families necessarily spent from 20 percent to 50 percent of the year living by the houses of backlanders, sharecropping with them, a humiliating and deculturating experience. The Canela must have felt that they might no longer be Awkhêê's chosen and protected people.

Two events of 1956 further undermined Canela morale and provided them with a grievance, justifiable in their view. First, the Indian Service rescinded its policy of paternalism to Indian communities. Reinforced by the death of Rondon in 1958, this change in *civilizado* "generosity" made it appear to the Canela that the *civilizado* had reneged on Awkhêê's social contract. Second, the bridge across the Alpercatas River at Campo Largo was built, so material goods poured into the area, increasing the material culture gap between the *civilizado* and the *índio*. Thus the Canela found it even more difficult to hold onto their belief in their cultural superiority, as they had so convincingly done during the time of Nimuendajú.

Deserted by *civilizado* help, demoralized by seasonal endemic hunger, and diminished and overwhelmed by the Brazilian's culture, the Canela were ready to listen to some good news which would redress the wrongs they were suffering. Surely, Awkhêê would not forget his people.

The Canela still believed in remarkable transformations of their own. Culture heroes, such as Sun, Moon, Star Woman, and Awkhêê, had changed themselves into other entities and had transformed inanimate objects. Moon had even created death, and Awkhêê had moved a mountain. When the Canela prophetess, Maria, spoke within the context of these beliefs, many Canela were ready to believe her. She was bringing welcome good news—relief from misery. If the *civilizado* had reneged on the social contract, surely Awkhêê would reissue it in favor of the Canela, his chosen people.

The welcomed prophecy carried the force of "divine intervention" to many Canela. Maria had the political skills, the force of character, and the courage to exert power. She chose young male and female leaders wisely, so that she had total obedience from her group of "employees." She was able to use them to dominate the tribe through the fear of humiliating punishments. Thus many Canela turned away temporarily from relying on the efficacy of a broad set of mixed social beliefs, including *civilizado* and *índio* orientations, to relying on the efficacy of a narrow set of earlier beliefs, based on instantaneous world-transforming powers. The new model for the Canela was the *civilizados* rather than the ancestors. The Canela had come to discredit their old way of life and were caught between two worlds. They had come to feel that the Brazilian urban world was preferable to theirs, at least in certain important respects which had to do with material culture and social hierarchy.

The defeat by the ranchers on July 10, 1963, must have been psychologically devastating. Great hopes were shattered, five Canela lay dead, and the dry forests of Sardinha, after the move, were utterly depressing. Members of the age class of Chief Jaguar's Coat (in their 40s), and the older age classes, were too inflexible to adapt to the forests. However, the members of the age class of the younger Thunder (in their 30s) were ready to change, and they had a leader who had favored accepting the ways of the backlanders for at least a decade. Thus the youths were ready to open their consciousness to urban ways found in Barra do Corda, so close to Sardinha. The most important opening of consciousness was toward putting in larger and more productive farms, and as a result, some of the younger families experienced a touch of the affluence they had wanted to gain through the messianic movement. However, the great surpluses, lifting the Canela completely out of economic deficiencies, came in the mid- to late 1980s, again led by the younger Thunder.

In the 1970s and early 1980s, the Canela began to participate in pan-Indian cultural and political activities. Though they could not give up tribal animosities and rivalries, they nevertheless were aware of the benefits to be gained from some cooperation with other Indian nations.

NOTES

7. Pacification (*pacifição*) is the term used by Brazilians to refer to the process of bringing a warlike tribe under the peaceful control of Brazilian authorities, local or national. By "Brazilians" I mean peoples of direct African, European, and Native American origins, including peoples of mixtures of these origins who have grown up in or who have adopted one of the Portuguese-Brazilian national or regional cultures. I use "Indian" rather than "Native American," because this is the Brazilian practice. The Canela say they are *índios* (Indians) and are proud of it. The Canela are aware that they and their ancestors were Brazilian before the arrival of the "Brazilian" settlers. The Canela say, "*Sou brasileiro legítimo*": I am the real Brazilian. Thus, "Indian" refers to a cultural rather than a racial distinction.

8. These surviving Timbira tribes are the Canela (also known as the Ramkokamekra), Apanyekra (*apán:* piranha), Krahó (*kraa-hô:* paca's [a rodent's] hair), Krīkatí (*khrīīkati:* tribe-large), Pukobyé (*pùkhop-yê:* yam plural/people), Gavião (falcon), and Apinayé (no translation). (The Gavião are northwestern forest Pukobyé.)

9. Canela research assistants use *khrīī* (village) to talk about the unit of people which live in one of their villages. This same unit is their *nação* (nation), when they talk in Portuguese. I find it convenient to use "nation" and "tribe" interchangeably, except when I use "nation" for the great village unit of earlier times and "tribe" for the much smaller Canela village unit of current times. I prefer "tribe" to "community" because Timbira units, as I have come to understand them through studying Canela war stories with groups of Canela research assistants, were relatively isolated and self-sufficient, especially in contrast to the Kayapó or the Yanomami.

10. See Steward and Faron (1959:22–23) for the Gê and other linguistic groups of South America.

11. These linguistic terms are from Rumsey (MS). See W. Crocker (1990:57–59) for a summary account of the current Gê-speaking peoples.

12. The nations which were at peace with each other traded occasionally. They sent small trading groups to each other, just when they needed to do so, to obtain necessities for certain festivals. Thus, they traded more for ceremonial adornments such as resin, feathers, chalk, and purple body paint than for food. Their more regular inter-village (i.e., international) contact was made through raiding their enemies annually in June and July.

13. The "closed" savannahs, known to geographers as "cerrado," are a principal vegetational type of Brazilian landscape. Cerrados are found in the highlands between the great tributaries south of the Amazon. In contrast to the "open" savannahs of Kenya, the closed savannahs of Brazil are grassy with short trees of 5 to 30 feet standing 1 to 20 yards apart. Thus vision is limited, though passage anywhere through closed savannahs by horse or jeep is almost unobstructed.

14. North of Barra do Corda and Grajau are deciduous dry forests, which shed their leaves during October. The famous Amazonian tropical rain forests slowly begin to take shape 75 miles to the west and north, beyond the Pindaré River.

15. Curt Nimuendajú was born a German, but became a naturalized Brazilian. He is Brazil's foremost anthropologist of the first half of the 20th century, and his magnum opus was on the Canela, *The Eastern Timbira* (1946).

16. "Canella," which is written "Canela" in modern Brazilian orthography, was applied to three separate tribes by local Brazilian authorities during the last century: the Kenkateye (*khen-katê-yê:* mountain enemy plural), the Apanyekra (*apàn-yê-?khra:* piranha-plural-people), and the Ramkokamekra (*ràmkhô-khãm-mě-?khra:* tree-resin grove in plural Indian-children: Indians of the resin grove). The Kenkateye, who split off from the Apanyekra in the middle of the last century, were massacred and dispersed by local cattle ranchers in 1913. The Apanyekra have long been separate from the Ramkokamekra, having been traditional enemies. Nimuendajú wrote (1946:28) that the Ramkokamekra believed they were not any closer to the Apanyekra culturally than they were to the Krahó (geographically adjacent former enemies) and the Čakamekra (geographically adjacent friends, the Fox people).

17. See Nimuendajú (1946:29).

18. See Ribeiro (1815, 1819a, and 1819b).

19. See Nimuendajú (1946:34).

20. See Nimuendajú (1946:150), translated from Ribeiro, Memoria . . . , Nos. 19 and 22.

21. See Nimuendajú (1946:153). ⸰

22. See Hemming (1987:183–187). The body build of the Timbira must be seen in contrast to the physique of the Tupi-speaking Indians living deep in the forests to the north of the Timbira, such as the Guajajara. The latter remind the Canela of Asians. An American missionary woman of Japanese descent living in Barra do Corda during the late 1950s was said by the Canela to be very much like the Guajajara. In contrast to the Guajajara, citizens of Barra do Corda see the Canela as being taller, thinner, more delicately built, less Asian, and more like "whites" (*brancos*).

23. See Hemming, *Amazon Frontiers*, pp. 187–188.

24. Johann Emanuel Pohl was a German explorer of the region along the Tocantins between 1817 and 1821.

25. Melatti (1967:21–31) presents an analysis of these pastoral and agricultural fronts, coming from the southeast and north respectively, and joining to cross southern Maranhão during the 1800s and 1810s, more as a pastoral front than an agricultural one.

26. Morse, ed., 1965, presents a history of Brazilian *bandeiras* in *The Bandeirantes: The Historical Role of the Brazilian Pathfinders.*

27. See Hemming (1987:184–185).

28. See Nimuendajú (1946:32) and Hemming (1987:185–186). Note the earlier name of the Canela's principal ancestors, spelled Capiecran by Nimuendajú and Kapiekran by Hemming.

29. This period of retreat and hiding from the settlers occurred sometime during the mid-1810s to early 1820s. The hidden valley (Vão da Aldeia: valley of the village) is near the Sítio dos Arrudas and the southwestern boundary of the present Canela lands.

30. Names of historical Canela, and of Antônio Diogo (Alligator's Tail) who died in 1960, are not changed. Names of most living Canela are changed to ensure individual privacy. Antônio Diogo was the living historical library to whom Canela sent me for knowledge about the tribe when I first arrived. I became his named-nephew's named-nephew, a special relationship. He provided almost all the information about the 19th century. Canela referred to their 19th century leaders by their Portuguese names.

31. See Nimuendajú (1946:33).

32. See Hemming (1987:177–179).

33. See Wilbert and Simoneau (1984:102).

34. See Nimuendajú (1946:240).

35. See Nimuendajú (1946:30).

36. For details of the group marriage ceremony, see Crocker (1990:264–265).

37. The younger Prùù-tsêt (path-burnt) was the disciplinary uncle of Three Streams and therefore was her protector and on her side in the interfamily legal trial. He, nevertheless, was able to maintain close contact with her objecting, jealous husband, Tsàà-tu (urine's deep-hole-in-the-sand), since these two men were age class mates. Thus Burnt Path, in the role of an age class mate, succeeded in reducing Urine Hole's anger and in bringing him home to his niece.

38. See Crocker (1984:68–69) for a more complete account of the reasons why the Canela age class marriage ceremony was terminated.

39. For the trend over 40 years of adolescents having sex with people of much older generations, see Crocker (1984:75).

40. For descriptions of the hazing and shaming act, through which elders forced young men into general submission, see Crocker (1961:78–79) and (1990:126). The Canela did not put on this mocking-hazing act for me in 1975; they put it on for themselves. They enjoy staging their ancient ceremonies, though the one photographed was an "empty" one, since the youth was not really being hazed for misbehavior during the act.

41. The term "moiety" literally means one-half (French: *moitié*) and is used frequently in anthropology to refer to customary divisions of a tribe into halves. The Canela have five moiety systems, which means they divide themselves, on different occasions, into halves in five different ways. The Canela moieties mentioned in this book are the Upper and Lower age class moieties, the Reds and the Blacks, and the Wet Heads and the Dry Heads.

42. Curt Nimuendajú's *The Eastern Timbira*, 1946 (357 pages, 42 plates, 16 figures, and 3 maps), written in German but translated into English by ethnologist Robert Lowie of the University of California, is one of the great ethnographic monographs of the first half of the 20th century.

43. Nimuendajú (1946:46–47) emphasizes how proud the Canela were of their nudity, though they would not offend city dwellers with it. He quotes a Canela female adolescent as saying that the visiting Guajajara Indian males should be ashamed of going into the plaza fully dressed.

44. As this book is in production, in 1993, I have learned another version of the third attack on the Canela as they passed Ourives. Indian Service agents Sr. Virgílio and Sr. Bento had written, in the 1980s, accounts of their years of service, which they gave to me to read. The agents said in their reports that they passed through Ourives in the morning rather than at night, and neither mentioned the potential attack. When I questioned another former Indian Service agent about the inconsistency between their accounts and what I had previously understood to be the facts, he said that the averted attack at Ourives was a popular myth. He said that such an attack was planned but that the ranchers promised the mayor not to attack if the Canela were removed from the area completely. History is made of such conflicting accounts. In this case, I now believe the less dramatic accounts of Sr. Virgílio and Sr. Bento.

2/Bonding Through Kinship

The Canela kinship system is the most obvious and the most all-inclusive of the three major sources of Canela bonding. Where people live and how they behave toward each other is strongly influenced by kinship. Above about 12 years of age, everybody in the tribe knows everybody else. Any individual's identity can be rapidly established by a brief conversation about his or her relatives. The kinship system, with its consequent behaviors, prevents the growth of privacy and the harboring of secrets. This kind of intimate knowledge about everyone in the tribe is also fostered by shamans' communications with ghosts and by extramarital sex practices, as will be discussed in the chapters to come. Unless Canela emigrate, they cannot detach themselves from their family or have a secret sex life. The Canela do not go off on tangents; the circle is the paradigm for village life. As we consider around-the-circle as well as across-the-circle bonds, we will see that the kinship system constructs an intricate net which allows some flexibility, but which weaves many connections holding the tribe together.

CONSANGUINEAL AND AFFINAL KINSHIP

Kin, affines, and "spouses" around the village circle   In tribal worlds, kinship is crucially important, far more so than in Western culture. The kinship system determines what kin (people related by blood) and affines (people related by marriage) call each other and furnishes most of the social structure of a tribe. Kinship creates expectations of behavior which are powerful guidelines even though individuals deviate from them in practice.

In the Canela world, for example, you address your uncle as *kêt*,[45] paying deference to him and expecting him to advise you, unless he is much younger. Within the category of uncle, you have at least two kinds, a "naming uncle" and an "advising uncle," and you are likely to behave somewhat differently to each. The naming uncle is the one who gave you your personal name, and the advising uncle[46] is the one who chose to discipline you as you were growing up. Because of such differences, you are not likely to behave the same way to all the men you call "uncle." Moreover, you have close uncles and distant ones, the proximity being a factor in how you behave toward them. Your many "uncles" have their individual characteristics, which again cause your behavior toward them to vary considerably. Nevertheless, as a Canela, you are likely to defer to most of the men you call "uncle."

In the United States, our behavior toward a certain category of relative, such as uncle, is similar, but there are many variations within that broad category. However, what is different from tribe to tribe or from culture to culture throughout the world is how human beings arrange their kin and affines into categories and how they address and refer to the people in these categories. The group of individuals whom human beings call "uncle," "father," "sister," or "granddaughter" and so on can be different genealogically from culture to culture. In the United States, for instance, we usually call our father's brother "uncle," but a Canela calls her or his father's brother "father." We call our father's sister's son "cousin," but a Canela calls him "father." A Canela won't behave exactly the same way to this relatively distant "father" as she or he would behave to an actual father (genitor), but the behavior may be similar in certain ways, especially if the actual father has died.

If you are a Canela, certain of your other "fathers"[47] replace your actual father in predictable ways upon his death. Moreover, your "fathers" have similar rights and duties in relation to you. For instance, your "fathers" are supposed to provide you with meat every now and then, just as your actual father should do all the time, unless he is quite old. Also, all of your "fathers" have sexual rights to your mother, at least in theory; in any case, they may act informally and joke frequently with her. Informality and joking are steps toward having sex for unrelated, opposite-sex individuals among the fun-loving Canela.

While behavior is not cast in iron by the term a Canela calls a relative, it is at least somewhat determined by it. This is sufficiently the case so that Canela individuals want to be able to call any outsider living continuously in their village by a term of address that helps them know how to behave toward that person. These guidelines for behavior may be seen as social structures.

When I first arrived among the Canela in 1957, the Canela needed to fill the social vacuum presented by my unrelatedness. Within two days a Canela woman, Waterfall, adopted me as her "sister" so that everyone else in the tribe would know what to call me—and how to behave toward me—through their existing relationships with her.[48] I can imagine a collective sigh of relief passing through the tribe as each individual heard that it was Waterfall who had adopted me. This solved each individual's problem of how to act in my presence, because they knew how to behave with Waterfall. When I returned from the Canela for the first time, relatives and friends in the United States expressed amazement that the Canela had adopted me into a family within two days. They thought that I must have been especially adept at integrating myself into the tribe. But I explained that my adoption was for the tribal members' convenience. Not all tribes adopt outsiders, but the Canela in earlier times had the custom of adopting Timbira-speaking Indians from other tribes. They had also adopted my predecessor, Curt Nimuendajú. I explained to my kin at home that when I was adopted as a certain Canela woman's "brother," I had thereby become part of the tribal kinship network. Each individual would know whether to call me "nephew," "son," "uncle," or even "husband," according to the appropriate rules of their system.

My Canela brother's wife, Khop-pêê (club-greased), addressed me as "husband," and therefore joked informally with me. So did my brother's wife's mother's sister's daughter, Tep-rã (fish's-blossom), since she was a "wife," another one of my classificatory wives. (According to general kinship reckoning in the U.S., she would be my brother's wife's first cousin.⁴⁹) Fish's Blossom joked boisterously with my brother and me because she did not live in our house, but Greased Club joked conservatively with us because she did live in the same house, being married to my brother, Falcon's Sight. Thus, behavior between "spouses" varies with physical and social distance as well as with genealogical distance. Behavior also varies for these reasons between "uncles" and "nephews" and between "fathers" and "sons," as well as between individuals in most other reciprocal kinship address and reference categories.

On one otherwise ordinary morning in Escalvado village in 1975, my 52-year-old characteristically shy brother Falcon's Sight amused us all when he carried out his joking role as a "spouse." He grabbed his distant "wife" Fish's Blossom, 37, and, throwing her on a mat, proceeded to suck her breasts while she screamed playfully, struggling to push him off and get up. My kin and hers gathered around in a circle, enjoying the wrestling match, cheering on one or the other contestant, and reveling in the fun. But Falcon's Sight could only have done this with Fish's Blossom in public. If done in private without a woman's consent, this kind of behavior is considered abusive. In earlier times, such "spouses" as Falcon and Fish usually would have had sex, when most opposite-sex Canela who were unrelated did so, but such practices, though not forbidden, are less frequent today. Greased Club might get jealous and, angry at her husband Falcon and her "sister" Fish for having hidden sex with each other, but nobody would support her hostility toward them, especially not in the interfamily judicial hearings or in the tribal council.

Roles in my Canela sister's household   At the time of my adoption in 1957, my sister Waterfall was 31 and her husband Macaw Bone was 40. Other significant individuals in our two-room house of palm straw were Waterfall's full sister Ha-pôl (on-fire), 29, Waterfall's first cousin (her "sister") Amyi-yakhop (self-searching), 22, and Waterfall's daughter Lake Lover, 14. Self Searcher's husband was Khen-yawên (hill-flattened: mesa), 35, On Fire was unmarried, and Lake Lover's husband was Kuhê-ʔkhũm (boil's-vapor), 20. However, Mesa and Boil's Vapor were not strong presences in the house, because they had married into it rather than having been born in it. Macaw Bone had married into the house also, but since he was older than the other men and had married the oldest female born in the house, he exerted considerable authority over these other "married-in" men. (See Figure 1.)

The three older women of the house had about eight children living with them. In the 1950s, approximately 60 percent of the children born to Canela women died before they were 9, mostly of dysentery and dehydration. My niece Lake Lover had been married for two years but had not yet conceived.

Macaw Bone directed the efforts of the two other married-in men when collective work was necessary in the separate fields of all the household's adult women, though each man worked for his own wife and family most of the time. Macaw Bone also directed the feeble efforts of his mentally handicapped oldest son Kô-ʔkanãl (water-endures), 21.

By 1966 Macaw Bone had three sons-in-law, so Self Searcher and Mesa moved out to join Khen-tapi (hill-climber), Self Searcher's "sister," a second cousin in this case. Hill Climber was not married, but had four children, and was living with her married sister one house away clockwise along the village circle.

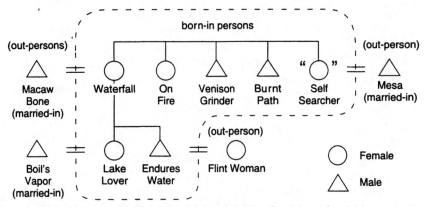

Figure 1. Married-in's versus Born-in's in a partial representation of my adoptive household.

Macaw Bone also managed most of the household's other economic activities. He was much more demanding with his young sons-in-law, who were married to his daughters, than he was with Mesa, who was married to his wife's "sister." He never sent Mesa on personal errands such as fetching a firebrand from the hearth to light his cigarette, but he sent Boil's Vapor and his sons-in-law on the most trivial errands such as getting used paper from me or matches from the post. One time he sent Mesa to the backland Brazilian community of Bacabal, 10 miles to the west, to obtain a pig for his daughter Lake Lover's belt-winning rite so that everybody in the whole household could eat and enjoy themselves.

Waterfall organized the women to carry out the domestic chores. Nevertheless, she deferred to her two brothers Poo-katwè (venison-grinder), 35, and Burnt Path, 28,

Women of three generations of a household prepare manioc. A typical cooking fire with three rocks can be seen behind the carrying baskets.

when they came from their marital houses to govern their house of birth, advise its members, and settle any significant disputes. These born-in male members of the house, since they did not live in it, had little to do with its day-to-day economic subsistence. But these uncles had much to do with disciplining the household's younger members and with helping their parents in their more serious socialization problems.

The underlying purposes of the leading individuals of such a Canela household are to feed its members, raise its children, and keep its morale high. Waterfall's energy and good will seemed inexhaustible to me as she carried out these traditional purposes: seeing that vegetables were cultivated and brought from the garden, arranging the preparation of food at the one communal hearth, and lending a hand at raising everyone's children. The principal role of Macaw Bone was to provide meat for the household. He was one of the tribe's great hunters. At least once a week he supplied meat, often venison or even a partridge now and then, the most difficult game to shoot. Mesa was a slow runner and his vision was poor, but he was good at digging armadillos out of their deep holes. Boil's Vapor limited himself to the Brazilian backland hunting style of waiting in trees with a flashlight at night to transfix and shoot large rodents such as paca and agouti. Macaw Bone's role also included bargaining with visiting Brazilian backlanders for food such as beef, rice, and brown sugar, and goods such as tobacco, gunpowder, and lead shot. He also sent any one of his married-in men away on errands to obtain cloth, machetes, and medicines or other household necessities in Barra do Corda.

The uncles Venison Grinder and Burnt Path, as well as other "uncles," represented the family judicially in the tribal council and before the chief. They also hunted to supply game (usually deer) for their nieces' and nephews' rites of passage through life, such as puberty, belt-winning, and the postpartum release of the contributing fathers. But with characteristic Canela flexibility, Macaw Bone quickly stepped in to carry out the "uncles'" traditional duties if they were slow to prepare for the ceremonies of his household's children or for their judicial representation in the plaza. Similarly, if the "uncles" who were good hunters were out in the Brazilian coastal city world, as occurred at the time of his daughter Lake Lover's postpartum contributing father rite, Macaw Bone did not hesitate to go hunting for her in their place to obtain the necessary meat.

Otherwise Macaw Bone deferred to the "uncles," although he was older. In February 1960, I saw him sitting quietly in a corner making a new pouch for himself, keeping his nervous fingers busy, while the "uncles" and his wife discussed his daughter's ceremonial future. They decided to allow Lake to accept the role of one of the two Clown society's female associates. Macaw did not like to contemplate the fact that about 30 Clown society members would use his daughter sexually. Close opposite-sex kin are embarrassed to be made aware of their sexuality. This reluctance may seem inconsistent with the sexual freedom discussed in Chapter 4. The kinship system, however, does involve sexual inhibition. Macaw would want to ignore his daughter's sexuality in order to maintain his proper kin relationship with her. In contrast, her "uncles," being more removed emotionally, were not as sensitive, and thought it would be best for the Clowns to bring Lake down a bit in ceremonial rank. No men's society had touched her when she was winning her belt earlier, because she was one of the two ceremonially high Wè?tè girls.

Kinship terms and their roles   Lake Lover's husband, Boil's Vapor, had trouble with the male members of my Canela family since he was only a married-in man and a new one to us in 1957. The two uncles Venison Grinder and Burnt Path and Lake's brothers, as born-in men, interrupted Boil in conversations. They also took small items without asking from the thatch where Boil kept things wedged near his wife's platform bed, such as tobacco and razor blades.

Boil *addressed* his wife's male kin as *impàyyê,* which I will translate as "in-brother," while they in turn *addressed* Boil using *piyõyê* ("out-brother"). Boil *referred* to each of them as *i-pree,* my "in-person" or my "in-brother," since they were male. The "in-persons," with few exceptions, *referred* to him in return as their *piyõyê.* (See Figure 2.)

Boil remained silent in our presence most of the time. In fact, he *never* spoke to my sister Waterfall, his mother-in-law (*pãn:* senior "avoidance-woman": "avoidance mother"). Boil will have a junior avoidance-woman as well when he and Lake eventually have a grown and married son. Then Boil will also refer to his son's wife as *pãn* ("avoidance-woman": "avoidance-daughter"). He won't be able to speak to her or to her sisters and her many "sisters." Similarly, Boil could not speak to Waterfall's sister, On Fire, her same household's full sister; nor could Boil speak to Self Searcher, Waterfall's "sister" in the neighboring house. Similarly, Boil could not speak to Waterfall's other "sisters" (her more distant cousins) along the village circle of houses in both directions. In the same way, Waterfall could not speak to Boil but could refer to him as her *wawè* (her "avoidance-son"), and Boil's future daughter-in-law will not speak to him but will refer to him as her *khrã?tũmyê* (her "avoidance-father").

Full avoidance relationships are common in tribal life throughout the world. I first became impressed by the compelling force of this relationship among the Canela when Hanging Fish, 45, who was a "son" to me, though I was 33, invited himself into the room I worked and slept in while I was studying one morning in 1957. He explained, apologetically, that he just wanted to sit there out of the hot sun without disturbing me, but I questioned him. Hanging Fish said he could not stay in his own house that morning because everybody had left except his primary avoidance-mother, making them both very uncomfortable.

Hanging Fish told me that he never looked directly at his avoidance-mother's face. He would walk off the trail if she were coming, and he would delay bathing whenever she was near the water hole. Hanging Fish and his avoidance-mother would never exchange the same cigarette as the Canela commonly did. When it was necessary to communicate with her, he would speak to his wife and let the older woman overhear.

I received the full avoidance treatment when my wife, Roma, came to join me in the village in the 1970s and we lived together in a room in her adopted Canela kin's house. Before she had actually arrived, I had to remain in my sister Waterfall's house or in my brother Falcon Sight's house. Roma's kin would not let me move into our room to spend the night in their house without Roma. Since poor regional communications prevented my knowing exactly which day Roma would arrive, I carried all our things over to our room on several consecutive days, only to have to carry them back in the evening when she had not arrived.

On the first occasion of this sort, Roma's mother, my primary avoidance-mother, Star Woman, had to speak to me, because she thought I was going to spend the night alone in Roma's room. So Star Woman gave one of her unmarried daughters a lecture about how husbands stayed in their sisters' or mothers' house when their wives were away unless they had children, so that I would overhear and leave. I was so absorbed in my work that I did not overhear her at first, and when I did, I assumed she was lecturing her daughter. She raised her voice louder and louder, always speaking to her daughter, until I caught on and started to pack up our things. To offend your avoidance-mother is embarrassing.

Affinal Models
("in"– / "out" –)

Terms of Reference Between Marriage-Connected Houses

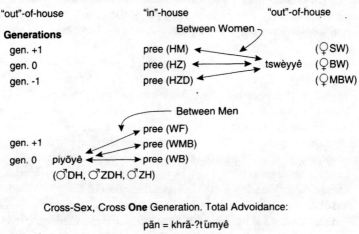

Between women-in-law, the "out-woman" (tswèyyê) refers to her "in-women" on three generations using the basic term **pree**.
Between men-in-law, the "out-man" (piyōyê) refers to his "in-men" on three generations using the basic term **pree**.

"in"-house		"out"-of-house	
HM	= husband's mother /	♀ SW	= woman's son's wife
HZ	= husband's sister /	♀ BW	= woman's brother's wife
HZD	= husband's sister's daughter /	♀ MBW	= woman's mother's brother's wife
WF	= wife's father /	♂ DH	= man's daughter's husband
WMB	= wife's mother's brother /	♂ ZDH	= man's sister's daughter's husband
WB	= wife's brother /	♂ ZH	= man's sister's husband
WM	= wife's mother /	♀ DH	= woman's daughter's husband
HF	= husband's father /	♂ SW	= man's son's wife

Figure 2. In-person versus Out-person terms.

In our house, Boil's Vapor got along best with his wife's sisters and "sisters" (On Fire's and Self Searcher's daughters), with whom he could joke sexually. Boil addressed and referred to each of them as "wife," which at their unmarried age consisted of calling them by their personal names. These girls were his "other-wives" (prō-?nō: wife-other). They in return called him by his personal name, Boil, since he was their "other-husband" (pyê-?nō: husband-other).

Spouses and relatively close "spouses" use teknonymy when full grown, whether they have children or not. Teknonymy is the practice of two related people speaking to each other by referring to their children. Thus, Waterfall called her husband, Macaw Bone, "Kô?kanāl-mē-hūm" (Kô?kanāl-his-father), or "Endures Water's father." And Macaw Bone called Waterfall "Kô?kanāl-mē-ntsii" (Endures Water-his-mother), or "Endures Water's mother." Couples who have occasional quick extramarital trysts use each other's personal names, but couples who are carrying on long-term affairs use the other "spouse's" oldest child's personal name (of either sex), just as if they were married.

During my research assistant group meetings in 1964, my special helper, the younger Thunder, 32, repeatedly called a very old informant, Pyê-?khàl (ground-spotted), 71, by her personal name. This intrigued me. I thought Thunder was being too familiar with his avoidance-mother's mother (his actual wife's mother's mother), whom I thought should be an "avoidance-woman" to him. But Thunder told me that in earlier times calling a woman "avoidance-mother" applied only to persons one generation above yourself, and that this custom was gradually being lost. (The sophisticated Thunder was well aware of many of these changes.) The loss of this personal name usage paralleled the disappearance during the 1930s and 1940s of the practice of adolescents having sex with far older men and postmenopausal women. I deduced that if adolescents could not have sex with these older people anymore, they also would no longer call the elders by their personal names. So I accepted that old Spotted Ground was Thunder's "wife" according to earlier usage. My young helper Thunder could behave familiarly with her even though the sexual basis for the familiarity had died out.

While my Canela research assistants could find no current examples for the corresponding male pattern, they assured me that an adolescent girl could call her avoidance-father's father (her father-in-law's father) by his personal name. Research assistants also said that the age span between sons and fathers is usually greater than that between daughters and mothers, which would make this practice unlikely. More probably, the girl would call her avoidance-father's father "uncle" (kêt), as younger people call almost all men in their late 60s and 70s. In the same way, they call almost all old women "aunt" (tùy).

The most frequent exception to the practice of adolescents calling old relatives and affines "aunt" or "uncle" is that a young wife is likely to refer to even her mother-in-law's mother (two generations above her) as her i-pree (my in-woman), no matter how old the older woman is.[50]

A wife, whether young or aged, refers to each of her husband's female kin as i-pree (my in-person), except for her husband's mother, her sisters, and her "sisters," whom she calls i-pree-kêy (my in-person senior). In return, she is their i-tswèyyê ("out-sister"/"out-daughter," depending on generational differences). "In-" and "out-" for women-in-law refer to those born *in* the house and to those married in but living *out* of the house (see Flint Woman in Figure 1). A bride continues to reside in her own mother's house and does not move permanently to her husband's and mother-in-law's house even when older. The behavior of this reciprocal relationship was harder for me to observe than most others, because my Canela sister Waterfall's sisters- and daughters-in-law lived in other houses. Occasionally, her sons brought their wives to work in our house, and I observed that the females of our house treated them well. Moreover, both my regular female and male research assistants spoke well of the female in-/out- relationship when we had group discussions about it. They said it is epitomized by collective work, good will, and cooperation, unlike its male counterpart described above for Boil's Vapor and his in-brothers (his wife's brothers and uncles). This male relationship, as we saw, is marked by petty harassment.

For several years, Waterfall's mentally handicapped son Endures Water and his older and more capable wife Khrùt-khwèy (flint-woman), 28, came to live with us, disregarding the generally well-kept rule of matrilocality, so that Endures Water's parents could give him moral support in his marriage. Flint worked well with the other women of the household and was treated substantially as if she were their kin instead of their out-sister or out-daughter. The Canela kinship system allows adaptations for special living arrangements.

One of the rites I liked most to record with my camera was one of the Canela's many steps into marriage: placing the wedding belt around the bride's hips, which takes place between a bride's female kin and her husband's female kin. During this rite, the bride's husband's female kin, her in-mothers and in-sisters, paint the body of the bride, their out-daughter or out-sister, with urucu while she stands on a mat in their house. Then they wrap the belt, a long line of cord, around her hips.

To make the cord for the belt, each one of the bride's female kin "rolls" tucum fibers on her thigh, forming many three-foot sections. Then the sections are twisted together forming an approximately 100-foot-long cord, which is sent over to the in-mothers and in-sisters. The cord is painted red by the bride's husband's kin, each woman running it through their urucu-coated hands in turn. Then they play out the cord as the standing bride rotates her body, thus winding the cord in many loops (about 80) around her upper hips. They tie the loops together in front, forming a knot, and the wedding belt is removed over her shoulders.

In former times, when the bride lowered her belt past her shoulders down to her hips each day, she would tuck two large leaves under the belt's knot. The leaves extended well below to cover her genitals. These days she wears the belt only for certain ceremonial appearances.

The belt is called an *i?-pre* (her-bond), the bond between the bride and her husband's female kin. Canela research assistants said the belt represents the bond between the two sets of female kin, its makers (the bride's kin) and its painters (the groom's kin). While *i-pree* (my "in"-in-law) and *i-pre* (my belt) are phonemically different, their meaning is similar.

Another close bonding exists between a naming-uncle and his named-nephew, usually his sister's son or his "sister's" son. (A similar but weaker bond exists between a naming-aunt and her named-niece.) A naming-uncle gives his little named-nephew a small set of bows and arrows. He teaches his named-nephew all his

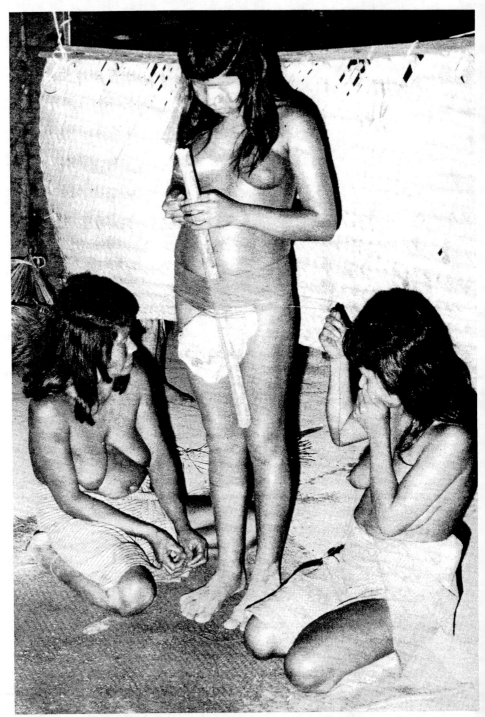

A bride's female in-laws hold the cord of tucum fibers while she rotates, wrapping the long cord around her hips, forming the wedding belt.

ceremonial roles and takes the youth to perform beside him during the transition period of several years. Then the uncle retires and lets his nephew carry on. The paired
naming-uncle and named-nephew used to be so close that they had sexual access to
each other's wives, and today they still address each other's wives as "spouses,"
though sex between them is rare.

I still wonder why my naming-uncle, Deer's Nest, actually my sister's "brother" (a
second cousin), called my first wife, Mary Jean, "wife" and referred to my second wife,
Roma, as his "avoidance-woman." Whatever his reasons, his choices demonstrate the
existence of customary alternatives. Canela women and men have many "other-
spouses." Some couples of this sort are "spouses," as reckoned through a particular series of kin linkages, and others are "avoidance-people" to each other even though the
series of linkages is identical. The choice can be made. Deer's Nest considered both
Mary Jean and Roma his named-nephew's wives. If he felt he could joke with such a
category of person, she was a "spouse." If he did not want to joke (and in earlier times
have sex), she was an "avoidance-daughter." I found many examples among the Canela
of individuals who had made such choices, consciously or unconsciously.

Committing "incest" with distant kin or affines is one of the ways many Canela
obtain their actual spouses, though they more often marry individuals to whom they
believe they are not related. Pairs of individuals can think they are unrelated in a society of this size (515 in 1975), because people are likely to forget certain sets of

A boy plays with the bow and arrow set given him by his naming-uncle.

kinship linkages by the third generation. In the Canela case, if the linkages are through males, people may not remember them by the second generation down. That is, a man and his father's father's brother's son's son *probably* do not know they are related, though they would be second cousins in most kinship systems of the United States. In contrast, a Canela woman and her mother's mother's mother's sister's daughter's daughter's daughter *usually* know they are "sisters," though they would usually be third cousins with us. In the United States, families are much less likely to keep track of third cousins. (See Figure 3.) For the Canela, Crow kinship patterns, matrilocal residence, and stress on the continuity of matrilines in long-houses are factors which place more emphasis on kin links among women than on those among men.

The closest bonding among the Canela, however, exists between siblings,[51] especially between sisters. Siblings are believed to grow off one and the same umbilicus. Consequently, all siblings have "blood" (*kaprôô*) that is "similar" or "equivalent" (*ipipēn*). Brothers tend to drift apart because they live with their wives in different houses at widely separate locations on the village circle, while sisters live in the same house or in adjacent houses along the village circle. Sisters are so close that respect between them does not have to be built up and maintained through the use of special terms of address and reference. Thus, sisters can call each other by their personal names, although senior and junior terms of address and reference are used when a serious difference arises. In contrast, brothers always use senior (*i-hà*) and junior (*i-yõ?hêw-re*) terms of address, as determined by relative age.

Opposite-sex uterine siblings, those born of the same mother, may call each other by their personal names when they are young and still close. If they have drifted apart, however, they practice teknonymy, though a different kind than spouses use. It is traditional for a sister and brother, whether uterine or classificatory, to give a name to one child of the other sibling, a child which is the same sex as the name-giver. Some opposite-sex siblings (and "siblings") may have exchanged

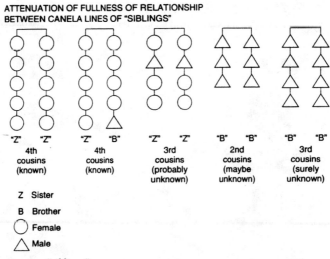

ATTENUATION OF FULLNESS OF RELATIONSHIP BETWEEN CANELA LINES OF "SIBLINGS"

| "Z"   "Z" | "Z"   "B" | "Z"   "Z" | "B"   "B" | "B"   "B" |
| 4th cousins (known) | 4th cousins (known) | 3rd cousins (probably unknown) | 2nd cousins (maybe unknown) | 3rd cousins (surely unknown) |

Z Sister
B Brother
◯ Female
△ Male

Figure 3. Knowing your "siblings."

names and others not. In any case, they all use the following terms of address: The sister calls her brother "my name-receiver's father" (*i túware-mẽ hũm*), and the brother calls his sister "my name-receiver's mother" (*i túware-mẽ ntsii*).

Name-exchanging takes place three times more frequently between non-uterine opposite-sex "siblings," to keep up the "siblingship," than between uterine siblings, whose "blood" similarity keeps up their relationship. The Canela male has an alternative to name-exchange with a distant "sister": He can make her his "spouse" through sex, if she is willing. He either exchanges names with her to maintain the extensiveness of his kin ties, or he has sex with her to increase his number of "other-spouses," who can be politically helpful to him later through their brothers.

When Thunder's "nieces" chose to have fun with him, they teased him mercilessly, sometimes saying he had few female kin because he had turned most of them into "spouses." His "nieces" proceeded to name most of the kin he had committed incest with, one after another, describing the occasions—common knowledge in the village anyway. Thunder was both embarrassed and pleased because being liked by a large number of "spouses," and keeping them all happy, was something to be proud of in the Canela world. Women with many "husbands" were also prestigious.

Because I was adopted by Waterfall, I was considered a name-exchange "brother." In 1960 I gave a name that I invented to her newly born son. I chose "Strong Locust" (*ku?tàà-tèy:* locust-strong), because locust trees are believed to furnish strength. In return, in 1970, Waterfall put her name on my step-daughter Tara, calling her Little Waterfall. As name-exchange siblings, Waterfall and I have great respect for each other. We talk to each other only when we have to, and we never joke. We have to talk quite often, however, since I live in her house when in the tribe, and she looks after many of my needs. As any Canela females do for their male kin or husbands, she sees that my domestic necessities are taken care of: the food preparation, the small amount of laundry, and the cleaning of my living space. Her abilities as female head of household win my highest respect.

One morning in 1959 an accident occurred that might have been a disaster for me. My three "nieces" from next door had playfully attacked me. We were throwing empty orange skins at each other, sneaking around from house to house to the amusement of all present. Trying to hit a "niece" by surprise, I threw a whole, mushy orange skin around a corner at her only to hit my sister Waterfall squarely on the side of the face. Silence filled the house, and I grew red and confused. I had insulted my principal ally in the tribe and broken one of the strongest Canela taboos. But Waterfall, great lady that she is, saved the situation after a pause by continuing to talk with one of her sisters as if nothing had happened. Soon I retired to my room, aghast at how she might have taken my mistake. I also realized how deeply I had absorbed at least two Canela values: respect for a sister and shame (*pahàm*) if that respect were violated.

Bonding around *the village circle of houses*   The network of kinship *around* the circle of houses bonds sectors of adjacent houses into "longhouses," while the network of kinship *across* the circle bonds pairs of "longhouses" for several generations, as discussed in the next section.

The Canela kinship system is called "Crow," because it is similar to the system of the Crow Indians of the North American Plains. In Crow systems, which are found all over the world, siblings of the same sex are often addressed similarly. As we have seen above, Falcon's Sight calls Fish's Blossom, his wife's "sister," "wife." Similarly, a woman calls her husband's brother, or his "brother," "husband."

Each society chooses which pathways of kinship linkages it wants to maintain. Maintaining these pathways often depends on the support of certain institutions. These institutions serve to keep the persons at the opposite ends of the pathways in contact with each other. The number of kin linkages, which all together constitute a pathway, between the speaker and the addressed person may be as many as 10 in some well-supported Canela relationships.

For the Canela, the village circle of houses is one of the institutions that supports the significant pathways of kin linkages which bond the society together. The other institution is the arrangement of the female kin living in these houses. By the word "arrangement" I mean the particular pattern of kin linkages which unite these female kin. These patterns are consistent with Crow kinship patterns. Kin linkages passing through males are not supported by the arrangement of females in the houses around the village, as will be shown later.

In theory, the principle that siblings are equal to each other—are called by the same kin term by certain other related people—is extended to a Canela individual's cousins of the same generation, *if* the reckoning of the cousinships is carried out through *all*-female linkages. The pattern of cousins being "siblings" is maintained for several generations down. Thus, an individual's mother's sister's daughter is this same individuals's "sister" (a first cousin to us). An individual's mother's mother's sister's daughter's daughter is this same individual's "sister" (a second cousin). An individual's mother's mother's mother's sister's daughter's daughter's daughter is this same individual's "sister" (a third cousin), and so on. (See Figure 3.)

In one extended family (see houses *aa* through *nn* in Figure 4), everybody was descended from one female ancestor, Amyiyakhop, an Apanyekra (a Piranha woman). Here I found "siblings" during the 1970 census-taking who were fifth cousins and still called each other "sister"—Thorn Woman, 23, in house *bb,* and Village Plaza, 28, in house *nn.* These women were teaching certain of their children to call each other "sibling" (sixth cousins in this case). The women of this great family extended over 14 houses, a segment of the village circle which contained 27 percent of the 52 houses. The village had 13 segments (called "longhouses") of this sort, the smallest of which was composed of one house.

Within her longhouse (*ikhre-rùù:* house-long), Thorn called many, though not all, of her "sisters'" mothers "mother" and her "sisters'" fathers "father." She called each of her "sisters'" children "child" and her "sisters'" grandparents "aunt" and "uncle," since no special terms exists for "grandmother" and "grandfather" in Canela. Thirteen such longhouses—each bonded internally through the same pattern of kinship reckoning (that is, through all-female linkages)—comprise the units found around the village circle. These unnamed longhouses, with known and traceable ancestors, are usually bound to certain longhouses *across* the village circle through another pattern of kinship reckoning.

To summarize, bonding *around* the village circle of houses starts with *same-sex* siblings—with two or more uterine sisters. Then the bonding around the village circle is continued with mother-to-daughter-to-daughter lines (called "matrilines") descending from each of the founding sisters down through the generations and spreading out

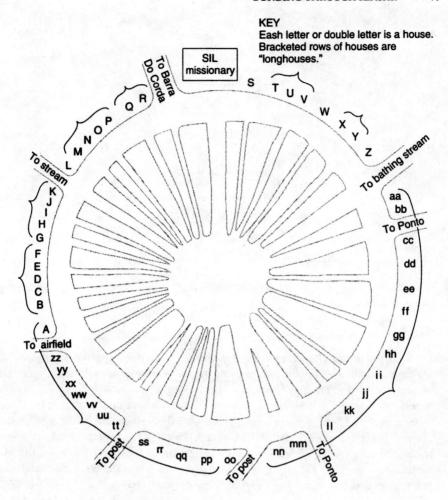

Figure 4. Village circle of longhouses (approximation, 1970).

from each of the founding sisters to form a longhouse. At each generation below the original sisters, the women are "sisters" to each other. On the first generation below, the "sisters" are first cousins to each other by our usual reckoning, on the second generation they are second cousins, and so on, as long as the matrilines last.

This mother-to-daughter-to-granddaughter structure is what holds a longhouse together internally (see Figure 5) through the generations. Marriage should not take place within a longhouse; in other words, a longhouse is "exogamous," so marriages internal to a longhouse are tabooed. When marriages do take place within a longhouse between distant kin, these marriages begin to terminate the longhouse. Longhouses also become weakened and shrink in size if few daughters are born to continue their matrilines. My special helper Thunder sometimes points with nostalgia to a location on the village circle where his natal longhouse had stood before the lack of female descendants terminated it completely.

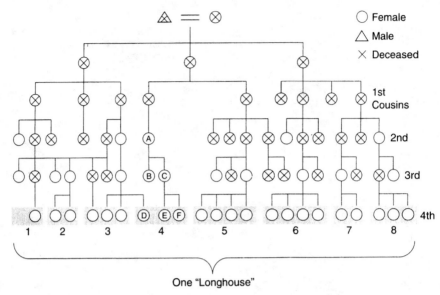

One "Longhouse"

Six women (A, B, C, D, E, F) live in house No. 4 with their men.

Figure 5. Matrilines in a longhouse (model).

Bonding across the village circle of houses   In contrast to the bonds *around* the circle, bonding *across* the village circle begins with *opposite-sex* siblings instead of *same-sex* ones. The pattern starts with a young man leaving his mother and sisters' house to go across the plaza to marry somewhere on the other side of the village circle.[52] There the young man procreates the first female of the mother-to-daughter-to-granddaughter lines which parallel through the generations the mother-to-daughter-to-granddaughter lines descending from the sister he left behind in his mother's house. (See Figure 6.) The first-generation female descendants of this young man and his sister (normally first cousins with us) are not Canela "sisters" this time, because they are not descended from *same*-sex siblings, who are called "parallel-cousins" in anthropology. They are descended from *opposite*-sex siblings, who are called "cross-cousins." As in Crow kinship, and in many other kinship systems, parallel-cousins and cross-cousins address and refer to each other using quite different terms.

Let's apply the different pattern for cross-cousins to the situation created by a young man, Whip, who crossed the village plaza to marry on the other side of the village. Whip's sister, Bat Woman, and all her female descendants call all Whip's female descendants "niece" (*hapaltswèy:* niece/granddaughter/female descendant), and all Whip's female descendants in return call all Bat's female descendants "aunt" (*tùy:* aunt/grandmother/female ancestor). The "niece" in the first descending generation below Whip refers to her "aunts'" sons as *i-pam* (my "father"), and the "nieces" in the still lower generations below Whip refer to their "aunts'" sons as *kêt* (uncle/grandfather/male-ancestor).

The across-the-village bonding described above joins two longhouses for about three generations, down to the second cousin level, rarely to the third and never to

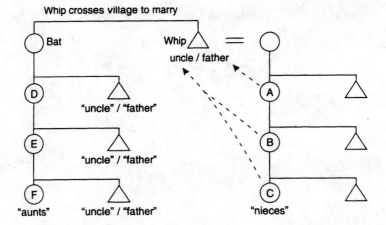

Whip crosses village to marry

Bat and her female descendants call Whip's female descendants "niece," and Whip's female descendants (A, B, C) call Bat and her female descendants (D, E, F) "aunt."

Whip's daughter Ⓐ calls Bat's male descendants "father," and they, in return, call her "child."

Whip's granddaughter Ⓑ and great granddaughter Ⓒ call Bat's male descendants "uncle," and they call her female descendants "niece."

Whip's male descendants follow his female descendants.

Figure 6. Across-the-village matrilines.

the fourth generation. Thus, a pair of across-the-village longhouses, which are united by a marriage on the first generation, should be exogamous for the next two generations.

The bonding *within* longhouses may continue for more generations than the bonding *between* longhouses. Actually, when longhouses become sufficiently long—when they consist of more than about two to four houses—they break informally into extended household units for the purposes of their youths' marrying across the village circle. Thus, every marriage creates a bonding between two longhouses, or between two extended households, which are said to be "across" the village circle from each other even though they may be next door to each other, as were Laker Lover and Boil's Vapor, temporarily, in 1957. This "across-the-village" bonding is massive. Figure 7 is a partial representation of most of these marital bonds in 1970.

In summary, the Canela tribe is integrated by matrilines originating from female parallel-cousins. These generation-to-generation structures hold the longhouses together internally. The longhouses exist end-on-end around the village circle and consist of from 1 to 13 houses. With husbands coming from other longhouses, marriages continue the matrilines within the longhouses down through the generations. Marriages also tie different longhouses together across the village circle.

The principal integrative building blocks for the kinship level of Canela social structure are the village circle of houses (which operates in space) and the matrilines based on Crow kinship (which operate through time).

The circle represents the village circle.

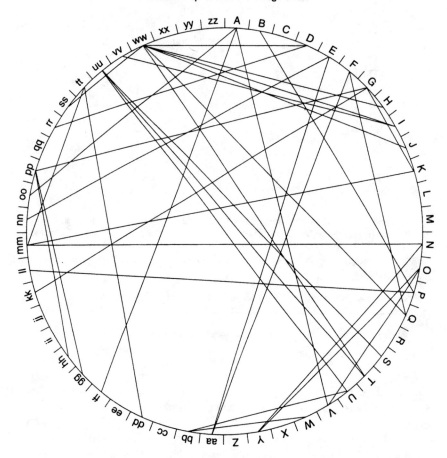

Letters and double letters represent Escalvado village houses.
Lines between the letters represent some of the marital connections.

Figure 7. Marital bonds across the village (actual—1970).

Joking behavior between aunts, uncles, nieces, and nephews Youths especially enjoy their "aunts" and "uncles" who live across the village plaza. They can be very informal with these "aunts" and "uncles" because of their social distance and because these relatives rarely assume responsible roles for them. While same-sex practical joking and teasing is common among such relatives, opposite-sex joking offers better opportunities for expressing the fun and sport the Canela seem to need so much of the time.

Belt Pulled Off, 62 in 1975, besides being my great kinship specialist, was my sister Waterfall's father's sister's daughter, our "aunt." I called her three sons "father" and behaved respectfully to them, though they were younger than I. On the other hand, I joked moderately with Belt and excessively with her three daughters, Single, 41, Alligator Woman, 30, and Silent, 27.

During June of 1975, while the husbands of these four "aunts" were clearing their fields, Aunt Belt invited me out to their field hut to spend Sunday. I brought my hammock along for an afternoon nap. However, my three young "aunties" may have thought I was sleeping too long. They quietly untied one end of my hammock and retied it to another tree so that my feet hung over a low fire. Fortunately, their unintentional jostling of the hammock woke me before the heat of the fire did. Then I had to get out of the stiff-rimmed, double-sized, deep matrimonial hammock (my size required a large one) without falling or stepping into the fire. My mock antics and verbal threats kept them laughing for some time.

An extreme example of "uncle" to "niece" sex-joking occurred one morning in 1979. Slippery Forest, 35, ordinarily a responsible and serious age class leader, caught his "niece" Long Woman, 10, and threw her on her back in the sand of the circular boulevard just outside my brother Falcon Sight's house. He spread her struggling little legs, lowered himself between them, and jerked his hips as if he were copulating. He had on long pants, however, which was unusual dress even for 1979, and she had on the usual wraparound cloth and panties. The young Long screamed with joy and continued wriggling to pretend to get away until Slippery Forest got up. The crowd was amused by the performance. At age 10, Long had learned enough about sex to mimic screams of delight rather than of fear or anger.

While the principal joking roles among the Canela are between the sexes—between "aunts" and "nephews," "uncles" and "nieces," and between "spouses"—a same-sex joking role also exists between males who have chosen to enter the traditional relationship of Informal Friends to each other, as discussed below.

OTHER FORMS OF "KINSHIP"

Besides the two kinship systems (the consanguineal and affinal), the Canela have several other interpersonal relationship systems of significance which involve the use of terms of address or reference: (1) Informal Friendship, (2) Formal Friendship, (3) name-set transmission, and (4) contributing fatherships.

Informal friendship Boys and young men become Informal Friends by participating in a ceremonial performance. Early one morning during the four-month initiation festival-pageants, the Khêêtúwayê (Ghosts) and the Pepyê (Warriors), boys and youths establish Informal Friendships with each other. They enter a swimming hole in pairs, side-by-side, and submerge themselves completely. When they emerge, still as pairs, they look at each other steadily. In the 1970s, they usually held hands when they emerged from the water, or they sometimes shook hands at the end of the rite, a Western adaptation.

The male pairs choose each other for their personal closeness and their desire to remain Informal Friends for the rest of their lives, unless a new relationship of higher priority, such as an affinal role, requires a change. Informal Friends call each other *i-khwè-?nõ* (my-group-one: the person of my group, or my age class).

Informal Friends formerly exchanged each other's wives for sexual purposes and still refer to each other's wives and children as "our wife" and "our child," using a special dual form, the personal pronoun *pa*. Extensions of this Informal Friendship

Youths emerge from the water as Informal Friends. The Canela use such spots in the stream for bathing as well.

system of address and reference sometimes spread through the Informal Friends' children, wives, and wives' parents to still further-linked kin and affines, thereby changing the usual pattern of the terms otherwise used in a longhouse and breaking up the mother-to-daughter-to-granddaughter lines.

Informal Friends take each other's possessions freely, without asking. They are constant companions and confidants. A war story tells of a youth who was shamed and disrespected by a sister. She did not consider him important enough to reserve and keep meat for regularly. He told his Informal Friend that he was going out of the tribal area and into the region controlled by an enemy tribe. Of course, the enemy warriors would kill him on sight, so this was an honorable way of committing suicide. The youth preferred death to living with his shame. The youth's Informal Friend felt obligated to accompany him, so they both were killed.

While the intensity of Informal Friendship behavior was considerably reduced by the late 1950s, evidence of the institution's continued existence surfaced almost every day in practical jokes. If a youth dumped a calabash of orange buriti palm juice on another youth's head, I thought they must be Informal Friends, but sought verification from research assistants when necessary. If a young man shoved another one into a young woman, who therefore screamed and moved quickly away, embarrassed, I suspected that the young man had pushed his Informal Friend into one of the latter's avoidance-women.

In a farm hut during the heat of the afternoon on the Wild Boar extramarital exchange day in 1958, Fox's Belly, 17, saw an opportunity to play a joke on his Informal Friend, Jaguar Head, 16. Fox's Belly was also playing up to his entire age class for their favor while they were lying around and resting with little to do but tell stories. No women were present.

Jaguar Head was lying on his back and snoring so loudly that he was disrupting the storytelling. Something had to be done to stop the noisy distraction. The offending person's Informal Friend often helps his age class in such delicate situations. Jaguar must also have been dreaming about some appealing woman because he was sporting a partial erection to everyone's amusement. In those days, some youths still went naked most of the time, especially out in the farms.

Fox approached Jaguar slowly, trying not to wake him, with the whole age class watching silently. Fox rolled back Jaguar's foreskin carefully and caught the noose of a light cord under Jaguar's glans. Then he dusted the glans with sand and rolled up the foreskin gently, stopping to wait each time the snoring lessened. Jaguar kept waving his hand in his sleep at what he may have dreamed was a fly settling on his penis, and the men had difficulty restraining their laughter. Finally, Fox, still holding the far end of the cord, positioned himself just outside the hut—and yanked. Jaguar sat up quickly to hear his age class roaring at him, and he searched the hut with his eyes for his Informal Friend, whom he assumed had played this trick on him, but could not see Fox. Jaguar would have to wait for some appropriate occasion to return the intimate compliment to their friendship, made in full confidence of its acceptance. However, he felt great shame that others had seen his glans, formerly the principal mark of male modesty in a naked world.[53]

The practical joke between Informal Friends that I remember best, however, took place repeatedly between the older Thunder and my out-brother Macaw's Bone. I first saw it happen during the informal meetings of an age class in the late 1950s and most recently during the formal meetings of the elders in the late 1970s. It was usually the irrepressible Macaw's Bone who reenacted the joke by tossing the first handful of sand in the more prestige-conscious Thunder's face. Then Thunder characteristically acted as if nothing had occurred, but later raised a hand to brush the sand out of his eyes, nose, and mouth. Maybe a half hour later, when Macaw's Bone had become unwatchful, Thunder caught him in the face with a return fistful of sand. I was always surprised at the accuracy and success of such assaults and amazed that otherwise dignified members of the elders would play such jokes on each other while the Council was in full session.

Formal friendship   The institution of Formal Friendship is extensive and very evolved among the Canela, so it can only be described in a summary manner here. Pairs of Formal Friends behave toward each other as avoidance affines: Full avoidance takes place between some pairs ("primary" ones: -*mpey*) and moderate avoidance occurs between other pairs ("secondary" ones: -*kahàk*). As a Canela, your primary Formal Friend decorates your body for ceremonial occasions and paints your corpse when you die, while your secondary Formal Friends have no prescribed ceremonial roles in relation to you, though they have many general ones. Your primary Formal Friends are considered "primary" because you carried out a special rite to originate this special status. The rite (*ntêê*) is performed before the house of a pregnant woman—chanting a song and giving food—to indicate that you would accept her offspring of either sex as your primary Formal Friend. Secondary Formal Friends are name-linked or ceremonially role-linked in origin. Such Formal Friendships may also be made during the swimming hole rite, like Informal Friendships, except that the pair enters and emerges from the water facing away from each other in shame and respect.

As a Canela, your secondary Formal Friends always support you when you are in serious trouble. Unlike your kin, however, your Formal Friends expect compensation for special services. They also withdraw from any competitive situation you are in. When I observed during log races that the individual log-carriers of both teams had slowed down, so that one was not attempting to pass the other, I knew that the two runners were Formal Friends.

When I was first with the Canela in 1957, Painted Leg was my primary Formal Friend. We never spoke nor looked each other in the face. Nevertheless, in 1959 during a trading day, Painted Leg spoke to me directly and looked up into my face, much to my surprise and sudden shock. She saw I was confused, so she quickly reassured me that a little talking was all right for us now, though joking still was not acceptable. She told me they had transferred the primary Formal Friendship between us to her newly born daughter, pointing to the infant in her arms. Now we were secondary Formal Friends. The helpful and flexible Macaw's Bone had performed the rite for me, but had forgotten to tell me.

During the Pepkahàk (Facsimile Warriors) festival-pageant, a wasp's nest is crushed with sticks to let wasps emerge near the hut in which the Facsimile Warrior troops are secluded. It is believed that because of the festival internment and its restrictions against food and sex, the Facsimile Warrior membership had entered into a ritually vulnerable state of being, so that wasp stings would harm them far more than persons in the ordinary state. To prevent the freed wasps from reaching the Facsimile Warriors' hut, secondary Formal Friends of Facsimile Warrior individuals station themselves around the hut and swat wasps that come by with large whisk brooms. The Facsimile Warrior members' Formal Friends always succeed in protecting the Facsimile Warriors by killing all the wasps, but usually some of the Formal Friends are stung.

A Canela individual calls her or his female Formal Friend *pintswèy*, while a male Formal Friend is *hààpin* (no translations). The general expression for Formal Friends is *khritswè* (lightening). These terms of address have priority over almost any other terms, including those used with close kin and affines. For instance, the older Thunder calls one of his sons *hààpin re* (male-Formal-Friend little). Consequently, the use of the Formal Friendship terms of address override most of the usual terms of address in longhouses. Such changes are clear to everybody for one generation, but often the change affects the second and further generations as well. That is, as a Canela, you sometimes do not call the daughter of your *pintswèy* what you should call her to continue the mother-to-daughter-to-granddaughter longhouse structure.

A special Canela pronoun, *yê*, expresses address and reference in the second and third persons, singular and plural, to all your Formal Friends and to all your affines who are not also your "spouses." Thus, there are two forms of "you" and of "she/he"[54] (*ka* and *yê,* and *kê* and *yê*).

Personal name-set transmission   Each Canela baby, whether female or male, receives a set of personal names from a name-giver, who is usually a female baby's father's sister (or her father's "sister") and a male baby's mother's brother (or his mother's "brother"). A personal set of names may contain one name or as many as 15, depending on the donor's memory and interest in conserving ancestral customs. In any case, the name-giver designates only one name in the set for the name-receiver to use and be known by. The name-receiver, however, passes the entire set on to each of his or her name-receivers, so the name-set goes down the generations "forever" (*nõ?nù?ti-mã*). This transmission of names occurs each time a name-giver exchanges names with a uterine or a classificatory sibling of the opposite sex.

A name-giver can either create a name on the spot when it is required for exchange with an opposite-sex sibling, or a name-giver can rely on one of the names already in her or his name-set. An example of name creation is the following: A woman who was angry at her husband ripped apart his half of the tied-together rods of their platform bed, leaving no room for him to join her at night. Later, remembering her great anger for her husband, she named her brother's daughter "Platform-bed thrown-down" (*pàl-rẽ*), possibly shaming her husband "forever." If Platform Down passes this name on to an eventual named-niece and this named-niece passes it on in turn, the name would be considered "ancestral" (*mãm mẽnkêtyê mẽnkaakaa tsà khôt:* early uncles' breath thing following: according to the breathing of the ancestors).

The transmission of male names is consistent with the consanguineal kinship patterns used traditionally in the longhouse, so it does not alter this pattern. However, the transmission of female names (from a woman to her brother's daughter) is not consistent with these kinship patterns, so such transmissions almost always alter the terms used in a longhouse, breaking up the continuation of the mother-to-daughter-to-granddaughter line which receives the passed-on name. For instance, a woman's brother's daughter's daughter should be this woman's "niece." But if this woman gives a name to her brother's daughter, this woman calls the named-niece's husband "husband," and their daughter "daughter" instead of "niece," terminating the mother-to-daughter-to-granddaughter matriline of "nieces." (See Figure 8.)

Contributing fathers   The Canela believe that once a woman is pregnant, any semen added to her womb during her pregnancy becomes a biological part of the fetus. Thus, children usually have one mother but several "contributing" fathers, or "co-fathers"—the usual expression in anthropology. While a child's father's brother and her or his father's sister's son are "fathers," among the other classificatory fathers, the child's contributing fathers are closer to the child in certain ways than these classificatory fathers. Like a "social" father, the one married to the mother, a contributing father observes restrictions against food and sex when his contributed-to children are sick, unlike the other "fathers." His children, in return, have to observe food restrictions when he is ill, to help him conserve his strength so that his condition does not worsen.

When a person is seriously ill, her or his immediate kin and spouse send messengers (usually able runners) to the sick person's absent one-link-away kin (parents, siblings, and children) to inform them that they must observe restrictions against certain "polluting" foods and against sexual relations which can also "pollute." Since

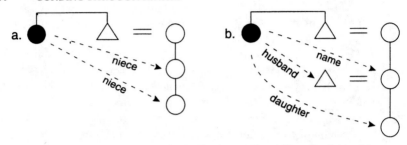

a. Usual: A woman calls her brother's daughter and granddaughter "niece."

b. After giving a name to her brother's daughter, this same woman calls her
named-niece's husband "husband" and her named-niece's daughter "daughter."

Figure 8. Female naming alters a matriline.

contributing fathers are included in this close group of one-link-away kin, messengers are sent to contributing fathers also. In contrast, messages are not sent to the sick person's father's brother (two biological links away) and her or his father's sister's son (three links away), though they are classificatory fathers.

Pregnant women usually seek good hunters, or good providers of some sort of food, to be the contributing fathers of their fetuses, since they believe such characteristics are inherited. These chosen men must give their semen to a demanding pregnant woman without hesitation, or they believe they may cause her to miscarry.

At the time of birth, only women cluster around the future mother, who sits on mats, leans back onto the abdomen of a sister, and raises her buttocks occasionally by pulling on a rope slung from an overhead beam. When the baby "falls" (*i?-pèm:* it-falls: is born), its father's mother usually "catches" it. This woman then asks the new mother, her "out-daughter" (her daughter-in-law), to designate the baby's contributing fathers for the sake of its health and survival. The new mother names the men who had sex with her several times during her pregnancy, and a child is sent to walk around the village circle to announce at pertinent doors the name of the designated contributing father.

These contributing fathers, pleased or compromised, have to go into a state of seclusion that is called "couvade" in anthropology. They have to live alone in a darkened compartment for some time, just as the social father does. Since the social father and the contributing fathers are all considered "biological" fathers in their relation to the recently born infant, they have to observe extensive food and sex restrictions against potential pollutions. This is done because these "fathers" believe their blood to be continuous with the baby's blood, so that if they allow their blood to become contaminated, they could also be poisoning the baby's blood. By eating certain foods or by having sex, these one-link-away "biological" kin could even cause the baby to die in its newly born and therefore very weak condition. The concept of pollutions will be discussed further in the next chapter.

A man may be embarrassed by his public designation as a contributing father, because he probably is living with his wife and his wife's sisters and their mother. These sisters may give him a hard time for not having been "faithful" to their sister, his wife. (Fortunately for him, his wife's mother and his wife's mother's sisters cannot even speak to him, being avoidance-women to him.) For these reasons, a contributing father may move at this time to the house of his own sister and mother to pass the period of the couvade's seclusion and to practice its requirements in a more sympathetic and supportive environment.

I do not use the anthropological expressions "genitor" and "pater" (the mother's husband) for the Canela, generally, because no one knows who the genitor is in the sense of Western science—the one whose sperm impregnated the mother's egg.[55] A Canela social father may be the genitor or just the pater, and any one of the contributing fathers, who may have been lovers of the mother before she conceived, may be the genitor or just a contributing father. A particular case involving a male homosexual illustrates this point as well as the Canela quantitative concept of procreation.

While three homosexuals were living in the tribe in 1971, only one of them was married. This homosexual and his wife, however, were taking a long time to produce a baby. Talk was going around that the young homosexual could not maintain an erection, but no one really knew whether this was the case because he refused to take part in the activities of the extramarital sex-exchange days. During these group occasions, the sexual abilities of both sexes were experienced by a member of the opposite sex, who subsequently discussed them so that any unusual sexual characteristics became common knowledge. However, in 1971 the young homosexual's wife became pregnant and gave birth to a baby girl, even though he had not allowed her to go out on the extramarital sex days.

In Canela thinking, the young homosexual, the social father in this case, was not considered at first to be one of the contributing fathers, even though he had the best opportunity to impregnate his wife. Later, however, people began to think the designated contributing fathers might not have contributed enough semen to be significant "biological" fathers, since the young homosexual had not allowed his wife to go out and about in the usual manner, collecting a sufficient amount of semen from each lover to make them biological fathers. The people began to think the young homosexual might have been the only biological father after all. Nevertheless, to follow custom and to play it safe, all the men declared by the new mother as having had sex with her several times during her pregnancy were considered contributing fathers—so that no significant pollutions could possibly reach the baby. Thus, Canela contributing fathership is an arbitrary quantitative concept, which makes the term "genitor" meaningless, unless we apply it in Western terms.

In order to test the Canela idea of conception further, I asked my most experienced research assistants, in the late 1950s and again in the 1970s, about an illustrative but fabricated scenario: What if a young man had sex with his wife once, left the next day for "the world," and was detained out there for 10 months? Could a baby develop to term in his wife and be born? (The Canela knew that the human gestation period is about nine months—moons.) I added that, being childless, his young wife in the scenario lived with her in-mother (mother-in-law) during this period and maintained a strict seclusion during his absence, not having sex at all. In the late 1950s, the research assistants said the wife would not become pregnant from the one experience with her husband, because it takes more than one sex experience to make a baby. However, by the 1970s, they declared that one sex act might create a baby, if it was a good act, but that the baby would be small when born.

Although the social father has to continue to maintain his restrictions against certain foods and sex (for about 6 to 12 months) to enhance the health and growth of the baby, the Canela terminate the couvade restrictions of the contributing fathers after about 40 days. At this time, the mother's female kin put on a special rite, the *mē hà?-khrēl* (they it-eat), to dismiss the contributing fathers. The mother, painted red, walks around the village circle to summon some of her "husbands," those that are her baby's designated contributing fathers. The social father and all the contributing fathers sit kneeling in her house around a large meat pie, holding eight-inch scratching sticks. At a signal, they dip the thin sticks into the pie and raise the morsels on the sticks to their lips, but do not eat them.

This act signifies abstention and thereby the concept of restrictions against certain foods and sex at critical times. As the biological fathers continue to sit, an "uncle" of the mother gives a formal lecture to these fathers, saying that they must never forget their responsibilities to their contributed-to child. They must provide

Women prepare a meat pie. They place meat cubes in a layer of manioc flour. After they fold the wild banana leaves over the flour and meat, they tie them with cords of buriti and bake the pies by placing them on hot rocks and covering them with earth.

their child with meat every now and then, and they must observe food and sex restrictions for their child when it is sick. Through this rite, contributing fatherhood is made a lifelong responsibility. Most villagers are looking on to witness the contributing fathers' dedication to their child. These villagers are certainly going to remember who the contributing fathers are and will make occasional remarks later if they are not living up to the responsibilities of their important roles.

Contributing father–child relationships extend beyond the two individuals involved, altering significantly the mother-to-daughter-to-granddaughter pattern of terms in longhouses. Through merely a contributing father relationship, individuals who may not be genealogically related at all in the Western sense call each other "sister," and their "siblingship" may continue down for several generations—matrilines in parallel with each other—changing the usual patterns in their different longhouses. (See Figure 9.)

KEEPING THE PEACE THROUGH ALTERNATIVE SYSTEMS

The various relationship systems which change longhouse patterns—Informal Friendship, Formal Friendship, female name transmission, and contributing fatherships—mix

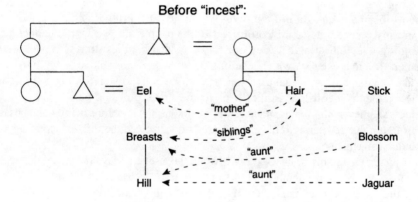

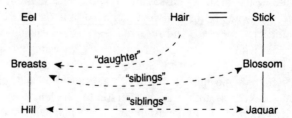

Figure 9. Contributed-to children alter matrilines.

with the consanguineal kinship system, breaking up the mother-to-daughter-to-grand-daughter matrilines. Nevertheless, this mixing of the various relationship systems adds to the overall social integration of the tribe. The various systems provide alternative bonding pathways between two individuals, helping to preserve communication and peace between them and their families. Thus, the various systems help maintain the high level of social cohesion which is so characteristic of the Canela. An episode which took place in my sister Waterfall's household in 1960 illustrates that interpersonal problems are often solved through the use of two different systems (or pathways) of terms of address and reference at the same time.

Lake Lover and her husband Boil's Vapor were not getting along. Boil had left Lake and had moved all his possessions over to the house of his mother, Sweet Potato's Wisdom. Besides the problems between Lake and Boil, an interfamilial problem was contributing mutual hostility to their relationship. Someone had seen Lake "talking" (flirting) alone with a man, Hard Bed (*pàl-tèy*), down at the swimming hole in the middle of the afternoon, when most people are sleeping or resting. Since the incident had become public knowledge and had therefore "passed shame onto Boil's face," he wanted a payment from our family to "erase this shame."

Waterfall and her brothers pointed out that Lake Lover had not gone off in the bushes to have sex with Hard Bed, so that her behavior did not warrant a significant complaint. Nevertheless, Boil and his family were adamant about receiving a compensatory payment. Burnt Path, who was Waterfall's brother and our spokesman (and my research assistant), promised Boil's people that we would cooperate in holding a legal hearing between our two extended families. In return, Burnt Path asked Boil to move back with his belongings as soon as possible to begin living with Lake once again for the sake of their two children, who were crying and missing their father. Nevertheless, Boil refused to cooperate. Boil said he was carrying too much shame (*pahàm*) on his face to appear in our house before being compensated through a public hearing. This exaggerated pride showed the influence of the backlanders' machismo.

Waterfall and her brothers knew it would take several days before all the appropriate persons could assemble to hold a proper legal "hearing" (*audiência: mē aypēn pa:* they to-each-other listen), and they did not want the hostile feelings to continue even for this short period. So we agreed to send one of Lake's two immediate uncles, Burnt Path, over to talk with Boil in a special way.

By coincidence, Burnt Path and Boil had been Informal Friends, but their joking relationship had been weakened by their later having become in-laws. Boil generally referred to Burnt Path as an "in-person" (*i-pree*), his wife's mother's brother, to whom he had to show considerable respect because Burnt Path partly controlled his wife. But when Burnt Path approached Boil in the plaza, he called him "Informal Friend" (*i-khwè ?nō*) and referred to the days of their roaming the savannahs together with their age class members, as they were undergoing initiation. With Informal Friendship invoked, Boil could listen in a friendly manner. Burnt Path expressed his sympathies for his Informal Friend Boil and agreed man-to-man that his niece, Lake, was not the easiest person to get along with. Thus, out of respect for their earlier Informal Friendship, and in keeping with their continuing membership in the same age class which requires mutual cooperation "forever," Boil gave in. He "came home to his children," as the Canela always put it; they do not talk about "coming home to a wife."

In the trial that was held a few days later, Alligator's Tail, 82, presided. After listening to witnesses from both sides and especially to Boil's "uncle" Standing Water, 71, who was representing him, Alligator's Tail rendered his nonbinding opinion. He maintained that while we, Lake's kin, were in the right according to custom, we nevertheless must pay Boil's kin reparations to keep the peace between the two extended families. Lake had not done anything offensive in merely talking to Hard Bed, or even if she had had sex with him. Nevertheless, since she had been so indiscreet as to flirt in a public place where she was likely to be seen by one of Boil's female kin, we owed Boil a "payment" to ease his shame. We (Lake's kin) would have to pay for Lake's lack of concern and respect for her husband.

Alligator's Tail pointed out that we, as a highly prestigious family, should give in to a family of low prestige—to keep them happy and to maintain peace in the tribe. Our Lake had been a Wè?tè girl, one of the highest ceremonial honors in the tribe. With our high honor keeping us "happy" (amyi?kĩn: euphoria), we had to give in to less fortunate families in the tribe to spread the state of personal and familial satisfaction to them.

NOTES

45. *Kêt* is used here for simplicity. Actually, *kêt-ti* (uncle-large [in physical size]) and *kêt-re* (uncle-small [in size]) are the terms used by the Canela.

46. The "advising uncle" of a young person is usually one of her or his mother's brothers. However, any man can choose to take on this special responsibility, including the young person's classificatory uncles, grandfathers, and men who are not in the *kêt* category. Thus, the advising (*to hapak-khre*) "uncle" is any man who takes on the continuous disciplinary role for a young person.

47. Quotes around a kinship term can indicate that it is to be taken in a classificatory sense, which means in the case of a father that he is a distant rather than an immediate father. Also, quotes around a kinship term are used to distinguish my Canela from my American relatives the *first* time they appear in a chapter. Later, no quotes are used for my immediate Canela kin and affines.

48. Since the Canela were living in two villages at the time of my arrival in 1957, they adopted me into a separate kinship network in each village. Thus, when the tribal schism ended in 1968, I had two primary families in one village.

49. "Cousin" is defined differently in various subcultures of the United States, and whether a person is one's first or second cousin, and so on, may be calculated differently.

50. A four generation matriline, the youngest female being Edible-vine-woman, 4, existed in my primary brother's household in 1975.

51. The meaning of the word "sibling" in Canela is revealing: sibling (*i?-khyê*: its-thigh/it-pulls). Both a human "thigh" and the act of "pulling together" on something are associated in Canela symbolism and festivals with individuals furnishing mutual support.

52. The Canela do not have exogamous moieties, as is erroneously stated in Nimuendajú's monograph (1946:79).

53. Only a man's spouse, and the "spouses" with whom he has had sex, can glance at his glans fleetingly without embarrassing him greatly. A man washes his glans under the water, so women and men present cannot see it.

54. In Canela, gender distinctions are not made through pronouns: *Kê* refers to she, he, and it; and *yê* refers to she and he. Gender distinctions are not made through adjectives either; but a few nouns are clearly sex-oriented. Most of the kinship terms of address and reference are gender specific, and separate terms for women (*pùyê*) and men (*mẽ-hũm-re*) exist at most of the stages of their life cycles, though not all. The suffix *-khwèy* can be added to a female's personal name, but no corresponding male suffix exists.

55. The Canela have no concept of the human egg nor of sperm. The male ejaculate (*hiràà*) joins female blood (*kaprôô*) in the womb to form a fetus, if enough ejaculate is accumulated. A woman and a man contribute equally to the fetus.

3/Bonding Through Meetings and Ritual

This chapter is devoted to ways in which structured individual and group activities with some degree of formality contribute to the social cohesion of the Canela. It is quite obvious that meetings and hearings designed to reach consensus and to resolve disputes help bring the community together. It is less obvious how the topics arrayed under the rubric of "ritual" connect to the theme of bonding. The chapter discusses the Canela beliefs in "other worlds," under the topic of "rituals," in order to explain the nature of ghosts. Through relationships with ghosts, shamans can know everything about any individual in the tribe, making secrets impossible. Relationships with ghosts lead to shamanic powers. Shamanic powers in turn contribute greatly to social control and conformity. The practice of maintaining restrictions against pollutions also supports the intricate web of connectedness we have seen in the preceding chapter. Kinship is reinforced by the concept of a common blood pool which must be kept healthy by restrictions against pollutions maintained by its members. Thus, the aspects of Canela "religion" discussed here do lead to tighter social cohesion. Canela "religion," however, is "this-worldly" in its orientation as opposed to the "other-worldly" folk Catholicism of the backlanders. Indeed, it is hardly recognizable as "religion" as we understand major world religions.

Canela rites and festivals are detailed in the rest of the chapter. The Canela are distinguished by their extraordinarily rich ceremonial life, ranging from single, almost imperceptible events to major festivals. Even those small acts carried out within the nuclear family unite the individual to the larger Canela community through the replication of what is believed to be customary. Group ceremony, whether rites or festivals, clearly increases group identity. Canela ceremonial life is not different from the ceremonial life of other tribal groups in this respect; but it is unusually profuse and a great source of satisfaction and pleasure to the Canela, adding to their conviction that Canela life is preferable to any alternatives.

TRIBAL MEETINGS AND JUDICIAL HEARINGS

The Canela have tribal meetings twice a day when they are assembled in their village. These occur at about seven in the morning and five in the afternoon. These meetings of male elders, any men from about 40 to 70, take place in the center of the

The chief exhorts the elders in the center of the plaza in the morning. A few younger men look on. Notice the relative nudity of the late 1950s.

village plaza and are led by one of the tribal chiefs, a man. A principal purpose of such meetings is to pick up contentious issues between extended families, which might disturb the peace, and to resolve such issues quickly if possible.

Another effect of the meetings of the elders is to provide male bonding for older men. Younger men find bonding through the lifelong age classes they belong to, each 10 years apart. These younger male age classes also meet twice a day in assigned places around the edge of the plaza. The meetings of the younger men seldom become formal, consisting largely of storytelling activities.

The plaza is the male place of the village; women dance in it and walk across it, but they never hold meetings there. Counterparts for female bonding are found in the village circle of houses, among the extended families where women control most activities. Women talk about activities of interest while they work in their extended family houses. They also meet and talk extensively with women of other extended families while fetching water or washing clothes down at the stream. There are no formal or informal tribal meetings for women. The circle of houses is the female place of the village.

Daily tribal council meetings   The first part of a meeting of the elders in the center of the plaza is quite informal. Men simply exchange news of the day about the tribe, about the backlanders, or even, though rarely, about the Brazilian nation. Much of what is discussed is simple gossip and serves the purpose of amusement. Men clearly enjoy sharing stories, often at the expense of women and backlanders, during this informal part of a meeting.

When the first chief, Jaguar's Coat, comes walking slowly down the radial pathway from his house and joins them, the small talk stops and the seating is rearranged, so no significant speakers are sitting behind the chief. Chief Jaguar's Coat opens the formal part of a meeting by changing the tone of the discourse and, formerly, by using a somewhat archaic vocabulary. He imposes the power of his office on the elders through his commanding manner. Nevertheless, he cannot take initiatives that fall far outside the consensus of the elders. He must convince the elders of the advantages of most issues; they definitely limit his power.

After the first chief has spoken at the meeting—or, in his absence, one of the other chiefs—the lesser chiefs speak in descending order of political importance. Then any man speaks who has a topic of interest, each one using formal tones and language.

Because the center of the plaza is a sacred place, little dissension can occur there. The tendency of the elders is to follow the chief or to make indirect statements offering alternative points of view, which the chief listens to carefully. These additional points may change the chief's point of view by the time he brings up the topic again at a later meeting.

I was impressed by the tones of good will which I almost always heard voiced at these meetings. Individuals who could not express good will usually stayed away or remained quiet. For instance, the older Thunder, the second chief, often held opinions that ran counter to the programs of the first chief, Jaguar's Coat. Thus, the older Thunder usually did not attend meetings led by Chief Jaguar's Coat, but he often led meetings in Jaguar's Coat's absence. Personal avoidances to prevent conflicts or unpleasant situations are typically Canela.

Topics which come up as gossip during the informal part of a meeting of the elders, if thought sufficiently disruptive of the peace, may be introduced at the formal part of the meeting or at a later formal meeting. Problems within an extended family are settled by the family itself, but problems between extended families are first discussed informally by principal older representatives of the two families, usually "grandfathers" or "uncles" of the plaintiff and the accused. If these family representatives cannot resolve the problem among themselves, or swiftly among the elders, they take the problem to a meeting in a convenient house of the extended family of either the plaintiff or the accused. There a "hearing" takes place, which lasts for as many mornings as are needed to resolve the situation. I will take up these hearings, or trials, later in this section.

Problems that are tribal in scope are the business of the chief and all the elders. However, it is only the Council of Elders, the Pro-khãmmã, a smaller and more select group of the elders, that puts on the great festivals, while the chiefs of the tribe just watch and cooperate. The great festivals last from two to four months and are complex pageants with many acts. They are supposed to be repeated in exactly the same way whenever they are put on, whether annually or every three to five years, depending on the particular festival. The details of an act that is put on only once in five years, or sometimes less frequently, may be hard to remember. Consequently, the elders debate what each performer must do, or wear, until they come to a consensus.

The Facsimile Warriors' festival, for example, takes place about every five years. In more recent times, however, longer gaps have occurred between performances, as between 1958 and 1970, and 1970 and 1979. In such situations the collective memories of the elders are strained to remember all the details of each act in the festival.

During the planning of the Facsimile Warriors' festival in 1970, one councilor of the Council of Elders said that in the Tàm-hàk (sensitive-falcon) act of the festival the membership of this society wore on their bodies only vertical white feather stripes. Another councilor argued that the Sensitive Falcon membership wore red urucu body paint between these stripes, as he recalled he had done in 1958 as a Sensitive Falcon member. However, my expert research assistant, the younger Thunder, not yet a member of the Council of Elders, spoke courteously to the elders at the council meeting about the work done with me in group sessions the year before. He said we had been working extensively on body adornments of festivals and on how and why they were used. He offered that we had decided that red body paint could not be worn at the same time as the *poopok,* the artifact hung down the back of each member of the Sensitive Falcon society during their performance.

Old-timers in my group of research assistants, in their 70s or early 80s, recalled performances of the Facsimile Warriors' festival that had taken place five and six decades earlier. They had helped us decide that the decorative cotton of the bamboo artifact, the *poopok,* should never *ever* be sullied with any paint, red or black. The *poopok* must remain whitened with chalk, enclosed in a clean box, and never used from festival to festival, in contrast to all other festival items. This is because white is the color of high ceremonial honor, and the Sensitive Falcons are the highest honor society of the Canela. The old-timers pointed out that if the Sensitive Falcons wore red between their white feathered stripes, the sacred *poopok* that each of them was wearing during the performance of their special act would be sullied by red paint.

I knew that the Sensitive Falcons had worn red paint between their white stripes in 1958, because I had a picture of myself "dressed" that way. Nevertheless, the mistake made by the Sensitive Falcons in 1958, as determined in my research assistant work group and thus learned by the younger Thunder, was not repeated in 1970, due to Thunder's explanations to the Council of Elders. The memories of the old-timers in my work group and their logic for why a *poopok* should not be defiled with red paint was convincing to the council in 1970.

This incident shows that the debates among the Council of Elders in the plaza when they are reconstructing a festival act are complex and detailed. It also shows how my work among the Canela had unintended effects. I had been trained not to interfere, teach, or prevent change. In fact, I was studying how changes took place, so I was glad whenever I could identify a change that was occurring. In this case, however, my studies were preventing a change that had already occurred from becoming instated permanently in the people's memories as "tradition." When the next Facsimile Warriors' festival was performed in 1979, the elders copied the performance of 1970, not the one of 1958. Thus, inadvertently, I had prevented the usual evolution of "tradition."

Another role of the elders, not just the Council of Elders, is to ease difficulties between members of the village and members of the backland communities of the region. In this role, however, the first chief, rather than the elders in general or the Council of Elders, has the principal responsibility and takes the initiatives for external relations.

One morning during the informal part of the meeting of the elders, one of them commented that he had heard a story that backlanders had waylaid a certain Canela couple as they were returning from the backland town of Leandro about 20 miles to the east. Backlanders had beaten up the young Canela male and then raped his teenage wife. The elder did not know whether the story was fact or rumor. Consequently, the elders turned to men who were uncles of the couple, individuals who happened to be present, but they too had heard nothing. The uncles left the meeting immediately, walked to the house of the couple, and started asking them questions. The young man's face was badly cut. He confirmed the story, but included few details. Fortunately, the backlanders had not physically hurt his wife beyond raping her, which is not as serious a matter for the Canela as it is in the United States. Canela women view access to their bodies differently.

Returning to the plaza, the uncles gave their report during the formal part of the meeting. The chief decided to send to Leandro two disinterested elders, who would be more diplomatic than the too involved uncles, to discover more about the situation and complain to the authorities there. The elders spent two days in Leandro, but no one there knew about the situation, except that the couple had gone on to Jenipapo, a community five miles to the south.

As the elders were returning home from Jenipapo, still with little news, they stopped at a farmer's house on the outskirts of the community. They knew this farmer sometimes sold illegal *cachaça* (cane alcohol). The elders bought some *cachaça* and asked the farmer if he had seen the couple several days earlier. The farmer said the couple had passed by there and bought *cachaça*. When the elders told the farmer the story of the rape, the farmer reported that just as the couple were leaving, two traveling salesmen with a donkey carrying goods had come by and bought *cachaça*. The farmer added that he had thought it strange that the salesmen had followed the couple, because salesmen coming from the south did not usually turn in the westerly direction of the Canela village; they continued north to Leandro.

Walking along this little-traveled trail, the elders could distinguish the tracks of the salesmen, the mule, and the couple. The elders "read" the tracks and decided that the salesmen had waited until the couple were thoroughly drunk and already lying down by the side of the trail before they attacked the youth and raped his wife. Of course, the young husband had not told the uncles that he had been drunk and that he and his wife had returned by way of Jenipapo instead of Leandro.

Since the assailants were itinerants, there were no authorities with whom a complaint could be placed to reprimand them effectively, so the chief and the elders had to drop the case. The chief knew that the authorities of Leandro and Jenipapo would have done little anyway, even if the assailants had been one of their citizens. He knew that the authorities would have claimed it was the Indians' fault, as usual, for having been drunk and therefore defenseless. They had left themselves open and thereby had become fair game. The chief and the elders believed, however, that it was the alcohol's fault, so even the couple could not be blamed.

"Hearings": Legal trials between extended families   One of the most notorious hearings between two extended families I ever recorded was between the family of a virgin of 11 or 12 years and the family of a married man of 25 with two children. As in the previous case, I will not mention names, even translated ones, to avoid considerable embarrassment for the married man in this account, who is still alive; the girl has since died. Thus, the married man will be "M," his wife "W," and the young woman "V."

I felt sorry for M because W was such a loudmouth. Extramarital sex was the custom, but W made a big fuss over any suspicion she had about her husband's activities with other women. Nevertheless, I was quite surprised when I heard that M had taken the virginity of young V, who was very beautiful and light of frame. Her breasts were barely coming out. I would have thought it impossible for any man to have sex with her—she was so small and fragile—but I knew that virginities were given at 11 to 13 years of age and that they were sometimes given or taken at still younger ages among some other Brazilian Indian peoples, such as the linguistically related Kayapó.

When young Canela women are behaving "correctly," they have their first sexual intercourse with a man who is unattached. Through this act young women become married, but the man's family can pay a fine to get him out of the marriage. "Unattached" here means a man without a child of his own, not a man without a wife. Unattached men may be married, and they may have fathered children in other marriages, but if they do not have a child with the woman they are married to, they are considered unattached. If an unattached married man had married his wife as a non-virgin, and if he then took the virginity of a young woman, he would have to leave his wife. He would have to marry the young woman whose virginity he had taken, according to current custom. However, if the married man had children with his wife and took the virginity of another woman, he was in deep trouble, and the young woman was in still deeper trouble. This was the situation of M, W, and V. Trying to resolve this problem, the leading uncles of the extended families of these three individuals held at least a dozen hearings (mẽ aypẽn pa: they to-each-other listen: audiências) over a period of six months.

Since M had two children with W, the usual way out of the conflict of loyalties would be for M's family to pay an acceptably large fine to V's family. Nevertheless, having lost her virginity, but not having gained a husband, V would find getting married more difficult. M made the situation much more problematical, however, by going to live with V in her family's house. By not paying the fine to get away from V and by going to live with V, M became married to V as well as to W. But the Canela have no tradition for polygyny; they think it is ridiculous. I used to hear M's age class mates, as well as his "other wives," teasing him as he passed along the boulevard, calling him Tomas. Tomas was a backlander, who, as a traveling salesman, lived in two communities several mule-traveling days apart. He had a wife and children in each community, though he was married to neither woman in the Catholic sense.

After M went to live with V and was accepted by her family (he was a good financial catch), the problem became compounded because W refused to have him back. She gave him a tongue-lashing whenever he returned for equipment or to see his children. But W's position was impossible to maintain, because the Canela do not allow divorces to occur while a couple are raising their own "biological" children. Nevertheless, the Canela held many hearings between spouses who were raising their own children. I assumed that even though such estranged spouses could only separate temporarily, their families nevertheless held hearings so the plaintiff could thoroughly air the complaints against the accused.

Since the Canela had made me a ceremonial chief of the people—a peacemaking chief—the elders sent me to visit W to get her to accept M's return for the sake of his children. I thought this assignment would be relatively easy to carry out, because I was on a joking footing with W, since by a quirk of kinship, she was one of my other wives. I asked my uncle Sticky Boar to visit her to see if she would accept a visit from me, and he returned saying that she would welcome me. W quietly listened to my explanations and request; nevertheless, she seemed more interested in using me to get back at M. She turned her loud-mouthing on me, demanding that I make him hear her objections. Obviously, I did not comply.

While it was within my role as ceremonial chief to help resolve such problems, I nevertheless decided to decline further requests to act as an intermediary. It was clear to me that I could not understand their personal problems sufficiently well, considering all the shadings and subtleties such problems always have. Moreover, it was more important for advancing my research to see how they resolved their problems by themselves. I could learn their ways better if I did not add my foreign influences. Besides, if I let an active role as a go-between develop for myself, such social bonding activities would consume more time than I could afford to give. If matters happened to go wrong and I was seriously misunderstood, my prestige among the Canela could plummet, and then my stay among them could be terminated by their chief and Council of Elders.

After many hearings led by uncles of the three parties, who summoned witnesses on all sides, and after we had heard the vitriolic complaints of M against W, W against M, and V against M many times, M returned to W, as everybody knew he would have to eventually. A man *cannot* leave his children who were born to the woman he is married to, for the sake of the children. The uncles decided that M had to give everything he owned to V's family, which in M's case was a substantial amount, including a horse and its equipment, machetes, axes, and shotguns. He also had to deliver a suitcase of city clothes, which in those days were rare possessions. W had to turn over half of her farm for V's female kin to use by pulling up manioc roots from it when they needed them.

These interfamily hearings can be seen as responsibly run trials, if the premises on which their decisions are based can be understood and accepted. All the hearings in this case took place in W's house, because it had a large room with two open sides, so many people could assemble inside or just outside in the sand to witness the proceedings. The location did not give one side or the other an advantage.

The main purpose of such hearings is to keep the peace between extended families. The Canela abhor and fear dissension. Justice is a lesser consideration than placating indignant and vocal plaintiffs. Moreover, the more ceremonially prestigious families are expected to give in to the less elite ones. Relative material wealth was also just beginning to become a consideration in 1959. Given these cultural assumptions, M and W did not have a chance of avoiding the payment of immense fines to V's extended family. Everyone knew this, but everyone also wanted to let the hearings run their course. The full public airing of injured feelings—from personal mistreatment to deeply felt shame—seemed to be what these hearings were arranged to provide.

During the first hearings, it seemed as if no one would give ground. M scored strongly on his numerous examples of W's harsh tongue, and several witnesses of both sexes supported him. M's numerous extramarital trysts had been carried out in a discrete manner, so W's complaints fell on largely unsympathetic ears. W's accusations were based on suspicions rather than on what anyone had seen and gossiped about. Thus, she had no reason to experience shame. Moreover, W's picky and unloving nature came through clearly, as she stood and made her unsupported accusations before 50 to 60 people.

V said very little, being so young and shy. Nevertheless, her uncles and mother presented her case well. They spoke repeatedly about the point, well-known to everyone, that V would be *na rua* (in the street), which they always stated in Portuguese, leading me to think this was a recently developed belief. They spoke of her as becoming a *rapariga* (whore), again in Portuguese, which to me was clearly an inconsistency with what I knew of Canela custom. Her uncles were playing on our sympathies by calling on backland customs.

V's uncles also spoke of her loss of virginity and that she would have gained nothing from this loss if M did not stay married to her. This point made more sense to me, according to my understanding of Canela custom. Young girls gave their virginity to gain marriage—it was traded—as was everything in Canela life, except between close kin and married couples. V's uncles also expressed how ashamed they were—"shame had been passed onto their faces"—because M was not offering to pay a sufficient amount to leave V.

What clearly "won" the case for V's uncles—though according to the premises of the culture they *had* to win—was the vehemence of their presentations, characteristic of people of low ceremonial honor. They were disturbing the peace of village life, hoping to get their way; they were capable of going around moping and complaining, if the case were not resolved very much to their favor. My research assistants, being of the elite, expressed it this way. V's family had to be placated, so that all the uncles of the tribe, essentially all the elders, could meet face to face every day in the plaza, enjoying each other's company in peace and harmony.

I remember well that I felt I had to watch and account for my own subjective reactions to these hearings. W had rebuffed my efforts, and I found her personality unappealing. These two facts may have accounted for my lack of sympathy for her. In contrast, I felt sorry for V but knew she would eventually get a husband; nothing is absolutely good or bad in Canela life. She was so young that her family could still keep her at home (i.e., off the street) for several years to improve her chances of getting a more reliable husband. They could keep her like a widow, not allowing her to go on the extramarital sex days. The first man to have sex with a widow after her loss, as with a virgin, is married to her by custom.

My observation made years later, and this could not have come from research assistants, was that M had managed to put W in her place during those hearings, so that their marriage could become more tolerable for him. Or, is my male bias showing here?

AFTERLIFE AND POLLUTIONS

The Canela are outstanding for living in the present and for their reliance on *this*-worldly projected procedures for living, in contrast to *other*-worldly projected procedures for solving human problems. "Projected" means *where our culture places* such activities, whether in the world in which we live or in the afterlife, on earth or in heaven, in the natural world or in the supernatural one. When a Canela shaman relies on *his own powers* to fetch the wandering soul of a person near death to bring it back to its body, this shaman is relying on his *this*-worldly powers, as is seen by the individuals living in his culture. When the Canela prophetess of the messianic movement, Maria, relied on Awkhêê as the authority behind her power, she was relying on a solution to problems of living people which she was *projecting onto* a Canela culture hero existing in a Canela "other-world." This was an *other*-worldly reliance.

I use the term "other-worldly" rather than "afterlife" most of the time, because I am discussing ongoing relationships—that is, simultaneous relationships—between individuals of the Canela world of the living and their other-world, not between the world of living Canela and their afterlife—a world that comes later in time. This simultaneous other-world of the Canela is populated by ghosts.

I use "ghost," "soul," "spirit," and "picture" (photograph) to talk of the entities of the Canela other-world, though the Canela use only one word, *karõ* (Portuguese: *alma*), for these four Western concepts. "Ghosts" are dead ancestors in the human form. I use "soul" to mean out-of-body living human forms which leave temporarily and return later to their living Canela human bodies. "Spirits" are out-of-object forms of zoological, botanical, and even mineral materials—animistic representations. Ghosts, souls, and spirits are invisible to ordinary Canela, but visible to Canela shamans.

It should not be surprising that the Canela use the same word, *karõ,* for both a photograph and a ghost. *Mẽ karõ to pôy* (plural-Canela ghost with returns) means "take photographs" as well as "return with a Canela soul." In the latter case, the Canela speaker would be referring to a shamanic ability described at the beginning of this section: that a shaman's soul had just returned from the other-world, bringing back the soul of a Canela in order to return it to its body, keeping the body alive; or in failing to retrieve the soul, letting the body die. The case of "take photographs" could be interpreted to mean, "I will come back from my little black box and give you a likeness of your body." Unlike many other peoples, the Canela are not worried about photographers stealing their souls and thereby reducing their energy or killing them. Canela individuals liked me to take their pictures, because they knew I would bring back copies for them on my next trip.

When Jean and I were with the Canela in October 1991, we heard about an extraordinary occurrence. A young man of about 14 years was dying of a stomach ulcer, dysentery, and dehydration. This was my diagnosis from what my Canela research assistants told me. The Canela believed in another diagnosis.

The young man's family believed that his soul had left his body and that it was traveling on the path to the ghosts' village. Thus, they summoned a shaman to try to return his soul to its body. The shaman caused his own soul to go out into the ghostly world, along the traditional path to the ghosts' village. There, the shaman's soul found the young man's soul in the company of the ghost of the shaman's aunt. The shaman's soul tried to bring the young man's soul back to the living Canela village, but the young man's soul physically knocked down the shaman's soul twice in rapid succession. Nevertheless, the shaman's soul kept working with the youth's soul, cajoling and persuading it to return, until the shaman's aunt's ghost told her nephew's soul to go home, saying that the youth's soul wanted to stay in the ghostly world. Thus, the shaman's soul returned to the Canela village empty-handed, the young man died, and his soul stayed in the ghostly world, becoming a ghost. My research assistants said that the youth just wanted to die and that this was why his soul would not come back.

Canela other-worlds   The Canela world of ghosts is only one of the Canela other-worlds. Individuals of the Canela culture maintain these other-worlds by projecting beliefs onto them, and, except for the ghosts' world, these beliefs place the other-worlds almost entirely in the past. The other Canela other-worlds are inhabited by culture heroes, and they are portrayed best in creation myths, war stories, and tales about the origins of festivals, some examples of which follow.

Creation myths

Sun (Pùt) created the Canela by walking out of a pool of a savannah stream, followed by a file of Canela individuals. He established the intelligent, ideal life in which work was carried out without effort: axes and machetes swung on their own, felling trees, cutting brush, and clearing the ground for gardens. Moon (Putwrè) modified the ideal world through his clumsiness and stupidity, creating death, floods, forest fires, and work: Because of Moon, men, by their own efforts, had to begin to swing axes and machetes to prepare the ground for planting gardens. Because of Moon's intervention, short fruit trees grew tall, so their fruit became harder to harvest. Moon also created the individual body characteristics which are less preferred by the Canela—kinky instead of straight hair, darker instead of lighter skin, and squatter instead of taller bodies—by walking out of a pool with a file of these accepted but less prestigious types following him. Sun ascended to the skies, taking Moon along with him, because he felt badly about the incest and fighting occurring among his people. Sun wanted to distance himself from the partially evil Canela nature, caused by Moon's interventions.

Star Woman (Katsêê-ti-ʔkhwèy) came down from the skies and showed the Canela all sorts of edible fruits and plants, which they began to collect or cultivate for the first time. Then she returned to the skies with one Canela male she loved, and they became the twin stars known to us as Castor and Pollux.

Awkhêê was born of a Canela mother, but he had remarkable other-worldly powers, which he used playfully as a child. For instance, he turned himself into a jaguar to scare his siblings, and then into an anaconda (a large constrictor water snake) to scare them again. However, his "uncles," the elders, took a dim view of such activities. Awkhêê's remarkable abilities threatened the uncles' power, so they connived to kill him. They pushed him off a cliff, but Awkhêê turned into a leaf and floated to safety. He saved himself in similar ways several times. Finally, the uncles pushed him onto a bonfire, but Awkhêê jumped out. Then they surrounded the fire and kept pushing him back onto it from every side. Seeing how determined they were, Awkhêê let them succeed. So he turned himself into a cinder and disappeared from view.

Several days later, Awkhêê's mother, longing for him, went to see the location of the bonfire. Instead of ashes, she found a farm with a white house. Horses, cattle, pigs, and chickens were roaming about. Awkhêê had turned himself into the first *civilizado* and had created the backland society and economy. Awkhêê welcomed his mother and showed her the new world he had constructed. He told her to go back to their people to summon his uncles.

When the uncles arrived at the white house, they became afraid of Awkhêê and the new world of the backlanders. Awkhêê welcomed them and told them not to be afraid; he wanted to help his special people, the Canela. He offered the backlander and the Canela the choice between the way of life of the shotgun or of the bow and arrow. Awkhêê was disappointed and disgusted with the Canela when they chose the bow and arrow. In anger, he sent them wandering for years with the belief that they were poor and socially inferior to the backland *civilizado*. This belief justified their dependency, so they could "beg" demandingly and still retain their self-respect. Through this myth, it became their right to be totally supported by the *civilizado*.

The Canela have a number of other myths, like "Jaguar and the Origin of Fire," which I believe the Canela have outgrown. I say this because their storytellers seldom recite these accounts, and when they do, old men tell them as if these stories were about another people, though admittedly about their ancestors when they were still *índios brabos* (Indians wild). The story of Awkhêê, however, was almost the only one they told as if it applied to the present—about why it was their right to "beg."

War stories

Stories about war heroes illustrate a number of Canela values and abilities which were prized years ago and are still admired, though with some ambivalence due to the change in times.

Khrùt (flint) persuaded an "uncle" to go with him on a raid of an enemy people to avenge the death of another uncle (his mother's brother), but the real reason was to prove his manhood and to gain the status of war leader. Flint and his uncle traveled inconspicuously and swiftly for several days and penetrated enemy territory successfully without being discovered. Leaving his uncle behind on a knoll, Flint slipped into the enemy village at night and killed one man, taking his war bonnet of macaw tail feathers. As he was leaving the village, enemy warriors shot at him, but, using his shamanic abilities, Flint dodged all the arrows and escaped into the darkness. Flint found his uncle waiting on the knoll, and running all the way out of enemy lands, they returned to the Canela village safely. Arriving home in the late afternoon, Flint laid the enemy's war bonnet on a mat before the elders and showed the blood still on his hands. After a number of weeks of seclusion and diet to rid his system of the blood pollution introduced by killing a man, Flint presented himself to the elders and they declared him a *hààprāl*, a war leader.

Flint had avenged his mother's brother, killed an enemy warrior, shown skill and courage in raiding, demonstrated his shamanic abilities, and proven his endurance in running. He also returned with the proof of his deeds, a valuable enemy artifact of feathers. The first three of Flint's deeds have seldom been carried out since pacification, but the last three are valuable assets today. Shamanic curing is valued by everybody, endurance running is respected in hunters, and arriving in triumph from cities with expensive goods is a justification for the trip. During the early 1970s, Chief

Jaguar's Coat came back with a truck given the Canela by the Indian Service, justifying his chieftainship.

Tales about the origins of festivals

For most of the festivals, a young Canela male (or two youths) went off to an other-world of the past where they saw a festival which they then taught to the Canela after their return. For example, Pore-?tèy (ear-plug capable) and his companion were sent by the elders across a great river to check on the growth of their people's vegetable gardens at the winter village. While Ear Plug and his companion were swimming, Ear Plug was swallowed by a large water snake, but his companion escaped to return to his people. As Ear Plug lay in the great constrictor's stomach being digested, the Fish people around the anaconda felt sorry for him. They entered the snake's mouth to introduce slime, which caused Ear Plug to pop out. Then the Fish took Ear Plug to the world of their village under the river, where their festival was just beginning. There, Fish were dancing in human form. Ear Plug carefully memorized all that the Fish were doing and taught the Canela the Fish festival upon his return.

Ghosts' world: Lesser than the living world

Ghosts inhabit a contemporaneous village on the same level of the earth as the Canela. In contrast, culture heroes inhabit other-worlds, largely projected onto the past: (1) above the level of the living-Canela world, such as the world of Star Woman; (2) on the same level as the living Canela, such as the world of Flint; and (3) below the level of the Canela, such as the world of the Fish people. Culture heroes are not ghosts; they do not go through the Canela human process of death. Sun, Moon, Star Woman, Awkhêê, Jaguar, Flint, Ear Plug, and many others exist in their own right as beings in Canela belief, whether myths, war stories, or festival origin-tales.

Ghosts, who have left their this-worldly bodies (*i?-khre-?khà:* its hollow's/space's cover/structure) forever, inhabit a village to the west of the living Canela world, but they also wander around the living Canela world so that everything a Canela does is seen by some ghost. While ghosts in their own village are believed to enjoy themselves moderately, Canela research assistants believe they would not enjoy being a ghost. For instance, ghosts carry out almost all the same activities that alive (*hĩũá*) Canela undertake, but living Canela believe that ghosts experience less pleasure in each activity. For instance, the water ghosts drink in their other-world's village is warm instead of cool, their meat is relatively tasteless, their sex is less invigorating, and festive activities are less fun. Thus, Canela prefer to be living in their present world, which they believe is far more enjoyable.

Ghosts eventually turn themselves into animals, which turn themselves into still smaller animals and even small plants, so that they eventually cease to exist as living entities. Thus, ghosts are not immortal; their life spans are finite. I maintain that the lack of a concept of immortality coincides with the Canela preference for their this-world of the living over their other-world of ghosts.

Ghosts never go to the other-worlds of the Canela culture heroes, though living Canela in origin-myths of festivals traveled to these other-worlds, and they returned to the Canela this-world as living Canela. Most baptized Canela believe they go up to the folk Catholic heaven upon death.

The advantages ghosts have over living Canela are that they can travel simultaneously throughout all of time and space and that they know instantaneously what any one ghost has seen individually while moving around among living Canela individuals. Thus, ghosts serve as an all-knowing source of information for shamans (*kay*), and all good shamans can converse with ghosts. In contrast, ordinary Canela do not have access to this other-worldly source, because contacts between ghosts and ordinary Canela result in the latter's death, so that they become ghosts too.

Examples of shamans' activities are that they can summon ghosts when they need to know who stole a machete and where it is, and when they need to know what sex or dietary restriction was broken by a Canela individual and where in the body of this individual the resulting pollution is. Another example of shamans' activities is that they can summon ghosts when they need to know whether a certain witch (also a *kay*) cast a spell (*hũũtsùù*) of illness on a victim, the shaman's client, and what sort of a spell it was. These activities of shamans are explained by Canela research assistants as undertaken on the individual shaman's own initiative and responsibility (*amyiá-?khôt*), and therefore rely on his this-worldly abilities.

Shamans can "see" arriving enemy warriors or approaching plagues days in advance on their own initiative—a this-worldly ability—though ghosts might warn them well in advance—an other-worldly intervention.

Canela relationships with ghosts   A strong opposition exists in Canela thought between their this-world and their other-world of ghosts. If a ghost appears to an ordinary Canela as an apparition in human form, the Canela has not long to live. This means that the ghost desires the Canela and that the Canela desires the ghost, which most often occurs between spouses parted by death. The Canela other-world of ghosts is a hostile one to the ordinary Canela, who carries out mourning practices to lessen or eliminate most memories and feelings for the deceased, even for a spouse or child. The Canela truly live for the life of their this-world and feel sorry for relatives who have had to move on early to the less gratifying other-world of ghosts.

Ordinary Canela are not only sorry for ghosts, they are afraid of them. If a Canela goes down to the stream at dusk to fetch water, ghosts may injure that person fatally. If a messenger runs 50 miles to the city of Barra do Corda alone at night, he carries a protective device which ghosts do not like, such as a tail feather of a macaw parrot. Taken collectively, these harassing activities of ghosts tend to make Canela want to move around in groups for safety rather than to act as individuals.

Unlike the ordinary individual, the Canela shaman has developed powers to communicate with ghosts. Thus, shamans bridge the Canela this-world and their other-world of ghosts. Nevertheless, an old shaman who understood the earlier shamanic practices, the older Deer's Nest, astonished me by stating firmly that he looked down on the ghosts he dealt with and that he was their master—they were serving him.

Becoming a shaman: Ghosts' choice

Ordinary Canela become shamans through two distinctly different ways. First, a youth who wants to become a shaman carries out extremely careful restrictions against eating certain foods which are believed to have a high level of "pollution." Meat juices, not solid meat alone, carry this degree of pollution (*hīī kakô ?-khên:* meat's liquid it-bad), but meats of certain animals are more polluted than others. Pollutions already in an individual, through eating polluted foods' liquids, are transmitted to other individuals during sexual intercourse through the sexual fluids of either sex. Consequently, an individual who aspires to become a shaman avoids on his own initiative the more highly polluted foods and sexual intercourse with the individuals who have sex most frequently, those in their teens and twenties. The concept of pollution is quantitative, and, therefore, relative.

Ghosts like and are attracted to relatively unpolluted, that is, to relatively "pure," individuals. Ghosts will choose their time to visit such an individual in a dream or in the wakeful state. A youth may be very pure from carrying out long, careful, and extensive restrictions, as they say, but a ghost, nevertheless, may or may not choose to visit him. Thus, the initiative is up to the ghostly world; it is not up to the individual who is trying to become a shaman no matter how hard he tries.

Women seldom become shamans, because it is believed they rarely have the strength and persistence to maintain sufficiently high restrictions against pollutions to attract ghosts who would transform them into shamans. Nevertheless, there are at least two Canela myths about the activities of female shamans, and one of my best female research assistants was a shaman.

If a ghost decides to make the aspiring youth a shaman, the ghost visits the youth in animal or human form. The ghosts issue instructions, which, if maintained, enable further visits by the ghosts. These are other-worldly interventions. The instructions have to do with maintaining high restrictions, keeping out more and more pollutions, increasingly purifying the body. If the youth carries out the instructions well enough, the ghost eventually gives him "powers" (*hūūtsùù*), which the youth carries in his body, usually in the left armpit. Thereafter, the youth as a shaman uses these powers on his own. He does not have to summon a ghost to empower himself, though he may summon a ghost to obtain needed information. Thus, the bestowal of "powers" is other-worldly, while the use of powers is this-worldly, though the source of information may be other-worldly. Research assistants vary as to whether a shaman can on his own summon a ghost to appear or whether he has to wait for a ghost to happen to appear. The more traditional shamans say they can summon ghosts, being more self-empowered, while the more folk Catholic-oriented shamans say they have to wait, being more subject to the other-world.

The second way of becoming a shaman occurs when an individual is very sick and possibly dying. Then ghosts may choose to visit the sick individual to cure him or her. If a shaman thinks that such a visitation is likely to occur, he orders Canela families to vacate the part of the village in which the sick person lives and to leave him entirely alone in his house for a night. Dogs may have to be tied up or taken to a farm, because their barking would scare away the visiting ghosts. If the village is sufficiently quiet, the ghosts might choose to come during the night. If they do, and if they choose to cure the sick person, this cured individual has become a shaman and will possess powers to make certain kinds of cures, which he can use on his own initiative and responsibility. Again, the initiative of bestowing "powers" is other-worldly, while the use of the powers, once they are received, is this-worldly. The maintenance of such powers by self-purification, through the practice of careful food and sex restrictions to prevent pollutions from entering the body, is a this-worldly and individual endeavor.

Culture change

To me, the Canela this-world and their other-world seem to be two worlds. To the Canela, however, they are one continuous world of existence, even though its beings are antagonistic. The Canela living world and their ghosts' world are *one* world, though they can make the distinction between "my" two worlds through their choice of verbal expressions. The importance to me of this distinction, nevertheless, lies in the fact that as the Canela adopt Brazilian backland and urban ideas and practices, they are giving up the this-worldly self-reliance of their prepacification state for the other-worldly reliance of backland folk Catholicism. This backland attitude is best expressed in the ubiquitous expression *Se Deus quiser,* . . . (If God should wish it, . . .), which constitutes a very other-worldly reliance and dependency. The Canela individual is little by little giving up a do-it-himself or -herself approach to life's problems for a basic reliance on the fatalism of the regional backland Brazilian.

Do-it-yourself empowerment   When giving public lectures on the Canela, I am often asked about Canela religion. My answers inevitably perplex the audience, because the usual Western view of religion leaves the Canela without a "religion." The Canela had no god or gods to whom they prayed to transform conditions on earth to their advantage, such as asking for rain to terminate a drought. Today the Canela follow to a considerable extent a folk Catholic religion with its struggle between God and the Devil (*Satanás*). Some Canela say that earlier they had Apuyayê as a single god. They do not mention Awkhêê in this capacity. However, Apuyayê is not connected in a systematic way with any remnant beliefs, festivals, or practices, so I suspect Apuyayê was an early term for the folk Catholic Christian God.

While the Canela have what seems like an excessive number of festivals and rites, they do not worship a supernatural being when practicing any of these ceremonies. Their ceremonies are this-worldly in the individual's mental projection onto the place of responsibility for the action—onto the individual him- or herself. For instance, when a shaman tries to repel an invasion of grasshoppers, he uses his own powers to perform an ancient rite with a song, and the grasshoppers do or do not go away.

"Prayer": For self-development, not for supernatural intervention

Finally, after years of working with younger Thunder, my best Canela research assistant, he declared on his own, much to my disbelief, that parading and singing in a certain formation, the Haakrel, was *rezar*—to pray. I knew the Haakrel is performed in three of the great "summer" festivals, so I turned immediately from the subject being researched by the group to fathom what Thunder meant. I anticipated that this was going to be one of those rare occasions that are so intensely gratifying in field research—the moment of working through to the discovery of a new concept—but I was disappointed. I asked Thunder to describe in physical rather than abstract terms what the Haakrel meant for him. He said it was like crossing a marsh by stepping on firm mounds so that he would not get his feet wet. He said that most of the words chanted in the Ḥaakrel were "strong" ones; that such words were not far apart in the song; and that proceeding from strong word to strong word was like crossing a marsh on prepared stepping stones.

Strong words refer to long-lasting, endurance-oriented, and solidly structured items. These may be certain cultural practices, certain animals and plants, and certain mineral objects. The Corn festival will last "forever" because if the family line which possesses this cultural practice dies out, the Council of Elders will transfer the possession of this festival to another family line, ensuring its continuity. The armadillo endures the heat of the noontime sun, wandering around on the scorching savannah sands while most other creatures, including most Canela, rest in the shade and take naps. Rocks that are hard to break up and glass that survives fire without changing shape are also "strong" (*?tèy*).

I began to realize I was dealing with self-affirmation and positive thinking, so I began testing the negative side of the concept to understand it better. It occurred to me that the dark blue palm fruit after which a youth called Kaapêl-tùk (bacaba-dark) was named was indeed notably squishy; so I asked Thunder what would happen if this youth sang about bacaba fruits. Thunder became somewhat distressed and said that such a song existed; that long ago a youth kept singing this song in spite of many warnings so that he grew weaker and finally died. Thunder said that it was all right to be named after such a "soft" item, but that a person must not sing about it or he would become like the item.

When I first heard Thunder use *rezar* and connect this word with the Haakrel, I expected that I had finally discovered a ceremony during which the Canela communicated with entities of one of their other-worlds, either to worship them or to ask things of them, but this was not the case. The Canela were "praying" for self-strengthening through a this-worldly practice. Each singer was doing it himself or herself for himself or herself. No priest or shaman was involved. Thus, "discovering" the use of the Haakrel did not change my position on Canela religion: that it is largely this-worldly and does not have worship or prayer in our usual Western sense.

Pollution control by food and sex "restrictions"

The Canela believe that many pollutions are out there in the world they live in, though their pollutions take quite different forms from Western ones. Instead of smoggy air, leaded tap water, and carcinogenic foods, the Canela believe that all meat juices are "polluted" to some extent, some meats more than others (*hīĩ kakô ?-khên:* meat's liquid it-bad). Generally, gamier meats are more highly polluted than domesticated meat products, male meats more than female ones, and internal organs more than long muscles. Meat juices of the male forest deer are very polluted, while those of a domesticated female chicken are not. Chicken soup is almost harmless. Canela also find pollutions in certain vegetables and fruits, but only to a small extent.

Canela pollutions enter the body through food consumption and through sexual intercourse with an already polluted person. The system of a healthy, strong individual can endure a considerable degree of pollution, but when that same person becomes ill or very old, his or her system handles already internalized pollutions less well. Babies, also, are especially vulnerable to pollutions. These vulnerable individuals should eat only relatively pollution-free foods, or the body becomes weaker and the person could eventually die. Once a person is weak, he or she should not have sex, because pollutions which may be in the sexual fluids of the partner may be transmitted, making the sick person weaker.

The problems of pollution are shared by the nuclear family, because the Canela believe that all kin who are just *one* blood-link apart share most of the same blood (*kaprôô*). (The Canela explain kin ties in terms of blood distance just as we do, though we should be talking about genes rather than blood.) Canela parents and children share the "same" blood (i.e., substance), as do siblings, being *one* link away from each other. Thus, they are in the same blood "pool." Long-term spouses, or even long-term lovers, have come to be part of the same blood pool. Sharing perspiration, body heat, and sexual fluids transforms blood differences between spouses into similarities. Thus, when any person becomes sick, the members of the same blood pool must take measures to prevent new pollutions from entering their bodies. These protective measures are called "restrictions" (*mẽ ipiyakhri tsà:* Canela's restrictive device; Portuguese: *resguardos:* protections), which are similar to, though somewhat different from, taboos.

When Lake Lover, 8, the daughter of my Canela sister, Waterfall, fell ill of severe dysentery and dehydration, her parents and siblings became cautious, avoiding sexual intercourse and foods which carry pollutions. However, her grandparents, uncles, aunts, nephews, and nieces, being *two* blood-links away from Lake Lover, did not change their practices. They did not have sufficient blood equivalence with Lake Lover, though they shared some blood with her, as all kin do. In contrast, Lake Lover's *one*-link-away relatives knew that by ingesting pollutions, they would be causing these pollutions to spread through the blood shared in common to the blood of Lake Lover, making her sicker, possibly eventually killing her.

Consequently, Macaw's Bone, her father, paid a machete to a runner to find her brother Pèp-re (electric-eel little), tell him about the illness of his little sister, and insist that he must carry out careful restrictions to save her. The messenger ran four miles to Electric Eel's wife's farm, but was told there that he and his family were staying at a certain backlander's house in Bacabal. There they were sharecropping to have manioc products to eat during the coming months of scarcity, since their supply had run out. The messenger then jogged the eight miles to Bacabal, where Electric Eel's wife told the messenger that her husband had gone off into the world, who knows where. She said he was falsely jealous of her attentions to another man.

The messenger knew he had come to the end of his search. Electric Eel could be moving through any number of cities in greater Brazil. If Electric Eel ate "heavy" foods or slept with prostitutes who happened to have eaten polluted foods, those meats which Canela consider *encarregado* (charged, loaded), he could be weakening or killing Lake Lover back at home. His distance away from the tribe made no difference. Thus, Canela individuals traveling away from their people's area were usually careful about what they ate and with whom they slept.

This concept of blood's relative similarity—of shared blood, of blood equivalence (*kaprôô pipēn:* blood weighed-equally)—among *one*-link-away kin is supported by the following belief. The Canela hold that all siblings come off of the same umbilicus at birth, and that a woman has only one umbilicus. Thus, siblings must be born with the same blood, though life's experiences, especially sex, will cause their blood equivalence to diverge later. Research assistants drew a woman's belly in the sand for me. It had a protruding umbilicus from which many siblings were hanging like pieces of fruit. They drew this picture to convince me of the correctness of their belief. Contributing fathers, men who have introduced sufficient semen into a pregnant woman they are not married to, are considered one-link kin to her fetus. Thus, they too have to maintain restrictions when the "child" they contributed to forming is sick. In return, such children hold restrictions for their contributing fathers for the rest of their lives.

This need to maintain restrictions for one's siblings, parents, or children serves as a constant reminder of the existence of such one-link relationships, as they are defined "biologically" by the Canela. While parents and children, or sisters, do not need to be reminded of such reciprocal responsibilities, contributing fathers and contributed-to children, as well as married brothers, need to have such bonding reenforced, since they live in different houses according to the village plan.

Bonding through "blood" is extended through a person's grandparents, uncles, aunts, nephews, nieces, and grandchildren, and through to these relatives' children and descendants. Maintaining restrictions for these two- and further-link-away relatives, however, is not necessary. The blood held in common among these relatives has become sufficiently diluted by other blood entering the blood pools through marriages that pollutions cannot be transferred between such relatives. Nevertheless, the recognition that some blood is held in common between such relatives bonds them together in the same longhouse and across the village plaza so that the awareness of potential incest prevents sexual contacts between such kin and thereby the termination of such relationships.

Self-empowerment through maintaining "restrictions"

At almost every transition stage of their lives, Canela men and women maintain careful restrictions against the entry of pollutions to attain the new state. At puberty, boys and girls are secluded for a number of days to help them learn how to maintain such restrictions. In the Warriors' festival (Pep-yê: warrior-plural), boys are interned in cells in their maternal houses for as long as three months, where relatively nonpolluted foods are provided by their families. During this period they are supposed to grow physically and morally strong, and to learn the practice of restrictions to help them develop in other transitional stages of their lives. When a young woman wins her ceremonial belt, she is secluded for four or five days during which time both she and her "child," her belt, gain strength through maintaining restrictions in preparation for one of her most important marriage rites, when the belt and woman are painted red by her female in-laws to indicate their greater acceptance of her. When a young man wants his recently pierced earlobe holes to heal, and to grow in size as larger wooden pins are inserted, he is secluded in his maternal house with his "children," the pins, to maintain careful restrictions for about two weeks to ensure his and their growth.

The most important practice of restrictions takes place outside of formal rites, especially for men. Not long after puberty, a male adolescent is supposed to maintain thorough restrictions for one to three years, depending on how determined he is to become an enduring runner and skilled hunter, or formerly a great warrior. During this period he smears charcoal indiscriminately on his body to indicate his condition and to make himself unattractive to young girls and women. This maintaining of thorough and extensive restrictions is an act of self-empowerment. I believe that self-control developed in this way generalizes to most other activities in Canela living. When my Canela research assistants spoke with great respect of a strong, tough, middle-aged man and his accomplishments, they invariably added that he maintained a high level of restrictions for a long time when he was an adolescent.

The effects of maintaining "high" adolescent restrictions are described in the story of Pàà-tsêt (forest-clearing burnt). For some unknown reason, Burnt Forest Clearing lived with his grandmother alone in an isolated valley far away from his people through the years of his puberty. Since he had no sexual contact with women and since his grandmother fed him largely pollution-free foods, he grew remarkably strong. When Burnt Forest Clearing and his grandmother moved back to live with their people, he won all the foot and log races easily. No one could contend with him, since he was so able. However, his traits of endurance and strength attracted young women, who flocked around him wanting sex. After much sex with them, he lost his special abilities and began to lose some races. He became a regular Canela young man, though an especially strong one.

Use of shamanic powers   Besides communicating with ghosts to obtain information for the people about approaching plagues and enemy raiders, and about the locations of stolen objects, Canela shamans both cure sickness and cast spells of sickness. They also make definitive pronouncements about the injurious activities of ghosts, the weakening effects of broken restrictions, and the damaging spells of antisocial shamans, whom I call witches.

Curing: Social usage

When shamans first receive their powers from ghosts, these powers serve to cure very specific illnesses, most of which are believed to be "intrusions" into the body. Some shamans are snakebite masters, others cure problems from broken restrictions, and others try to cure pains of internal organs or even tuberculosis. In any case, they lay hands on the patient's sore area, blow smoke on it, and suck out the intrusion.

One morning during the late 1950s when I was working alone on my research materials in the house of my mother, Dove Woman, two messengers burst in and talked in an emphatic manner. I knew immediately from their tone that I would have to stop working and comply with whatever was called for, as if their summons were a military command. My brother Burnt Path had been bitten in the right hand by a rattlesnake and was in a farm hut on the next stream to the east, the Dove Stream, only about four miles away. I put generic anti-snake serum ampules, syringes, needles, alcohol, matches, and the metal box for boiling everything into my carrying bag and started running off with the messengers, soon slowing down to a jogging pace. I wondered if I would get there on time. Burnt Path was one of the uterine brothers of my special sister, Waterfall. I could not fail this test; I must save him.

Arriving at the Dove Stream farm hut out of breath and exhausted, I was relieved to see that my help would not be needed immediately. Burnt Path was sitting

A shaman sucks illness from a patient's back.

up. Khlúwa-tsù (arrow-decorated), the old snake master, was already attending Burnt Path. I greeted Decorated Arrow, Fish's Plant, and others, and was pleased to realize that Decorated Arrow had actually welcomed me. We were on generally good terms, but in this context he could feel that I might disapprove of his medicine. Apparently, this was not the case.

Decorated Arrow had applied a tourniquet of string on the lower arm well above the wound on the patient's finger and was sucking on the wound, spitting out the blood. Then he went out of the hut and over to a small tree, on the back side of which he placed something he had just taken out of his mouth. I assumed that this was the intrusion he had just sucked out. Then he returned to Burnt Path and applied a poultice to the wound and tied it onto the hand with string. He talked to Burnt Path very quietly for a while and then turned to me, saying it was my turn to use my medicine. I remember feeling deeply relieved, but my medicine was not ready, since I had been watching Decorated Arrow's treatment so closely—always the ethnologist.

First I put alcohol in the lid of the small metal box. Then I propped up the box above its lid on the supports provided and put water in it. Finally, I pulled the plunger out of the syringe and placed the needles, plunger, and syringe in the water. All the equipment for sterilizing the needles and syringe was now set up, so the last act was to light the alcohol in the lid to boil the water. I found I had to shield the flame of the burning alcohol from the breezes to keep it from going out, but finally the water came to a full boil. I let it boil for five minutes before withdrawing the equipment.

The Canela were watching the preparation of my medicine with interest, though they had seen similar activities carried out at the Indian Service post. They believed that injections were more powerful medicine than pills. Nevertheless, I almost always gave pills, since I was not an M.D., though I had been a premedical student. However, during the late 1950s, backlanders and Indians expected urban-educated people to give injections, so I had to learn to comply, but gave shots only in the large muscles of the arm or leg. Disposable needles and syringes did not exist; neither did AIDS.

Burnt Path's lower arm was somewhat swollen, so I injected the nonspecific anti-snake venom serum into his upper arm—and waited and waited. Presumably, the venom would spread up Burnt Path's arm and I would have to give three or four more shots, as the instructions indicated. But after two hours the venom had not spread, Burnt Path's eyes were clear, and the swelling had subsided somewhat. Probably, Decorated Arrow had arrived early enough to suck out most of the venom.

I asked why they thought the bite was made by a rattlesnake, so they showed me the rattles. Then I casually wandered out of the hut and meandered indirectly over to the far side of the tree where I had seen Decorated Arrow place the intrusion, the illness he had sucked out of Burnt Path's hand. Wedged into the bark of the tree was a small piece of paper folded several times. It was a piece of my notepaper, which the Canela borrowed for making cigarettes. I felt conspicuous while walking out to the tree, as if I were defiling something sacred—as if I were questioning the efficacy of Decorated Arrow's medicine. I felt very guilty. However, I was taking a chance for ethnology. Although people watched me, no one said anything. I was taking the situation more seriously than they were.

What had happened? I was totally confused. I had administered only one of the several injections that should have been needed, since my serum was not rattlesnake specific. Was it really Decorated Arrow who had cured Burnt Path? If so, what use had he made of my piece of paper? Did Decorated Arrow believe he had to have something foreign in his hand that people could glimpse for them to be convinced of the cure? I knew this was a question I could not ask Decorated Arrow or any other Canela shaman, or I would get a meaningless answer. Even today I do not know the answers to these questions.

Witches' spells: Antisocial usage

The Canela have only one word for "shaman" and "witch"—*kay*. Most Canela shamans are "good" and are known as *curadores* (curers) in Portuguese, but a few turn antisocial and throw spells (*hũũtsùù*), it is believed, and are known as *feitiçeiros* (witches). I will use "witches" only in this negative sense.

Nobody knows for certain who is a witch, and no one would admit to being one. When carrying out my census of the Canela in 1975, I asked all male adolescents and adult men whether they were *kay*. This was a proper, unembarrassing question to ask. To become a curer and to earn a reputation for having cured a number of people was considered a great service to the community and very prestigious. About 20 percent of the men claimed they had *kay* (psychic) abilities, but they usually modified their claims, saying that they had more powers when younger, or that they needed to undertake thorough restrictions to bring back their currently reduced powers.

My Canela research assistants were hesitant to say that any particular man was a witch. (Women seldom were curers, and I have never heard of a female Canela witch.) To actually say that so-and-so throws negative spells is a terrible accusation.

Nevertheless, my research assistants indicated quietly to me that a certain man was generally considered a witch. He had caused certain individuals to become sick and several had died. My research assistants gave me the victims' names in hushed tones. Nimuendajú (1946:238–239) mentions this same man as being a witch, and I was surprised to find him still alive during the late 1950s, though he died by the late 1960s. People avoided him, but gave him everything he asked for, being afraid of his powers. I found his eyes wandering when I talked with him, as my research assistants said was characteristic of a witch.

A witch "throws" a spell of illness into another person, where it is lodged in a certain place as an intrusion, making the victim sicker and sicker. Witches are said to throw spells when they do not get their way. The victim's kin call in a curer who, if he has strong *kay* abilities, will know who the witch is and see exactly in the body of the victim where the intrusion is and what it is, such as a lizard or a beetle. The curer, if he is not powerful, may have to consult ghosts to find out such information. To the extent that the curer has the power to cure the victim, the illness reverts back to the witch who threw it, making him sick. But the witch cannot go to a curer for help, because a curer sees a witch as being evil. This is why I was surprised that the witch mentioned in Nimuendajú's book was still alive more than 20 years later.

When I returned to the Canela in 1978, I was sad to learn that my naming uncle, the older Deer's Nest, had died. He had been a good research assistant and privately had taught me much about shamanism. I was shocked when I learned how he had died. The Canela reported that one of his eyes had become infected and swollen so that little *bichos* (animals) crawled in and out. They confided that he had died of an illness he had thrown into a victim which had returned to him, making him very sick. I knew my naming uncle had been a good man. He always went around beaming with good will and high self-esteem. To me he generally epitomized the highly favored Canela expression *amyi-khin* (self-liking: joy, euphoria). Nevertheless, I knew he was a powerful shaman, a good curer. How could it be that he had turned evil? Did the manner of his death prove he was a witch? An ordinary Canela would never be able to say this to me, but a shaman could definitely declare what had happened. But would the declaration be the "truth"?

Shamans' pronouncements create "social facts"

Powerful shamans live a life that is quite independent of chiefs of the tribe, though they have little political power. They are not leaders of the community, or of any group, except when they are conducting a village-wide curing ceremony to ward off the arrival of a plague. Their power and respect comes from how they use their special knowledge, from successes of their curing abilities, and from the fear that they may become, some day, antisocial witches.

When someone becomes ill, shamans are usually expected to know something about what has happened. The person may have broken certain food and sex restrictions, been injured by a ghost while wandering alone, or be ill in the urban sense and need urban medicine, which a shaman cannot furnish but may indicate.

While carrying out the Brazilian national census of 1970 for the Canela, I had to ask a number of intimate questions of many Canela women. I had to know about

their miscarriages, abortions, and why their babies had died, to the best of my limited abilities. Sometimes, I spent over an hour patiently questioning one woman
with the help of a special research assistant to determine reliably the history of her
fertility. One time, when I asked a woman why a certain one of her babies had died,
she was clearly evasive. My research assistant, trying to be helpful, shocked me
when he said abruptly, even though she could hear him, that she had killed this baby.
Knowing that the Canela do not have infanticide of any sort, I tried to remain cool,
hoping I had not uncovered a murderess. The woman remained impassive, apparently accepting the statement, so I turned up my courage and asked my research assistant what he could possibly mean. He said simply that she had broken her sex
restrictions while the baby was only a few months old, so the baby had grown sick
and died. He said that the older Deer's Nest had revealed this, so that everyone was
sure what had actually happened.

I knew that it would be futile to ask the woman if this were true, because the reason for the death of this baby had become a social fact—history. More than likely, if
she had not believed the "accusation" before the shaman's pronouncement, she had
come to believe that she had "in fact" committed the lapse soon after the pronouncement. Nothing she could say could alter what was accepted and believed by
her people. There had been no trial, because a shaman's pronouncement is always
right. Either the older Deer's Nest had "seen" what had happened on his own or a
ghost had told him what had occurred. No possibility existed for her to deny information backed up by an other-worldly source. Her uncles had no opportunity to
come to her defense. On the other hand, there was no this-worldly punishment for
losing a baby in this way. People just remembered her as a not very responsible
woman.

Shamanism as the ultimate social control   After the Canela executed a witch
in 1903, the authorities in Barra do Corda intervened. Then the Canela knew they
could no longer execute witches. Nimuendajú reports that after that time, they were
afraid witches would take over the tribe and do much damage, but this did not occur.
Among a people who do not have a police force and do not have agents to carry out
the "decisions" made at hearings between extended families or by the chief of the
tribe, the fear of sorcery takes the place of such agents. When a young man defied
the decision of a hearing in 1960 and would not return to his wife or make the payments specified by the consensus at the hearing, and when he also defied the orders
of Chief Jaguar's Coat, people said that eventually some witch would get him and
he would die a horrible death. Fear of sorcery was the final law enforcement. By the
1970s, however, the fear of sorcery had almost disappeared. While many men believed they had *kay* abilities, people were little concerned about their becoming
witches.

This-worldly versus other-worldly religious activities   Although folk Catholicism pervades Canela thinking these days, the Canela formerly had no god, did not
worship or pray to any supernatural being, and did not try to influence supernatural
entities to bring about improvements in their harvests and living conditions. (I ex-
empt their messianic movement of 1963 as being a product of their modern circumstances.) Thus, it may seem that the Canela have no religion. Social scientists,
however, do not accept such a point of view and answer that if one looks far enough

into the social system of any culture, one will find religion. The Canela "religion" was so thoroughly this-worldly, while many of the world's religions are so otherworldly, that one must expect to find the Canela religious system to be quite different.

While I do not want to go into a definition of religion, because such definitions vary from specialist to specialist, I do hold that the simple concept of a belief security system may satisfy a number of specialists, though certainly not all. The Canela belief security system met most of their needs as a hunting and gathering society with some agriculture. There were no floods, earthquakes, volcanos, droughts, famines, social disasters, or drastic plagues in the area that a more complex religion would help them understand and protect themselves against. Snake bites and seasonal warfare provided the worst insecurities. Their belief system explained the origins of "good" and "bad" aspects of life, through the myth about Sun and Moon. Star Woman's myth explained the origin of vegetables and fruits.

A religion not only provides a sense of security, but also a sense of community. The emotional needs of the individual as well as general bonding is supported by Canela festivals and rites. Festivals as sources for role models provide one dimension of most religions.

A religion usually furnishes sufficient challenges to infuse direction and meaning into individuals' lives as found in the Canela initiation festivals and in the pollution and restrictions system. Pollutions are internal "enemies" to be overcome. They enable individuals who are strongly motivated to discipline themselves, and they bond the nuclear family into a cooperative unit that must work closely together.

A religion usually supplies social structures which set free necessary human expressions such as joy, as well as controlling them for the safe continuity of the society. Canela social structures are outstanding here. They provide settings for ample recreation in the form of athletics, social dancing, and extramarital sex. Through extensive recreation, hostilities are reduced and gratification is acquired. Recreation is not usually considered religion, but Canela recreation supplies some human needs that religions often furnish. This discussion touches on only a few aspects of other religions. It is not intended to be exhaustive, but rather to show that, among the Canela, what religions often provide takes secular and this-worldly forms.

LIFE CYCLE RITES

Every people of the world marks transitions such as birth, marriage, and death with one or more rites. Other life passages that are usually marked by a ceremony are personal naming, puberty, and first childbirth. Still other passages may be adolescent induction into religious responsibility, assumption of legal adulthood, and the step into retirement. Most life cycle rites mark moments in the lives of individuals that are more cultural than biological in both timing and meaning.

I will describe two Canela life cycle rites in detail: the ear-piercing rite that boys of 9 or 10 undergo to socialize them into obedience to the elders, and the cluster of rites associated with death and mourning. At both of these life passages, the individual's relationship to the tribe is defined in various ways. In very small tribes, life cycle rites are usually handled by the individual's extended family. In a large tribe such as the Canela were in the past, from 2,000 to 4,000 members, some life cycle rites are handled by the whole tribe. Festivals represent the tribal level of celebration for the Canela. The Ghosts' festival, for instance, forms boys into an age class which will last their lifetime. Young adolescent women earn their ceremonial belts through service in a men's society during a great "summer" festival. The rites surrounding the birth of a baby, on the other hand, are carried out within the extended family. The reader will recognize that many of the events described elsewhere in the book are in fact life cycle rites, such as those involved in socialization for sex, the various steps into marriage, and the establishing of other relationships such as Informal Friendship, Formal Friendship, and contributing fatherhood.

Ear-piercing rite: "Opening" boys to knowledge and compliance   One morning, when light had arrived but not yet the sun, I left my hammock earlier than usual. Instead of listening to taped recordings in Canela to help train my ear, as I usually did in the early morning, I put the strap of my super-8 camera over my head to the further shoulder and hung my 35 mm still camera in the same manner from my other shoulder. Then I put the strap of my carrying basket over my head so that the basket hung down in front. The basket was made like a western woman's purse, though larger, and it held a hand-size tape recorder, extra film cartridges, 35 mm film, and tape cassettes, as well as a hand-size clipboard with carbons inserted between every third page to make on-the-spot duplicates of my notes in speedwriting.

Heavily armed, I walked rapidly over to the house where I had been told a male ear-piercing rite was to take place. As I was arriving, Ro-?tii-pôl (anaconda-large-burning) joined me. The night before, Burning Anaconda had agreed to help me cover the ear-piercing rite. With his essential interpretive help, I felt prepared to face most foreseen and unforeseen occurrences.

Slippery Forest greeted us with an expected *Ka apu mẽ mõ* (you along plural go), and I returned with a *Ka tsa* (you stand), the usual greetings referring to the other person's activity. Slippery Forest explained that his son, Ka-?hàl (it-enter) was old enough (about 9 years) to have his ears pierced. Slippery pointed to the ear-piercer, Tsùù-khè (decoration-smelly), who was preparing his equipment on a mat in a spot behind the house that would be out of the sun's rays that would soon appear. I could identify Enter It, because his mother, Wakhõõ-khwèy (coati-woman), was cutting away the hair around his ears with scissors. Enter It's mother's brother's first cousin, Enter It's classificatory "uncle," Mesa, was in charge of the occasion, because he was Enter It's naming uncle. The rest of Enter It's nuclear family, and the ubiquitous little boys from other families, completed the cast of characters for the performance.

When Coati Woman had finished cutting Enter It's hair, she placed him, sitting on his ankles, on a mat behind their house, as the sun was beginning to appear on the other side. Smelly Decoration approached Enter It and fingered both of his earlobes, massaging them as if to soften them. Then he squatted by him, and from cotton on a small stick carefully dabbed a dot of red urucu paint onto the center of each of his earlobes. Mesa squatted by his nephew to inspect the location of the red dots. I remember thinking that Mesa would never let the dots' placements stand, because he would have to maintain his authority. A discussion between the two men followed, and Smelly slightly altered the position of one of the dots.

The objective was to pierce a well-centered hole through each lobe. The holes were to be stretched first by inserting wooden pins, then by increasingly larger round wooden plugs, and years later by increasingly larger wheels of wood or even chalk stone up to three inches in diameter. The resulting loops of flesh and skin, like wide elastic bands, hold the dangling wheels in place. Whenever the wheels are not worn, the loops are hung over the top of the ear.

With the locations of the dots on the earlobes approved, each character in the performance assumed his or her position. Enter It remained patiently on the mat, looking impassive and resigned. He knew he must remain motionless throughout the operation, showing no reaction of any sort, or great shame would be part of his people's memory of this occasion. Those witnessing the operation would tell others,

A mother supports a youth during the ear-piercing rite. The youth's ear holes will gradually be stretched to accommodate plugs like the ones worn by the ear piercer.

constructing his persona, bonding him further to his people for better or worse. Enter It's mother, Coati Woman, knelt behind his back, holding his shoulders to remind him instantly with a word should he wince. The squatting Smelly edged closer to Enter and drew the mat holding his equipment to his side. Two of Enter's sisters, squatting on either side of him, smeared red urucu paint along the side of his face, from his nose across his cheeks under his eyes, almost to his ears. When finished, they moved away to join the encircling crowd.

I had created an artificial situation by requesting that one quarter of the circle of people around Enter It be left open for my filming. Burning Anaconda, my assistant, was continuously clearing little boys out of this area, where I had placed the mat with my equipment covered with a towel to protect it from the low-blown sand. I had already taken a number of high ASA still shots of the scene, and especially of the placement of the dots and the relocation of one of them, but I was careful not to hamper Smelly Decoration and Mesa's movements, staying outside their area of activity and relying on telephoto shots. Now that there was enough light I could begin the super-8 sound filming. Every now and then I retreated to my mat to speak observations into my tape recorder or to draw spacial relationships on my clipboard. For other occasions during which chanting took place, I usually placed my high-quality tape recorder on a stool, but I had already seen this rite several times and knew no singing was involved. Anyway, my sound camera would pick up some of the words exchanged.

Mesa stood beside the squatting Smelly and bent over to look along the wooden awl in Smelly's right hand. This was the signal that the performance could begin. The awl was made of a red hardwood (*pau brasil*), which had been filed to a sharp point. With its hand-gripping end, it was close to one foot in length. Smelly firmly secured Enter's left earlobe with his thumb in front just below the dot and his first two fingers behind the earlobe. Smelly placed the point of the awl on the dot and waited for a moment. Then he thrust hard and rotated the awl clockwise and counterclockwise until I could see two inches of the point showing on the further side of Enter's earlobe. I was watching Enter's face through the filming lens, and saw no tensing on his part. Anaconda told me that the pain began later. However, I thought that the way Smelly had pinched the earlobe to secure it would have been painful in itself. With one earlobe successfully pierced, the quiet that had descended on the family group during the moment of anticipation was broken and everybody began to talk. The tension was over; young Enter It had behaved like a man.

Smelly withdrew the awl from the left earlobe and put red urucu paint into the wound with a cotton swab. Then he inserted into the new hole its first wooden pin, Enter It's "child." A half hour later, Smelly created the other earlobe's hole and inserted Enter's other "child." Coati Woman put a sheet of fine white cloth over her son's head, and then she and her "brother," Mesa, conducted Enter to his cell of confinement in a corner of her house. The cell was made of old mats which were held erect by tall stakes thrust through them and into the ground of the house.

Mesa lectured his nephew to remain in the cell until "his children" (his earlobe pins) had "grown" sufficiently, which was for about two weeks. Before then he was to emerge from his cell only in the evening or during the night, if possible, and only when nature's functions called. He was to move around outside his cell always with the white cloth covering his head to protect himself from the ill effects of the sun, and he must avoid stepping on leaves or small sticks because they could injure him. He was now in a sensitive state so that he was vulnerable to injuries from a number of sources. Anthropologists would say that Enter It's society had placed him in a liminal state in which he was not part of the world of daily living. In this ceremonially special state he was vulnerable to harm, but he and "his children" would grow more rapidly in this state than if they were still in the world of daily living. His mother, Coati, would provide him with foods that were unpolluted, or low in pollutions, so that they would not hinder his growth and the growth of his children.

Mesa gave Enter a little bag of unshaped wooden pins and a knife. He told his named-nephew—Mesa had given Enter It one of his many names—to fashion earlobe pins which were to be slightly larger every day. Mesa said he would come around each day for the insertion of the new, larger pins and the cleansing of the wounds with fresh urucu paint. I knew Mesa would take advantage of Enter's confinement to tell him stories about the ancestors that would teach him to grow up into a fine Canela. Large boys Enter's age spent much of their time with their age class, playing or carrying out communal activities. Enter's seclusion provided Mesa with an excellent opportunity for personal instruction. His "captivity" reminded me of driving to schools and later colleges with my active son in the front seat. He could not get away, so we had wonderful talks.

If the ethnologist asks Canela males why their earlobes are pierced and wheels hung in their earlobe straps, they will say that the adornment enhances male beauty and that women are attracted to men who go around with large, painted ear wheels. They told me in male-shared glee that women give themselves more readily to such men, showing what they meant by thrusting their right forefinger through a circle made by their left thumb and forefinger. Nevertheless, while accepting this generalization, the ethnologist knows that deeper reasons for male earlobe-piercing must exist.

From a lengthy study of key Canela words and phrases, I know that the verb *khãm hapak* (in ear) means to hear/listen/understand/obey/perform. The suggestion here is that in earlier times when a young Canela heard an order, he performed it automatically: that in their quasi-military society, hearing was doing. Taken alone, this observation would prove very little. However, I know also that *to hapak-khre* (make ear-hole) means to "advise," that *ha-?khre pey* (its-hole good) means to "know," and that *i?-kuni* (it's-whole) means "it is whole/complete/virginal." The imagery here— and I did get my Canela research assistants to confirm this—is that information (advice) enters through the ear holes into the head; that good, large, well-opened ear holes lead to building up knowledge and compliance; and that unopened ear holes (virginal ones) lead to stupidity and lack of obedience. (Similarly, a virginal girl is a useless one, as are virgin forests.)

Taken in this semantic context, and with my general knowledge of the Canela as a quasi-military society, I see the male ear-piercing rite as a symbolic opening up of these older boys to receive information from their elders and to become obedient to them. It is a socialization rite which takes place not long before puberty to introduce older boys into the more adolescent world of obedience, while they are withdrawn temporarily from the activities of living in an age class. To my Canela research assistants, such an interpretation was food for thought and not denied, but they could not express this interpretation themselves. This ear-piercing rite may be the Canela parallel institution to Catholic or Protestant confirmation or to the Jewish bar mitzvah.

It is important to examine what each member of the cast of characters in the performance represents. Usually, the rite takes place in the boy's maternal home, but it is run by the boy's naming-uncle who is the representative of the boy's home to the greater society, especially for ceremonial purposes. The uncle calls in an ear-piercer, who is a nonrelative and who represents the greater society. Thus, this ear-piercing rite and its subsequent seclusion keep the boy at home, while calling on the greater society for a service. Other Canela rites take the boy and girl out of the home and into the greater society at large, creating the separation from their families that bonds them to the larger community. The tribe as a whole is more important than the individual and his or her family.

Death and mourning as a cluster of rites   The final rite of passage is death and mourning. Again, there is insufficient space in this book to describe completely this important passage with its many rites and acts, but I want especially to describe mourning, since it is important to understanding the Canela's extreme orientation to living for the present. Moreover, mourning is an excellent exemplification of bonding, since the relationships among individuals in kin groups are reenacted and solidified during mourning as well as the relationships with the deceased's Formal Friend.

Wailing: One aspect of mourning

The most conspicuous aspect of mourning is the wailing done primarily by adult women over 30 who are close kin of the deceased. Only a few men can wail, which involves singing in a high-toned yodeling manner, including words of personal meaning to the mourner. The wailing by the close kin, sitting around the cadaver, starts as the first rays of sun appear above the houses or landscape in the morning. The wailing continues for two to four hours as the sun rises.

The close kin remain wailing around the cadaver as the principal Formal Friend of the deceased and his or her close kin, the Formal Friend's associates, prepare the corpse for burial and dig the grave. The Formal Friend and his or her associates are nonrelatives of the deceased by definition and self-selection. The close kin continue to wail as wave after wave of more distant kin of the deceased walk across the village in family groups from different houses to wail and bond with the closer kin of the deceased, squatting on their ankles around the cadaver.

When the Formal Friend's associates have dug and prepared the grave in the cemetery about half a kilometer outside the village, they return and walk briskly to the house of the deceased with old mats, ropes, and a pole with which to wrap, tie, and sling the corpse. As pallbearers, they will carry the cadaver on the pole to the cemetery.

The deceased's Formal Friend's associates usually have to pull the close kin away from the decorated cadaver. The mourners are wailing so intensely that they are not aware of what is going on around them. Consequently, most of their material goods are taken at this time by people from other houses. When a death occurred in my Canela family's house, my Canela sister, Waterfall, used to stuff a few family valuables for safekeeping in my private room before the wailing started.

Her husband and other close kin mourn over the body of a young woman.

As the pallbearers carry the corpse out of the house, hung horizontally on a long pole, the wailing reaches a dramatic crescendo. The very seriously bereaved, such as fathers for small sons, have been known to do somersaults, landing on the back of their heads, breaking their necks. Associates of the Formal Friend are on the alert to swiftly intervene and stop such attempted suicides. This scene is the most emotional and frenzied of any that I know of among the more characteristically self-controlled Canela.

When the pallbearers return about an hour and a half later from the cemetery, having buried the corpse, the wailing breaks out again. The associates of the Formal Friend of the deceased tear out some of the walls of the palm thatch house and sweep its floor, so cleansing breezes can pass through.

During the following days, before the gravediggers are paid for their services, the bereaved individuals may break out wailing as the sun appears in the morning and as it sets in the evening. Wailing may also break out as close or distant kin return to the village from farms or from travel and come to the house of the bereaved. The very severely bereaved, such as the mother of a favorite child or the wife of a lifelong spouse, wail with every individual returning to the village they have not wailed with yet. Each time I returned to the Canela, my Canela sister and mother used to wail over me, pushing me down to kneel on a mat, my head bowed. Once, when they did not wail over me at all, I had to investigate the situation to learn why. I had thought they were wailing only to honor my return. But I found out that each time I returned, they wailed over me for a deceased person they were remembering, not just to honor me. The time they did not wail over me was when no close person had died during my absence of a year.

A few days after a Canela burial, depending on how long it takes to gather the necessary items of payment, the bereaved family pays the deceased's principal Formal Friend, the gravedigger, for his services and for the help of his associates. At sunset, members of the extended family of the deceased sit on the edge of the boulevard just in front of their house. One of their leading mothers' brothers summons the grave-digger by chanting out in a formal manner for him to appear. Soon the gravedigger walks solemnly along the village boulevard and arrives before the assembled family with several helpers following him. The principal spokesman of the deceased's family tells the gravedigger in formal language of exhortation to take the items laid on a mat, which might include an axe, two machetes, a cast-iron cauldron, a shotgun, several cuts of cloth, and a half-meter section of tobacco wound into the form of a rope.

As the gravedigger and helpers pick up and walk casually away with the items, the kin of the deceased break out wailing again; the most severely bereaved sustain the wailing for about 10 minutes. Then their principal uncle calms the last mourners and lectures the group for about five minutes. The thrust of his lecture is always to say that the living must forget the deceased and that they must live for their surviving relatives, especially their children. The principal uncle stresses that it is danger-ous to remember the recently deceased. If the mourners remember him or her too intensely, the deceased might return as a ghost to claim their lives. Then they would not be able to take care of their surviving children.

If strong memories of the deceased still persist in the thoughts and feelings of a deeply bereaved woman, the latter's primary female Formal Friend goes with her to all the locations in and around the village where the associated memories are strongest. A woman may intensely remember where she went bathing privately and had sex with her deceased husband, or where she pulled up weeds with him on their farm. She goes to these places with her Formal Friend, and the two women wail to-gether for some time. The Formal Friend listens to the bereaved woman's memories as she wails, and the Formal Friend wails with her to help keep her wailing longer.

The Formal Friend is a nonrelative, and therefore she is not bereaved. Neverthe-less, she manages to wail with tears and nasal fluids falling on her thighs. Such wail-ing activities, including the facilitating services of the Formal Friend, are believed to help a deeply bereaved person forget a loss and to live in the present for the sur-viving members of the family.

One time in the late 1950s a Brazilian backland farm woman complained to me that when she had lost her small son, Canela women of one family came to her and compulsively wailed by her side, expecting to be paid for their wailing. The back-land woman had failed to understand that the wailing Canela women were trying to help her forget her loss and that this was a service as well as an expression of care and bonding. These Canela women had stayed with the backland woman's family many times, working there for food, and they had remembered her lost son. They were carrying out the role of Formal Friends to the backland woman, helping her wail and cry so she would forget her loss—a service which was always paid for back in the Canela village. Of course, it also might be true that the Canela women were hungry and had thought of a legitimate way, from their point of view, of obligating the backland woman to feed them.

Rather than relying on an *other*-worldly intervention, such as praying to a saint and asking him to relieve the anguish caused by the loss, as a backland Brazilian woman of the Canela region does, the Canela women were relying on a *this*-worldly practice, wailing, to help the backland woman live for the present and the immediate future.

ANNUAL AND GREAT FESTIVALS

In their festivals the Canela reinforce the norms for behavior in their culture, though they sometimes do this paradoxically by acting out the opposite of the norms. Teaching the mores of Canela life and associating them with the pleasures of feasting, singing, joking, and sex, the festivals are both didactic and celebratory. At times these dramas present symbolism that is so deeply held in a Canela's subconscious that my Canela research assistants could not provide any sort of interpretation of them. This has to be left to the ethnologist who, after years of study, may be able to offer valid interpretations.

The nature of festivals   Canela festivals are really pageants which are acted out in the "same" way every year or every time they are put on. I put "same" in quotes because the Canela believe they do not make changes, though, of course, they occasionally do. Festivals go on for a day or several months. The long ones consist of several phases, and each phase consists of many acts in the theatrical sense, and each act consists of many events.

It is hard for the Canela to remember every event of every act of these complex and lengthy pageants, but the members of the Council of Elders try to do so by holding meetings before each festival phase and meetings each evening to be sure of what is going to occur the next day. Often, the councilors summon the actors to appear before them in the plaza to assign them roles and instruct them how to carry them out. More than one role may be carried out by the same person, who has the right to do so either through matrilineal inheritance, through personal name connectedness, or through previous assignment in an earlier performance of the same festival. In any case, most performers need to receive the order to carry out their traditional role or they do not carry it out when they are supposed to do so. For instance, the owner of the Hardwood Log ritual, Paa-pôl (our-fire), knows that only he or his younger brother through matrilineal inheritance can go out and cut the pair of hardwood logs (*pàlrà*) required for this race, but he has to be summoned to the plaza and ordered to do so by the Council of Elders. Only he can judge the propitiousness of the day of the ritual by noticing whether chips fly near his eyes or whether wasps buzz around. If they do, he may judge the time is not right to put on the ritual and report this to the council in the plaza in the evening.

Relative status and the sisterly role portrayed in the Firebrand act

Most Canela cannot read, but they can observe the roles carried out in these festival acts. In the Firebrand act of the Facsimile Warriors' festival, young girl associates of men's societies are given firebrands by the sing-dance master. The girls throw these burning sticks at one of the young men who are circling around in the center of the plaza carrying pots, machetes, shotguns, or other common objects. A girl's mother chooses the item her family needs and a girl throws the stick according to the manner of her ceremonial rank: Low-ranked girls throw viciously to hit and hurt, while high-ranked girls throw to hit the ground near the youth carrying the item her mother wants. Thus, the role differences among ceremonial ranks are demonstrated in the festival act for the young to practice and learn, and these behaviors are supposed to be carried over into daily life. The ceremonially high-ranked Wè?tè girl in my family took care to behave with forbearance, and if she did not, she was reminded of who she was.

Another event in the Firebrand act is that whether or not the young man was hit, one of his sisters rushes out of the crowd to throw water from a gourd onto his shoulders, exemplifying the role of sisters to brothers—one of administering to them when they may be hurt.

Mothers-in-law hold strings tied to sons-in-law

An act that I like to describe, and show slides of, is the one in which the interned initiates of the Warriors' festival march around the village boulevard with strings attached to their waists held by their mothers-in-law, portending their future service, almost slavery, to these women.

Clowns, as individualists, support the right by doing the wrong

During the Fish festival, the troop of Clowns govern the festival proceedings instead of the Council of Elders. The Clowns represent individuality in contrast to conformity. While the Clowns sing the songs of the dignified and proper Facsimile Warriors, they sing out lewdly worded statements between each song. They end each session in disharmony by walking separately back to their houses and by singing out of tune and time with each other. These are negative kinds of performances that the

Women hold strings of palm straw tied to the necks or waists of their sons-in-law as they march around the boulevard.

establishment-oriented Facsimile Warriors would never carry out, since they accept the governance of the Council of Elders. The superior Facsimile Warriors even stop singing—they withdraw disdainfully—when mild opposition presents itself in the form of a barking dog or a loudly crying baby.

The most hilarious act of any of the Canela festivals may be the special performance by the two female associates of the Clown male troop, who are chosen partly for their willingness to please men in extramarital sex. During the middle section of the Fish festival, on one very special late afternoon on the edge of the plaza by the Clowns' improperly constructed hut, the Clown women do everything in the wrong way. They have a pulp doll, the baby of one of them. Its mother drops it so that it cries. But the Clown women let the baby cry, not picking it up. One Clown woman pretends incest with her brother, in an exaggerated demonstration which makes the crowd roar in laughter, as the sister partly resists.

An interpretation that research assistants could not provide

After years of studying and analyzing the Canela festivals, their myths, and the meaning of many of their key expressions, it became clear to me that the Canela rarely see people or issues as opposed to each other in an extreme manner. The Canela prefer moderation, and they like opposing situations that can be modified

One of the Clown society's two female associates. By doing everything wrong (the crooked house, the mishandled doll), the Clown associate implies what is right.

into complementary ones, not unresolvable ones. This aspect of their world view—
one of their values—can be found as patterns in their festivals, but my Canela research assistants could not point out such an abstraction. In the case of the Facsimile
Warriors' festival, they could merely say that the Facsimile Warriors' troop are opposite to the Clowns' troop of the Fish festival, because the Facsimile Warriors and
the Clowns do things in opposite ways.

I can see, however, from my perspective, that on a scale of extremely "good"
to extremely "bad" behavior, the Facsimile Warriors are only quite good and the
Clowns are only somewhat bad. In contrast to this moderation, the ceremonially
high-honor-ranked Sensitive Falcons, who are all Wet Heads (mē ka-khrā nkoo:
they of-head wet), are held in extreme contrast with the ceremonially low-honor-
ranked Dry Heads (mē ka-khrā nkràà: they of-head dry). However, the expression
of these extremes appears only in two acts of the Facsimile Warriors' festival,
while the Facsimile Warriors and the Clowns appear every day in their respective
festivals. Thus, the Facsimile Warriors and the Clowns are models for behavior,
while the Wet Heads and the Dry Heads represent extreme parameters that are not
realistic models.

The annual ceremonial cycle   The Canela annual festivals are put on every
year, during a period determined mostly by environmental aspects of the season.
For instance, the Red and Black racing season begins when the buriti palm fruits
ripen (October), and it ends when the bacuri fruits mature (January). The Canela
also have great festivals, one of which is put on each year during the "summer,"
May through September, though two of them may start as early as late March.

Canela research assistants say that their year starts in September, when heavy
dews and occasional light rains end the dry summer and start the new growth
sprouting on bushes and trees. At this time the grass of the closed savannahs turns
from brown—and from black where burned—to light green, and wild flowers appear in abundance. One surprising flower pushes its way directly out of the sandy
soil, without the benefit of a stem or leaves for support. I find the change in the appearance of the savannah vegetation to be delightful. The Canela appreciated this
beauty and talked about their longing for it when they were living away in the dry
forests of Sardinha between 1963 and 1968.

The Canela do not mark the beginning of their environmental year with any
event, and research assistants did not announce this "spring" as the beginning of
their year swiftly and with certainty. Thus, I believe that no fundamental beginning to their year really exists. Similarly, the annual cycle of their ceremonies and
festivals has no fundamental beginning or ending, though certain points are distinctly marked. For instance, during a September or October afternoon, the year's
"summer" great festival is terminated, and during the next few minutes, the first
act of the Red and Black log racing season begins with a race of the young males
of the tribe divided according to Red and Black moiety membership.

Red and Black moiety relay log racing brings "spring"

A man or woman is a Red or a Black depending on the membership of the name
he or she was given within a few days of birth by a mother's "brother" ("uncle")
for a male, and by a father's "sister" ("aunt") for a female. The season of the

Reds and Blacks is called the Mẽ-ipimràk, meaning "they change and change," or "they bring about renewal." Thus, this expression can be associated with the "spring" of the year, with the appearance of fresh new growth, even though this spring comes just *after* their dry summer. The Red and Black log racing season expresses the spirit of renewal through the structure of the various performances. First, the Blacks race against the Reds carrying small hand-held cylindrical pieces of wood; but with each new race during the following days, the Blacks make these "logs" slightly larger until they become long trunks of buriti palm trees, requiring four men to lift them onto one man's left shoulder. Then he jogs off with it for as many minutes as he can stand the weight before he turns around to pass the log onto the left shoulder of the next racer on his team. After a great race with large logs fashioned in the Black cylindrical manner, and painted black with longitudinal stripes, the Blacks surrender their dominance to the Reds, who race first with small hand "logs" shaped like disks with the central point of the cross-section painted with a red circle. On each ensuing racing day, the Reds cut larger disk-shaped logs until these logs reach about 250 pounds. Then the Blacks take charge for several weeks, and finally the Reds take charge once more. Thus, this pattern of growth and change—renewal—is repeated four times, though the logs do not "grow" the third and fourth times. The season terminates in late January.

Age class moiety log racing; logs of 300 pounds

The day following the last Red and Black race, the Canela race according to a different arrangement, that of the age class moieties, the membership of which is by age class. The men of the age classes in their teens and thirties race against the men of the age classes in their twenties and forties. By their fifties, men retire from log racing, which may have become too strenuous for some of them. They race in their age class moiety divisions, with some exceptions, until the end of the summer festival season, when the Reds and Blacks take over again.

Agricultural rituals increase the crops

During February or early March, the Canela put on the Grasshopper and Sweet Potato rituals and then the Corn ritual. The ownership of these three annual rituals lies with a certain family and is inherited matrilineally. If the female line in this family dies out, the ownership of the ritual is transferred to another family by the Council of Elders, thus ensuring the ceremony's perpetuity.

The Canela liken their Grasshopper ritual to the *carnaval* of the Brazilians. Members of the extended family that owns the ceremony form a file in the plaza late in the evening. As the file arrives before a master sing-leader with a gourd rattle, the members separate from the file one by one, carrying out strange antics until all the file members have clowned before the sing-leader, amusing the crowd. The membership hop like grasshoppers, show whitened faces like clowns, and perform unusual behavior that they think the Brazilians carry out during their *carnaval.* The hopping is supposed to help the sweet potato crop increase.

In the center of the plaza during one of the Corn ceremonies, a member of the ritual's owning family tosses out shuttlecocks made of corn husk for youths to bat up into the air with their hands as many times as possible, thus helping the corn crop increase. Whenever a shuttlecock touches the ground, a new one is thrown out by a member of the owner's family for the young men to keep up in the air for as long as possible.

Hardwood log racing ritual forecasts summer amusements

When it is time for a great summer festival to be put on, from late March to early May, depending on the festival, the Pàlrà (hardwood) ritual is performed, the principal feature of which is a race with two great hardwood trunk logs instead of the buriti palm trunk logs (*krówa*) of all the other races during the year. Pàlrà racers run according to the age class moiety division. The right to initiate the Pàlrà ritual is passed on matrilineally in one family. However, representatives of the ceremonially governing group of the summer festivals control the race for the first time during the yearly cycle. That is, representatives of the two Wè?tè girls, two Tsù-?katê-re (decorated-artifact master little), give the signal—a word—for starting the race.

Ceremonially elite Wè?tè girls ensure peace

The two Wè?tè girls serve the opposite age class moiety from their fathers', as "sisters" to the opposing moiety instead of as "other wives," as is the relationship of all the other pairs of female associates to their men's societies. Thus, each Wè?tè girl, starting at about age 6, serves the males of half the tribe, providing water and playing the role of peacemaker. If, on a certain day, the two moieties' racing teams compete too fiercely, challenging and rechallenging each other to an additional race, tiring each other out, a little Wè?tè girl is likely to appear walking along the boulevard from her house toward the men, with her mother or older sister carrying a bowl of food behind her. As soon as the men of the racing teams see her approaching, they feel relieved of their obligation to win and they stop their activities. They form a circle in the boulevard around the bowl and each awaits his turn to scoop up a handful of rice mixed with bits of meat. Their Wè?tè sister has "pacified" them.

During the summer great festival season, which is known as the Wè?tè season, the members of the age class moieties spend much of their time together in large rooms built onto the houses of the two fathers of the Wè?tè girls. Here they chat, prepare themselves for racing, and occasionally eat food provided by the Wè?tè girls' families. They address a Wè?tè girl's parents as "father" and "mother," and her sisters and brothers are addressed correspondingly. Along with the four girl associates of the internment festivals, the two Wè?tè girls form a group of six ceremonially elite girls, an honor which they retain for the rest of their lives. They are known as *pep-khwèy* (warrior-female), a great honor.

The Wè?tè-showing ceremony turns on passions

Several weeks after the termination of the Pàlrà ritual, one of the five Wè?tè season's festivals is put on; but first the two Wè?tè girls must be sent in a ceremony out

Wè?tè girls decorated with falcon down and urucu.

of their houses into the boulevard for all to see. Their appearance signals the people to enter into the spirit of the summer festivities, which include a number of occasions for extramarital sex. The opening festival, the Wè?tè Pipēl Tsà (Wè?tè-showing occasion), lasts for two days. During the first in a series of acts, the men and women are parted. They sing defiantly against the opposite sex in mass formations which circle around each other in the plaza. The next day, the women go "hunting," normally a male activity, taking half a dozen male associates with them. They proceed to take turns having sex with the men. Of course, they chose men whom they know to have great sexual stamina.

Upon returning from this hunt in the late afternoon, the male associates hang the meat of the game they have killed from a 20-foot pole. The women of the village, acting in a mass, bring down the pole the men are holding and grab the meat selfishly in group chaos. This act of disorderliness symbolizes the spirit of the Wè?tè season as one of extramarital sex in contrast to one of marital orderliness. Thus, the women go to one Wè?tè house as if they were men, and the men go to the other Wè?tè house in opposition to the women. Canela research assistants assured me that some married couples scarcely see each other during the two to four months of a Wè?tè summer season. My observation is that such separations depend on the closeness of the couple, the close ones not parting often. Such separations also depend on how modern a couple is, the very modern ones not parting at all.

The Wè?tè season is terminated when the Red and Black season begins on October. At this time, a ceremony called the Wè?tè Pimtsul Tsà (Wè?tè-concealing occasion) indicates that no more "fun" is allowed. Actually, private trysts continue but the publicly sponsored occasions do not, except for one during the Red and Black season.

"Summer" season festivals enhance extramarital sex   A few days after the Wè?tè-showing ceremonies open the summer season, the members of the Council of Elders allow the appropriate social group to put on one of the five festivals of the season. They are the festivals of the Ghosts, Warriors, Facsimile Warriors, Fishes, and Masks. These five Wè?tè season festivals have similar structures but different content and purposes. They have opening, middle, and terminal phases. The Canela open a summer festival dramatically with an act that is supposed to be a surprise, though everybody knows something is going to happen.

The Ghosts' festival: Kinship reenforced

In the case of the Ghosts' festival (the Khêêtúwayê), an elder suddenly runs out of a house in the late afternoon, when everyone is assembled and waiting in the plaza, brandishing a two-to-three feet long staff for everybody to see. The staff is painted red and pea green, the green being glued-on parakeet down. Upon seeing this sign, everybody knows the Ghosts' festival was the choice of the councilors, and within 30 minutes, the boys of the youngest age class of the tribe have been "caught" and interned in two large cells, which are hastily constructed for the occasion. This is the first time that many of the boys have lived away from home and have been disciplined by nonrelatives, appointees of the Council of Elders—two troop commandants, two file leaders, and others.

During the middle phase of the Ghosts' festival, these leaders march the boys in two files from their cells on opposite sides of the village circle out into the center of the village plaza. There they sing a set of special songs about six times a day. These songs are believed to attract ghosts, who created the songs in the first place. Though the souls of the singing boys are in danger of being snatched away by the encircling ghosts, the boys' souls are held secure in their bodies by female relatives grasping their rib cages from behind and by the boys' wearing headdresses sporting long macaw tail feathers, which scare ghosts away. The boys'·uncles are stationed just behind the boys' female relatives, also helping to keep the ghosts at bay.

Warriors' festival: To learn restrictions and group living

The middle section of the Warriors' festival (*pep-yê:* warrior-plural) for adolescent males stresses the importance of maintaining restrictions against pollutions in order to gain personal strength. The youths are interned in beehive-shaped cells (like wombs) in their maternal homes and fed carefully by their families. At first they are

Boys with macaw feather headdresses sing in the plaza during the Ghosts' festival.

fed small amounts of unpolluted foods (never meat) until they have grown lean and strong. Then they are fed large amounts of relatively unpolluted foods until they put on weight and presumably strength.

Near the end of their seclusion, their naming-uncle's men's society calls upon each individual "nephew" in turn. The youth is harshly summoned out of his cell, and an uncle demands to know if the youth is ready to go out into the savannahs to fight the enemy should he appear in force. The youth, knowing his role at this moment of the pageantry, answers no.

Later, the youths, when considered strong enough to race with great logs, are let out of their cells together as a troop. They are exposed to the effects of being out of doors and among people only in stages. It is believed that from the beginning of their long internment they had become very sensitive and therefore vulnerable to all sorts of "injurious things" (*kurê tsà*), such as sunlight, twigs, the odor of sex from women, and the evil eye of witches. Thus, they must be shaded from the sun, supplied fresh leaves to sleep on, and kept away from women. The youths must also be shielded with mats from the eyes of villagers as they pass around the village for their food. Each additional day that they are out of internment, their vulnerability diminishes, so they are shielded less until the protective mats are finally omitted. They are out of the ceremonially dangerous condition which helped them to grow rapidly.

Canela research assistants explain that the young adolescent initiates learn through their internment how to maintain high restriction against pollutions, which they supposedly carry out during the rest of their lives. The practice of restrictions is the means by which any youth makes himself a more effective hunter, runner, and formerly a warrior. Self-respect is acquired largely in this way. Maintaining a high level of restrictions is how ghosts may be attracted so that an internee may become a shaman. In a world where *this*-worldly solutions are important in contrast to *other-*

Youths shield themselves from the villagers' view with mats as they pass around the village for food during the Warriors' festival.

worldly ones, this Warriors' festival and its internments for adolescents—a youth undergoes two and sometimes three Warriors' festivals—become very important for the maturation of the individual.

One important aspect of the Facsimile Warriors' festival, though it is for adults instead of adolescents, is its return to practicing food and sex restrictions, so that the older male members have an opportunity to regain life's force through their own efforts, but facilitated by the environment of their internment.

I agree with the interpretation of the Warriors' festival which my research assistants offered—that it is for an internee to learn to undergo restrictions. But I would add an observation they were not able to provide. Once secluded in a womb-shaped cell, alone or with a sibling, for a kind of rebirth into relative maturity, the internees are believed to have become especially "sensitive." Belief in this special ceremonial condition and its consequent personal dangers makes the internment far more significant for the individual. Violations of the internment conditions could be personally dangerous. Thus, the initiate is likely to take the internment more seriously and to learn the practice of restrictions better.

Preparation for a festival's final phase: Hunting

The final phase of any of the five summer Wè?tè season festivals involves special activities for three to nine days. During this period, Canela do not like to leave the dramatic festivities to hunt or fetch food from their farms, so they amass sufficient quantities of food in advance. These five great festivals are called *amyi-khĩn* (self-liking: euphoria), and without a sufficient supply of food no Canela can feel such a state. Thus, to build up supplies for this festive state, the village has to disperse, the men hunting for two to three weeks in their age class moiety divisions, and the women staying on their farms extracting and processing manioc roots.

The supply of two to three weeks' game is cooked and smoked over low fires. The other alternative to such extensive group hunting is to oblige visitors, or the resident anthropologist or missionary, to purchase several head of cattle and a number of sacks of rice and manioc flour (*farinha*) from backlanders. The Canela thinking, which I agree with, is that the outsider gains so much from watching, filming, and recording festivals that he or she must pay appropriately. Canela lose self-respect if something is taken from them without sufficient return.

Festival of Masks: "Begging" supported

The Festival of Masks is called the Ku?khrùt-re-?hô these days, though Nimuendajú claims it was called the Kô-?khrit-hô (water-animal's straw-mask) earlier. Its terminal phase may be the most dramatic and enjoyable spectacle for the outsider who knows little about Canela life. During an initial phase of a few days, Masks society male members induct their girl associates and other members. During a middle section of about six weeks, the Mask members weave their life-size masks in a lean-to several kilometers from the village. Then, to open the terminal phase, Masks society members march in single file inside their large masks, entering the village in the early afternoon.

A mask ranges from five to six feet tall and is about three feet wide. Its height depends on the size of the wearer and the size of the "doughnut" of palm straw he

A hunter returns from the savannah with a small deer.

The Masks march toward the village from their lean-to in the savannah.

wears on his head. This doughnut supports the horizontal bar holding up the material of the mask, which covers the bearer completely. The upper part of a mask is
made like a woven mat. The lower part, from the waist down, is made of loose
lengths of shredded palm straw reaching the ground to form a skirt. A slit in front of
the wearer's face allows him to peer out, and he can manipulate this opening by
pulling the attached strings, making "facial expressions." Spear-like poles of hardwood about seven feet long are tied onto the back of the mask and extend diagonally
upward to represent horns.

As the festival's terminal phase opens, the 30 to 40 Masks march in single file
through the closed savannahs along a trail from their lean-to toward the village,
raising a small cloud of dust as their feet shuffle through the sand. These feet are
the only human parts that are visible to the villagers, except for an occasional
glimpse of an eye or nose as the man inside the mask slightly parts the opening to
see what is going on. The Masks' two female associates march in their slightly
smaller masks near the front of the file after the leading Khen-pey (mountain-
beautiful) Masks.

The masks' "faces" are painted according to the kind of mask they are, and each
one of the dozen kinds behaves in a slightly different way. The Khen-pey Masks are
the leaders, so they move sedately and slowly, and their faces are minimally painted,
with only a large black horizontal stripe just below the transverse supporting bar. The
Tôkaywêw-re Masks have two eyes which are three concentric circles, and the Espora
Masks have two circular eyes with points all around to look like spurs. These two
Masks run around in the boulevard, playing jokes on each other and having a great
time. The Little Bad Mask (*i?-hô-?khên:* its-straw-bad) is made irregularly by the
Clowns, and it runs about trying to steal things from villagers.

Each kind of Mask has a slightly different sort of grunt or squeal to express itself. The Masks are viewed by the Canela as being nice little creatures, which are
not quite human, but are amusing and playful pets with definite personalities. The
Masks represent the creatures (*kô-?khrit:* water-animals) which were seen on the

banks of the Tocantins River years ago by Canela visiting the Krahó Indians who live there. As such, they could be fresh-water otters, though the origin myth of the festival reports them as being larger and fiercer, and with murderous horns.

As the Masks file into the village, women approach them, wanting to be their "mothers." If the man in a mask sees a female relative approaching him, he avoids her, knowing that sexual relations are a possibility with the approaching "mother." If a nonrelative approaches, the Mask does not avoid her, but allows her to tie a short chain of beads to one of his "horns." Then he goes off, running and playing around the boulevard, dodging other Masks. Occasionally, two pairs of feet are seen sticking out from under the skirt of a mask, and the smaller of the pair has to be the feet of one of the "mothers." At night such a pair drift off behind the houses into the darkness for mutual pleasure.

On the second evening of the terminal phase of the Masks' festival, just after dark, each family lights a small bonfire in the boulevard in front of the family house. The Masks dash water on their skirts and file past these fires, each Mask trying in turn to put each fire out by a swish of the skirt. If it succeeds completely, the fire must remain out. However, a partly extinguished bonfire can be nursed back by family members between assaults.

The Little Bad Mask plays a special role. Made by Clowns, this mask is painted irregularly; its skirt may be hitched up on one side, and its horns may be crooked and small. The Clowns make this mask somewhat differently each time the festival is put on. As Clowns, they must do the job unevenly and improperly. While most villagers are watching a performance in the boulevard or the plaza, the Little Bad Mask sneaks into a house from the side or the back and steals something, such as a small pot or a machete. According to the script, the Little Bad Mask really wants to be caught in the act. If a woman of a house is not sufficiently watchful to catch him, he may do something "careless" to attract her attention, such as knocking over a water gourd. Once the woman sees him, she gives chase, screaming at the Little Bad Mask, who tries repeatedly to attempt a theft and to receive a scolding, much to the amusement of the villagers.

A feat the Masks try to perfect is entering a house door sideways, one horn after the other, without spearing the doorpost or the thatch around the door with a horn. They try to accomplish this feat faster and faster and vie with each other in the eyes of the watching villagers for the most skilled performance. Running across the boulevard up to the house chosen for the contest, they dip the leading horn in time to enter the door, and they lower the rear horn in time to avoid tearing the thatch. Considering the weight and unwieldiness of the masks, and the wearer's obstructed vision, this feat requires dexterity and practice. The spectacle continues all morning as the villagers watch and voice approval or disapproval.

As the demonstration is about to terminate, the Little Bad Mask enters the game, but never succeeds, of course. He must do everything incorrectly. After several Masks have demonstrated their perfected art of house entry, the Little Bad Mask takes his turn. However, his horn pierces the thatch on one side of the door, not letting him enter the house at all, but pinning him to the thatch. His ridiculous efforts to extricate himself amuse the crowd.

A Mask deftly maneuvers to pass through a doorway.

After failing to enter the house several times, the Little Bad Mask, pawing the ground, charges madly at the house like a bull blinded with rage. If he succeeds in doing what is "traditionally" correct, he breaks his leading horn on the door post, while the villagers collapse in delirious laughter. In a final attempt at entry, the Little Bad Mask trots up to the door, drops his entire mask onto the boulevard, and walks through the door as a man, standing proudly erect. This breaks up the crowd into convulsions of laughter, approval, and delight. This independent Clown will not do it the establishment's way, but he will enter the doorway in his own special way, and he will make the entrance with dignity.

All Masks except the Beautiful Mountain ones spend much of the time begging from the villagers, though less outrageously and shamelessly than the Little Bad Mask. All Masks can put on several facial "expressions," such as entreaty, joy, and shame, by manipulating the facial slits with internal strings. They rub the facial slits together for impatience and thrust their horns up threateningly for anger. When they want food, they manipulate their faces in the begging style, thrusting up the lower facial edges and grunting. When a piece of food is put on the stick extended through their facial slit, they bring it inside the mask and grunt and dance around with glee. When they beg but are refused, they appear to wilt as they twirl around and down to the ground, bowing their faces and horns to the sand, grunting piteously. It was impossible for me to refuse these endearing creatures.

Portrayal of status and state through drama

Interpretations of such performances have to be subjective. My Canela research assistants could give little help here. I see the Festival of Masks, however, as a cultural justification for begging, as an acting out of the message of the myth of Awkhêê: that it is all right for the Canela to beg.

As some Americans say, "I am going to the 'little boys' room," or "I am going to the 'little girls' room," for going to the toilet, relegating the undignified act to children, the Canela relegate the act of direct, unabashed begging to creatures that are somewhat less than human. Masks do not speak, but they are likable, they have a good time, and they are almost human, since they experience joy and shame. The Little Bad Mask seems even more human than the other Masks, since he won't obey the authorities and since he does transform himself into a human to maintain his dignity and to get his way. If nothing else, the Canela are flexible and pragmatic.

Another view of how the Canela see themselves is found in their treatment of animals. The Canela have pets, such as parrots, monkeys, wild boar, and emus (South American ostriches). These animals are treated with tender loving care and raised from as young as possible. They are also fed well until they die or escape, and so their treatment is similar to the way Canela treat their children. Dogs, however, are not treated as pets, possibly because backlanders do not treat them well. But Canela treat them even worse, scarcely feeding them and hitting them with a stick or foot whenever they come near. Canela say that if dogs are fed well, they won't be fierce hunters, which may be true. Nevertheless, I see the Canela as treating dogs in the way they feel the backlanders are treating them. While Awkhêê's myth justifies their inferior social position, the Canela must still feel badly about the inferiority thrust upon them, so they unconsciously pass this misery along to dogs, the only entities they can consistently abuse.

When photographing each Canela house from several angles during our short stay in October 1991, a dog on the other side of the village from my wife's sister's house disturbed my focusing by licking my ankles. I was surprised, as Canela dogs usually cower near humans. I reached down and it let me pet its head. No Canela had to tell me that this dog had been raised by a non-Canela. I knew it had to be the dog of the German anthropologist, and so it was. I noticed that the house I was photographing was his, supporting my hypothesis. As in 1964, when my wife had raised a dog from a newborn pup with condensed milk from an eyedropper, this pet of the German expected affection, unlike any Canela-raised dog. While most Canela appear to have high self-esteem, their consistently poor treatment of dogs says something about how they really see themselves as a people.

Food distribution enhanced

Another interpretation of the Festival of Masks is that it reinforces the food distribution system in general, and the principle of generosity to all in need in particular. Compassion (*hapê: pena*) for those in trouble is a prime Canela value. Begging from the backlander and the urban *civilizado* is all right according to Awkhêê's myth. Expecting to receive food from individuals of the same status when in need goes a step further and comes close to being supported by the Festival of Masks, though the Masks are of lesser status. Such aggressive "begging" without embarrassment, as some categories of Masks portray, is consistent with the economic necessities of Canela life.

Meat is spread on palm fronds for distribution.

Hunters do not kill game and produce meat every day for their families, so families in mourning, or with members who are very ill, often lose most of their crops and have to rely on the compassion of others. Generosity with food occurs automatically among members of the same household and is expected to occur among extended family members, as among most Amazonian peoples. Melatti claims the Krahó Indians distinguish between kin and non-kin by whether food is exchanged freely. Among the Canela, however, this "generosity" is extended even to non-kin when they are hungry and when they come and *ask* for food. I do not call this aspect of the Canela food distribution system "begging," because I view it positively as a very important element in societal survival. Giving food to those in need provides occasions for the givers to express compassion, the value which underlies Canela bonding for survival as a tribe living in a single village-community.

The Wè?tè-concealing ceremony limits sex to trysts

The various acts of the terminal phase of the Festival of Masks are completed in three days, so the ceremony to close the summer Wè?tè season, the Wè?tè Pimtsul Tsà (Wè?tè-concealing occasion), is put on. The final act of the Wè?tè-concealing ceremony—the Wè?tè girls' deactivation act—consists of erecting a log called the Kô?khre (water's-hole/hollow: a spring) vertically in the boulevard directly before the house of one of the two Wè?tè girls. This five-foot-high log of buriti palm has a large rectangular trough cut in it, which is burned black and faces toward the plaza for all to see. This empty trough is said to represent the absence of the Wè?tè girls' spirit of fun expressed through singing, dancing, and extramarital sex. The color black represents this "fun."

   The erection of the Kô?khre announces that there is to be no more dancing and singing in the boulevard. Such recreation can take place only in the plaza until the Wè?tè girls are "shown" again the next year at the opening of the summer Wè?tè season. Until then, the villagers must return to emphasizing farming and family activities (the alternative color, red); they must return to seriousness.

The Kô?khre log marks the end of the summer Wè?tè season.

As an alternative interpretation, the log's name, Kô?khre, a spring, may portend the coming season, with its heavy dew and light rains, bringing the Canela "spring" to their savannahs. Taken in this sense, the color black may symbolize the coming control of the Blacks of the Mẽ-ipimràk season, the time for renewal. Symbols can be taken in several ways, but Canela research assistants could not help me with this second interpretation, possibly because they are living at a time when they simply accept their customs rather than in a period when they are creating them.

Interpretation of the great festivals   The Canela great festivals of the summer Wè?tè season can be interpreted in a number of ways, and their many acts can be interpreted separately. We have space to present only two or three interpretations of each festival.

The two initiation festivals, the Khêêtúwayê (Ghosts) and the Pepyê (Warriors), process boys into adolescents and then adolescents into a mature warrior age class. The Ghosts' festival reinforces family relations, as the initiates' female relatives and their uncles protect them from ghosts—the needed opposition—who would take away these initiates' souls as they sing songs which attract ghosts. In addition, families surrender their boys for the first time to the care of age class leaders appointed by the Council of Elders. This separation is like going to school. The councilors indoctrinate the boys, interned in two large cells, with dozens of stories about their ancestors. Ghosts' festivals are put on for the same group of initiates two to three times over a period of about 10 years.

Warriors' festivals continue the formal socialization of the initiates under the control of age class leaders appointed by the Council of Elders. Learning to take control of one's life is emphasized, through learning to practice a high level of food and sex restrictions to keep out pollutions—the opposition here—from one's body and therefore from the bodies of nuclear family kin, the individual's closest unit of bonding. An adolescent initiate's relationship to his naming-uncle and to the latter's men's society is emphasized, as well as the initiate's relationship to his own age class. These relationships take an initiate's reliance slowly away from his family and move it toward his society at large. The initiates, when they run together in a group, continuously shout *krôô, krôô, krôô* (meaning wild boar) in unison, suggesting that they go around fiercely like wild boar in a pack. The last Warriors' festival graduates the initiates into a mature age class, the purpose of which is to fight for the survival of the Canela as a people.

The Canela have three internment festivals. *Boys* and *adolescents,* as initiates, are interned in the Ghosts' and Warriors' festivals, while *adults* are interned in the Facsimile Warriors' festival, the Pep-kahàk (warrior-facsimile/secondary/false). Adult males of any age are interned to help them renew their practice of restrictions against pollutions. It is like going on a religious retreat to renew one's adolescent vows. Here, however, in the Facsimile Warriors' festival, more realistic kinds of oppositions exist: the sting of wasps, the cold of the night, and the Ducks, a competing men's society. In each case of opposition, Formal Friends of the Facsimile Warriors and also the Clowns, instead of their kin or their maintenance of restrictions, protect them from the supposed life's difficulty. It seems as if *both* opponents *and* facilitating agents have to be dramatized in a festival situation to make the socialization of its principal group more effective.

There is another side to the Facsimile Warriors' festival: the representation of ceremonial rank. The Facsimile Warriors manifest middle-to-high-honor ceremonial prestige, since their membership consists of both Wet Heads (high prestige) and Dry Heads (low prestige). The Facsimile Warriors perform every day and carry out their roles in an arrogant manner, wearing red and white, but never black. When they march in dignity around the village each evening to obtain their family-provided meals, they never catch anyone's eye, but look disdainfully ahead. Nevertheless, the Facsimile Warriors are not as aloof as the Tàm-hàk (sensitive-falcons), who are all Wet Heads, who perform only twice, and who wear only white items.

The Facsimile Warriors are contrasted with the Clowns, who are all Dry Heads and wear mostly black paint. The Clowns appear several times in secondary roles in the Facsimile Warriors' festival to help the Facsimile Warriors, but they run the Fish festival entirely on their own. The ceremonial rank held by individuals, because of the festival roles they inherited or acquired, somewhat determines their daily behavior. My closest Canela research assistant, the younger Thunder, could not manage his store properly to make a profit from it. This was because he could not refuse poor-risk individuals credit, being of high ceremonial rank himself. Thus, he always had to be generous.

The Fish festival, the Tep-yalkhwa (fish-talk/language), is completely dominated by the men's society of Clowns, once the Council of Elders (the establishment) allows the Clowns to put on their festival. The Council of Elders governs and directs all the other annual and great summer festivals, day by day, and even moment to moment. One sees councilors telling individual performers what to do just before they do it, especially in the great festivals that are not put on every year.

As stated before, the Clowns must do everything, at least partly, in a nonestablishment way. The Clowns represent the person's individuality against the establishment's required solidarity. In the terminal phase of the Fish festival, the Clowns compete against several kinds of Fish societies and water animal societies, such as turtles, stingrays, anaconda snakes, and river otters, but the Clowns *always* win—eat—their opponents. In the other great festivals, the competition is mediated before the end of the festival, but the Clowns, as individuals, must win; their victory is not mediated.

The victory of the Clowns is portrayed during the last night of the terminal phase of the Fish festival. The men and the female associates of the Fish society are in a weir (a circle of vertical palm fronds) in the center of the plaza. The Clowns start to enter the weir to catch and "eat" the Fish, but the Fish choose to escape instead. Each Fish is carrying a meat pie of manioc meal on his or her shoulder. The meat pie is wrapped in wild banana leaves and tied in a frame of supple sticks shaped like a fish. What follows is like a game of Prisoners' Base, in which each Fish tries to escape by racing from the weir to a house, a safe base, before a Clown snatches the meat pie off the shoulder of the running Fish. When a Clown is not looking, a Fish streaks from one house to another, or even back to the weir.

This act is not really a contest, because in the end the Clowns have to catch all the Fish. The Clowns pile the fish-shaped meat pies high in their spot at the edge of the plaza and sing a triumphal song. Competition and winning are anathema to the Canela, who live for problem solving and are devoted to mediation, but the Clowns

Men of the Fish societies race from the weir with fish-shaped meat pies on their shoulders.

epitomize Canela values by acting out what is held to be wrong—the smashing of social bonds—by winning outrageously and gloating at the demise of other Canela social groups.

4/Bonding Through Sex

The Canela sociocultural system is remarkably complex and varied with regard to extramarital sex activities. It ranges from private trysts arranged by individuals, to private trysts sanctified and carried out according to ceremonial customs, to group sequential sex which takes place on ceremonial occasions and even within the daily cycle of events. In the third case, women have sex sequentially with a number of men in prescribed situations. A woman may even have sex with three or four men sequentially in a completely casual and chance situation. To understand how Canela young people are raised into adolescence and adulthood to want to take part in and to enjoy such sexual activities may be very important to our understanding of the flexibility of human sexuality and the degree to which sex is molded by culture.

Our primary purpose, however, is to show how the Canela extramarital system provides yet another important arena for social bonding. Especially in earlier times, a man or a woman would have had sex with most of the opposite sex in the appropriate age groups who were not kin or formal friends. The sexual abilities of all members of the tribe are generally known through "gossip" or conversation. Thus, the Canela know each other with an intimacy almost unimaginable by us.

The ideal of generosity so important to the Canela is supported by extramarital sex. Individuals should be generous with their bodies as they should be with goods. Sexual jealousy and possessiveness are suppressed.

THE EXTRAMARITAL SEX SYSTEM, PUBLIC AND PRIVATE

Growth in awareness of the ethnographer When I first started living with the Canela, I was already aware of the festivals which separated spouses for extramarital sex. On certain ceremonial days, spouses go with different tribal moieties for feasting and log racing as well as sex. Thus, by nightfall, a person knows that her or his spouse probably has had sex with someone else, or with several other persons. Feelings are not hurt, however, because a spouse's sex partners are not identified and because the arrangement is sanctioned by tradition. Nimuendajú's volume describes the Warriors' initiation festival's Wild Boar day,[56] when wives of men of the Upper age class log racing teams amble out to a Canela garden's hut with men of the Lower age class moiety log racing team for feasting and sex, while wives of men of the Lower teams stay in the village for dancing and sex with men of the Upper teams. Nimuendajú wrote that extramarital sex practiced apart from such ceremonial occasions was "adultery" and cause for divorce.[57] As my research eventually

143

proved, Nimuendajú's view of the Canela extramarital sex system was erroneous, so I had some surprises coming as my field research deepened.

On my first trip[58] to the Canela, I asked questions about extramarital sex only to be countered by denials. Canela research assistants, who otherwise were helpful, assured me that Nimuendajú was wrong in saying that extramarital sex was practiced away from the village at a garden on the Wild Boar day. Who was lying? But "lying" was not the right interpretation, I decided. A more plausible explanation was that the Canela were being protective about their extramarital sex practices.

After several months, I brought out from my field trunk two large medical volumes, which I had brought with me because I had to be my own doctor. These volumes had colored plates showing all parts of the body, internal and external, female and male. I had concluded that the Canela were embarrassed by talking about sex with outsiders and that I needed to condition them, and myself, into being more comfortable about this subject. Indian Service agents had talked to me depreciatingly about Canela sex. "Women sleep in the village plaza with men who are not their husbands," an agent warned me privately in derogatory tones. He had observed this activity while wandering in the village several times after midnight. Later, a backlander took me aside and complained that Canela couples, when they lived by his house, sometimes crept under their large mats, moving them in sex, not caring about what was heard. *Bichos do mato,* "beasts of the forest," backlanders often called the Canela.

It had become clear to me that I needed to prove to the Canela that I did not think negatively about them because of their sex practices. I hoped that my use of the medical volumes' explicit pictures would help convince them I was not critical or prudish.

The Canela had had experience viewing and discussing illustrated books. I remember sitting on a mat by the door of my sister Waterfall's house to provide better light for the pictures and having a few Canela kneeling around me in the sand. Although I had intended to show the medical books first to men, women crowded around eagerly, pointing out and naming the sexual parts in the anatomical drawings. I remember my anxiety as I started asking them the names of various parts of the body, repeating their answers several times to get the pronunciation right: head (*?-khrã·* its [body's] ball), arm (*?-pa:* its branch), leg (*?-te:* its limb), penis (*?-hù:* its seeder), testicles (*n-kre:* its eggs), foreskin (*?-hù ?khrã ?khà:* its seeder's head's hide), vulva (*?-hê:* its [vertical] cleft),[59] pubic hair (*?-hê hô:* its cleft's pendants), clitoris (*?-hê ?khrùt-re:* its cleft's beak little). As well as learning the Canela terms, I was ridding myself of the inhibitions characteristic of my upbringing.

The Canela were interested in the photographs and diagrams, and groups frequently came by, especially women, to look through the volumes for entertainment. Soon, by joining these groups, I became at ease describing and joking about the color and shape of sexual parts. Such talk became easier in Canela than English, as I discovered when I tried to describe such joking back in the United States. After several episodes of fun with the volumes, I had convinced the Canela that I was not embarrassed by a discussion of sex and that I did not hold their sexual practices against them. Subsequently, Canela research assistants willingly furnished the intricacies and intimacies of their unusually extensive extramarital sex system. As I learned its patterns, I realized that Nimuendajú had been largely mistaken about one of the principal Canela concepts. His belief that they considered casual adultery untraditional had contributed to the Canela's need to hide most of the details of their extramarital practices from him, as they had always done from backlanders and later from Indian Service agents.

Public Extramarital practices   During my first year, the Warriors' festival's Wild Boar day feast was held in a hut on a garden clearing several miles from the Canela village of Baixão Preto. From the hut I watched small groups of young women disappear into the woods followed by groups of young men. An hour later these groups returned separately, the bodies of all individuals haphazardly decorated in charcoal stuck on with white latex sap. Such groups vanished into the bushes and emerged all afternoon, some individuals joining them more than once. Canela assistants denied sexual activity was occurring out there, but I did not believe them.

The next year, on the same festival occasion, Canela assistants confirmed that the groups in the woods away from the garden's hut were indeed having sex. Informants added that since each group had more men than women, some women satisfied several men. They said that the women of a group found separate bedding-down spots to which the extra men came in sequence.

I quietly savored the field victory that this new information brought me, but tried not to appear too interested or curious. I tried to strike a balance between being appreciative of the Canela fun derived from such practices and being matter-of-fact about the special knowledge Nimuendajú had missed. My training had taught me that if I appeared too eager to hear about their sex practices, they might bring an inflated number of examples to please me.

The black charcoal, stuck firmly but haphazardly with latex on bodies of individuals emerging from the woods, proclaimed the occurrence of an episode of extramarital sex. Men paint only women with whom they have just had extramarital sex, while women paint both women and men in any of the various traditional ways. Charcoal carefully applied on a man with latex was the daily work of his wife. All styles of body painting signal meaning. For instance, charcoal rubbed on loosely, without latex as a binder, announces that the individual is undergoing strict taboos.

On another annual ceremonial occasion, a Red versus Black moiety day[60] during my second year, adolescent women and adult men assembled 500 yards outside the village along a road at about seven in the morning. I had missed this Red versus Black episode the year before from not having been warned that it was taking place, though I knew of its extramarital sex nature from Nimuendajú's volume. Because it was the beginning of a formal occasion, the participants were painted in carefully applied solid black charcoal on latex, horizontal lines for the Reds and vertical ones for the Blacks. The precise traditional designs represented the two Regeneration ("winter") moieties involved.

By the time I arrived, a fence four feet high had been erected across the road so that no one lying or sitting on the village side could see anyone on the savanna side. Red women and men were on the village side of the fence in separate groups, while Black women and men lay or sat apart quietly on the farther side. Besides several Canela elderly observers and myself, only two male performers were standing, one painted in each pattern. The Red man asked several Red women in low tones which men they favored. Then he went beyond the fence to the Black side and tapped each chosen Black man with his wand. At the same time, the Black messenger walked in from behind the fence to tap certain Red men so that they would know they were a

Black woman's choice. These two male messengers, assistants told me, were asking women which men of the opposite moiety (other than their husbands) they wanted to go hunting with.

Later, the Reds and Blacks filed separately along a wooded trail, and women caught the eyes of the men they had chosen. The men were waiting for such meaningful glances. Later, small groups of individuals ambled off into the bushes eventually to pair off with their partners for the day. Individuals tried not to let their spouses see whom they were joining. Attempting not to be conspicuous myself, I kept watching women and men I knew to be married to see how careful they were being. Their care was minimal, but they did cooperate by averting eyes from the location of their spouses.

Canela research assistants said that once deep in the small woods scattered in the savannah, the man hunted, while the woman waited under a tree. If she were sufficiently pleased with the game he brought her, she might give him sex. That evening, sex or no sex, the woman made a small meat pie of the supplied game and passed it inconspicuously to her mother-in-law. The older woman accepted the pie, knowing that the meat was supplied by her daughter-in-law's lover. Then the mother-in-law supplied a bowl of meat and manioc to her daughter-in-law's lover's Red or Black group when it was assembled in the plaza that evening.

This meat pie rite represents the mother-in-law's acceptance of her daughter-in-law's customary right to be involved in extramarital sex on public occasions and in private trysts. Before this rite, the older woman might have taken her son's side if he were complaining about his wife's extramarital trysts and his consequent embarrassment and shame. And before this rite, the younger woman would not have gone on public ceremonial occasions, such as the Wild Boar and Red versus Black days, for fear of the vicious talk any of her female in-laws might spread against her. Now they could say nothing. They had accepted the marriage more completely, including the couple's customary full participation in extramarital sex.

A Ceremonial Chief sing-dance day[61] could occur many times during a year to install a singing chief, a town crier, or a protection chief of another Eastern Timbira tribe. Such sing-dance days were also put on to honor the visit of a high-ranking government official or to extract goods from the tribal anthropologist or missionary, who had to contribute an outrageous amount when so honored. I felt exploited when they did this for me, but decided they felt they were exacting a fair exchange for what they thought would be my future sale of books and photographs. Otherwise I would be getting a "free ride on their backs." The Canela feel they lose something essential, maybe dignity or self-respect, when they think themselves used without a proper return.

During every Ceremonial Chief day, the honored person, female or male, is painted red with white falcon down applied onto an adhesive resin base. This installation into a ceremonial position of respect takes place in the plaza, while the tribe spends most of the day performing sing-dances in separate male age class units. These male groups dance sideways around the village boulevard in single rows, facing out toward the houses. An Upper age class group dances slowly clockwise, arms around shoulders. They invite wives of men of a Lower age class to come out from their houses and dance with them, interspersed in the male row, arms around shoulders also.

A Lower age class of men dances counterclockwise and inserts wives of Upper age class men into their row. (See cover photo for a current enactment of this dance.)

During an hour of this Mē Aykhē sing-dancing, approximately 50 men collect about 10 women into their age class's sideways-moving rows. Then the men, perspiring and elated, take these women away for sex. The age classes of one moiety dance into a Ceremonial Girl's[62] house, enlarged and equipped with a special room for such a purpose, and the age classes of the other moiety drift to a secluded area along the village stream. Spouses are thus well separated.

My assistants said that the dances of these sing-dance Ceremonial Chief days arouse sexual feelings in participants, and I occasionally saw dancing males in the line brushing their hands casually over female breasts. In any case, this hopping and sidestepping around the boulevard, the rear foot crossing behind and ahead of the forward one, require considerable stamina. After I turned 40, I could not complete the long journey around the village circle even once. In contrast, Canela up to 50 years old completed it many times.

In the ceremonial house, members of the hosting family, according to Canela assistants, erect enclosures of light mats in their special room to screen each woman. Some sets of mats are placed around existing platform beds and some are strung up around piles of mats on the floor. By the stream, the women are separated by bushes so that any of the men who want sex can go, one at a time, to a woman who is not a relative, in-law, or Formal Friend without their activity being closely watched.

A similar arrangement is set up on tribal work days, when the elders decide most of the men will perform services together. They might cut open the vistas through the savannahs and woods along the tribal boundaries, work on the roads so vehicles will not stall in the sands, or harvest a family's field of rice. On such occasions, each age class moiety files out swiftly to different sectors of the work area. Three to five women are assigned by the chief to each moiety for the day. They flirt with the men while they work and chat with them while they eat light lunches in the early afternoon. Then the women, assistants said, walk out about 30 yards in different directions from their moiety's central location to prepare concealed, comfortable nests in the low bushes in which to please a number of men, sequentially. A man picks a woman he is not related to and walks out to her. He swiftly completes the sex act and stands up. Then the next man, seeing the first one stand, walks out to the woman's nest. She moves the nest slightly for each man so that he will not come into contact with any sexual secretions left on the grass from the earlier trysts.

This traditional placing of women so that men can go to them sequentially for sex also occurs at the end of a two-week hunting encampment away from the village. Such hunting trips serve to obtain enough meat so that the whole tribe can eat well during a 10-day festival without leaving the village. Again, the men are divided in two large groups by age class moiety, and the half dozen women assigned to each moiety are spouses of men of the other moiety. The women cook and prepare the meat throughout the hunting period but have sex with the men only after the last sing-dancing, during the night before their return to the village. To have had sex earlier might have polluted and weakened the hunters and spoiled their rapport with the game. Assistants say that game animals like hunters who are unpolluted by recently eaten "heavy" meat or by sex with women who are thus polluted. Animals like to approach hunters who are in such a state of relative "purity." Consequently, the hunters can easily kill them.

This arrangement for sequential sex also takes place informally on any day the men work in their age class moiety units close enough so that they can join each other to race back to the village in the mid-afternoon, each moiety team carrying a log. While such races, preceded by group sequential sex, do not occur every day, they are a potential element of the daily cycle of events when the members of the tribe are living in their central village and not generally dispersed to their gardens or to the houses of backlanders. These events are thus daily in nature, not ceremonial. While it is relatively easy to recruit women for ceremonial events, it is often difficult to obtain them for daily work occasions. These daily work situations therefore have usually lacked women in more recent times.

While the sequential extramarital sex arrangements described above place many men with a few unrelated women, the Festival of Oranges places about half a dozen men with 40 to 50 women for about 10 days. Women generally enjoy discussing among themselves how a certain man performs sexually, so the capabilities of most men are known to most women, just as the capabilities of most women are known to most men. Thus, the women can choose the young men with the greatest sexual abilities to accompany them in their quest for oranges and other foods for the Festival of Oranges.

When I was away from the village for several days on a mapping trip during my second stay with the Canela, my mapping assistant asked me the first evening if he could send for women from the village to help my work party members enjoy the night. Of course I said yes, hoping to witness activities usually hidden from me, since I could not participate in them. (Aside from my personal and professional ethics, Brazilian law was clear on this restriction, and Indian Service personnel would have reported infractions quickly and canceled my authorization to work with the Canela.)

Later that evening I remember feeling delighted at this opportunity for observation when four laughing young women arrived. After one of them, my assistant's long-term lover, had satisfied several men in the bushes, not quite out of my hearing, she climbed into my assistant's hammock which was hung on one of the same posts as mine. Between about midnight and five I was awakened six times by a rhythmic shaking which the common post transferred to my hammock. Six times I confined myself to listening, afraid to be caught peeking to collect field data, even though the night was dark. After what I had heard and felt that night, I was no longer surprised that the women usually sought my mapping assistant as one of their Festival of Oranges male companions each year.

One time when I asked about whether women were ever sexually aggressive with men, assistants told me a story of earlier times. Young Hole Grater was said to revel in having sex with as many women as possible. The young women decided to teach this boastful youth a lesson. Ten of them climbed a tree and one called down to him for sex as he was passing beneath. He spat on his hands and climbed the tree, grabbing at one then another, but each one said it was another who had called him. Finally, near the top, he cornered one girl, stretched her out on a branch, and had sex with her there, publicly and perilously, to the others' consternation. Further action was needed to humble this man.

Several days later, the same group of young women, hoping to teach Hole Grater a lesson and wanting to take advantage of his superior attributes, invited him into the woods. There they made a bed to lie in, and each one came to him in turn, lying down for him. Nobody can say these days just how many sex acts Hole Grater's erection survived, but he finally got tired, saying he was hungry and asking for something to eat to bring back his strength. However, the next woman in line insisted on her turn and would not let him rest. So she lay down and started pulling on his penis until it became erect (a totally uncustomary manipulation). Then she inserted it and they had sex one more time.

After this last attempt to humble him, they had pity on him and took him home to his wife. The news of his lesson reached the village and his wife's ears before he did, so she teased him when he came in the door. Nevertheless, Hole Grater rested a moment and ate something, and then demonstrated that he could do it one more time with her. He had not quite been tamed.

Private extramarital practices   A frequent cause of fun, when I was moving around with male companions, was the discovery of a sex tryst spot. The discoverer would gleefully summon his friends to the spot, and the group, thoroughly enthralled, debated what each mark in the sand indicated: her buttocks were here, his feet were there, his buttocks swung low here, and her head relaxed there afterward; the couple were in a hurry and did it quickly because there was only one set of relatively unblurred markings.

While I saw many tryst spots in the sands, I seldom was close by when sequential sex was taking place. However, I once found myself conversing with the men going to and from such an episode. The tryst had been informally arranged; it probably had occurred spontaneously. In the Canela village of Sardinha in the dry forests, the soil was sufficiently fertile within the village circle, unlike the soil in a savannah village, so that corn could be planted between the radial pathways leading from the circular village plaza to the houses on the circular boulevard.

Just after the performance of the Sweet Potato rite in March of my fourth trip, I was standing at the edge of the plaza of Baixão Preto where the young were sing-dancing, when Ràm (tree resin) emerged from the corn stalks that were growing between the plaza and the village boulevard before the houses. I overheard him talking to younger Thunder and gathered that a woman was hidden among the corn stalks, available for sex. Thunder, who was helping me learn about the rite, then disappeared into the standing corn. When he emerged two minutes later and was alone with me, I teased him for just having had sex, which he denied at first, as was the custom, and then admitted it privately to me, as my helper and friend. Electric Eel Girl was there, only 10 to 20 yards from the plaza, a woman in her late teens. Thunder said she had been lying there first with Macaw Bone (age 45) and was desirable because of her large vagina. He said that Resin (age 30) had spotted them, and so had joined them for sex, and that he had done the same. When Macaw Bone emerged from the corn, I teased him that I would tell his wife, my relative, which he knew from experience I would not do. Although he said nothing, he smiled.

I found the constant interest in sex remarkable. With sex so easily available, I wondered why the interest was so keen. At the beginning of my field work, young men discussed the arrival of panties as a threat to their easy access to women. Perhaps such lively interest reflected concern that sexual availability was waning. Possibly, extramarital sex was the principal joy in a society which offered few other excitements and many overwhelming social and economic discouragements. The principal societal sources of satisfaction other than extramarital sex are team racing with logs, daily sing-dancing in the plaza, performing festivals, hunting animals for food and sport, and providing for children, kin, and spouses. Nevertheless, except for the last one, all these sources of gratification among the Canela are accompanied by sexual activities.

Besides the festival-sanctioned and work-group occasions for extramarital sex described above, personally arranged trysts are also traditional and more frequently practiced. If a man feels a strong sexual desire for a woman, and if she is neither kin, affine, nor Formal Friend, he gives her a certain look as they pass, or he says, possibly, that he would like to pass his hand on her (*i-mã a-kuupên prãm:* me-in you-touch [I] need). She responds in kind if she feels the same way. Later, when the opportunity arises, he sends her a spoken message through a neutral person, usually a child of either sex who would have inconspicuous access to her, suggesting a location and time: for instance, down behind the locust tree which juts into the wet meadow left of the main stream when the sun is low.

Canela assistants assure me that women take the initiative as often as men. My best evidence for this occurred in May 1959 on the evening of my third return to the tribe. I had been paying my respects to the Indian Service personnel by having dinner at the post. After dinner, while slowly climbing the sandy hill back up to Ponto village, I heard the beating of a drum, a sound I had never heard in the village before. Off-pattern occurrences strike the ethnographer's attention sharply. The rhythm reminded me of the several backlanders' dancing festivals I had attended during the two previous years, and I knew from the sound that someone was beating an empty metal gasoline barrel.

Easing through the crowd in the larger of the two Ceremonial Girl's houses, I found Canela women and men paired and dancing bare topped in the embraced manner of the backlanders, shuffling their feet to the monotonous rhythm of a metal drum. No instrument or singing provided a melody. I realized that this was an historic event: a first occurrence of dancing borrowed from the backlander by the Canela, but only partly reproduced. After waiting in the crowded room for the pattern to repeat itself several times, I noticed that when the beating ceased for an interval, couples parted according to the backland custom. However, contrary to the custom, when the dancing resumed, it was the women who chose the men they wanted as their next partners. A year later, Canela couples were dancing fully clothed, often with shoes, to the music of an accordian. Only men were standing and choosing seated women after each break in the dancing. Now the adoption of the backland pattern was complete. But before this happened, it had seemed traditional to the Canela to have the women do the choosing.

LEARNING ABOUT SEX

Several nights after I was taken into Canela life, assigned an adoptive family, and given a corner in their house, I was awakened by soft noises coming from the rafters. Although it was dark, I knew there was a platform bed high up in the area the sounds were coming from and interpreted the moderate creaking as evidence that some sort of sexual activity was taking place. I wondered how the children of the

A woman sits on a platform bed. Mats woven of palm fronds provide privacy. Beds for younger women would be even higher. Possessions are stored under the rafters of the house.

house interpreted these sounds and whether the parents of the girl up there found the sounds appropriate.

Nimuendajú wrote that unmarried women receive lovers on such rafter platforms at night. Lake Lover was recently married, however, and about 14, so I wondered what was going on that was appropriate for her whole family to overhear. Waterfall, her mother and my "sister," rose to stir the fire, appearing not to hear the noises. Single Girl, 4, was returning from relieving herself just outside with her mother's sister Self Searcher following her. However, except for one slight turn of her head, Single Girl paid no attention to the noises. I concluded that little girls and boys grew up hearing their older sisters having sex, but I thought that I had better check this point with my research assistants in the morning. In this case, I thought (though could not see) that the young man who had climbed the notched pole to the high platform was Boil's Vapor, Lake Lover's new husband. Family members confirmed the next day that it was Boil's Vapor. He had departed quietly before dawn. Assistants said later that young couples seldom have sex in their platform beds, but only when overcome by great desire and only when they think every one else is sound asleep.

During my second stay among the Canela, in my adoptive sister's house, two preadolescent boys, Electric Eel and Fast Pig, were teasing Flint Woman, the new wife of their older brother, Endures Water. The boys were trying to pull off her wraparound skirt. She resisted, screaming with fun, while they persisted unsuccessfully. The smaller children watched the sex-oriented fun with delight.

A month later, again in my sister's house in front of all the children, the younger Thunder, an "uncle" to the children, called me to join him in having fun with our adolescent "niece," Kô-rên (water-spilt). We both caught her, and he tried unsuccessfully to suck one of her breasts while I tried to hold her securely, keeping her from escaping him. Spilt Water was strong, however, and managed to evade Thunder by ducking and wiggling. This traditional "uncle"–"niece" game was broken up when her wraparound skirt began to come off, turning the game into a serious embarrassment for her. Spilt Water had screamed in delight earlier, but with her skirt slipping, she began to scream in fear and anger, so we released her. Thunder accused her of being angry, a-khrùk (you-angry), a social offense which Spilt Water heartily denied, resuming her social good nature, at least in appearance. Younger Thunder initiated such fun and games only in a limiting familial setting.

I had qualms about becoming involved in such traditional games, even to the extent of just holding by the shoulders a "niece" whom I already knew very well. What if a backlander or an Indian Service agent saw what I was doing? What if a Canela innocently told a backlander or an Indian Service agent that they liked me because I was participating in the fun of Canela life in this way? Fortunately, this did not happen.

One day during the summer of my second year, while I was eating lunch in the open-walled part of my sister's house, a sex game occurred between Macaw's Bone, my sister's husband, and one of his "other wives," Three Forests Woman. Macaw's Bone had severely hurt his leg in the log race the day before, so he was spending the day in his hammock, hung in the open part of the house so he could observe all that was going on. Suddenly, Three Forests Woman dumped him out of his hammock, and rolled on top of him as he lay on the ground. The large woman grabbed his genitals. She was enjoying her advantage over the temporarily hobbled Macaw's Bone. The struggle went on for at least a minute until the Indian Service agent with another outsider barged in.

Fun had been had by all, except for the children of the household, who watched silently, unable to laugh when their own father was the butt of the joke. Nevertheless, the children witnessed the amusement and joy associated with sex, even if they could not participate.

Assistants said that in these sex games between "other spouses," "aunts" and "nephews," or "uncles" and "nieces," the women try to grab penises and the men attempt to suck breasts. These games occur only when many relatives are watching, ensuring that the fun does not evolve beyond culturally allowed limits. Nobody must get seriously hurt—either physically or emotionally. The older generations thus impose their authority over the younger ones by sugar-coating their discipline with the fun of sex. Women work off their hostilities to men, and vice versa, by cloaking their aggression in the amusement that traditionally surrounds sex.

In the village of Sardinha during my fourth stay, I had built up a group of Canela research assistants whom I could be sure were telling me the truth about almost everything. Thus, I could undertake the sensitive quest of reconstructing with them what their sexual mores had been in earlier times. I inquired into sexual behavior for several days with a group of both sexes, selected for their good memories and their superior abilities of expression. About six of us worked in a room with a window, with coffee and crackers brought to us in the middle of the morning and afternoon sessions. By this time it did not surprise me that little tykes of 3 and 4 years came back repeatedly to listen for minutes at a time, and that children of 8 or 9 spent half hours hanging on the window sill, attempting to follow our debates. Their parents were not concerned about what their children might hear.

One time, the younger Thunder got on the table in our room and demonstrated several of the positions used in sex, squatting for male ones and lying on his back with his knees spread for female ones. It happened that the table was near the window, so that Thunder's little "niece" of 9 years, Star Girl, could reach him through the window with a pencil in her hand. When she began poking him with it, while he was on his back demonstrating a female position, the group erupted into continuous laughter. Within two to three years she would be doing what Thunder was demonstrating.

Certain festival situations call for public parodies of sexual behavior which, while intentionally ridiculous, are really an expression of great joy. The joy is acted out in this way to honor one's Formal Friend. The sexual behavior thus mimicked, simultaneously comic and ecstatic, is witnessed by children and adolescents. The young thus see that sexual expression is the greatest joy that can be invoked to honor a Formal Friend.

During my first year with the Canela, an old man in his late 70s tried to take off an equally old woman's wraparound skirt in the boulevard in front of a house during the Warriors' initiation festival. He was doing this with exaggerated clumsy motions, expressing joy to honor his Formal Friend, an adolescent boy. Standing on a mat nearby, this initiate was being ceremonially presented to the adults at the end of his initiation ceremony's internment. However, the game was stopped when another old woman came up and hit the old man lightly on the back side with a stick. The second woman, as the old woman's Formal Friend, was protecting her. Children and adults had gathered around, enjoying the ridiculous pantomiming of the couple for several minutes, and were probably sorry he had not succeeded.

During the Closing Wè?tè festival of my eighth Canela trip, a woman who was a Formal Friend of one of the two ceremonial girls performing in the festival expressed her joy for the performer being honored, her Formal Friend. She jerked her hips, thrusting up an artificial male genitalia, made of two gourds and a graphically carved stick. On such occasions, some men formerly pulled back their foreskins for everybody to see the glans of the penis, as Nimuendajú wrote[63] and my Canela research assistants confirmed. Acting in the same spirit, a woman was reported in earlier times to have bent over to expose her vulva. Such acts were ordinarily forbidden in public as extreme immodesty but in these ceremonial occasions were customary. One assistant said that a certain woman in earlier times took a handful of grass, and rubbing it on her exposed vulva, pretended she was wiping herself clean after having had sex. Again, this was behavior ordinarily forbidden in public. An assistant reported that years ago one Formal Friend's rejoicing act went too far even for this traditional breaking of the usual behavior patterns. One rejoicing female Formal Friend of a performer went on all fours to present her vulva like an animal, while a male Formal Friend of a performer pretended to enter her from behind. However, before she could prevent it, he had succeeded, leaving her dripping and chagrinned.

Although some of the young people may be embarrassed by witnessing these public displays by their close kin, they cannot avoid the realization that the displays are expressions of joy and honor.

Socialization of virginal girls for sex   During the Fish festival, Hand's Blossom Girl, about 10 and still a virgin, but already an associate (*kuytswè*) of the men's

The Formal Friend of one of the two ceremonial girls wears artificial male genitalia in a public parody of sexual behavior.

Fish society, was ambling by the men's fire on the western edge of the plaza with other Fish society women just after running with them in a log race. One of the older men standing there, age 45, teased her, saying that she should not have sex with adolescent youths, but only with older men like himself. He added jokingly to me that she looked tired because she was having sex with adolescents.

Old Man was indirectly teaching Hand's Blossom Girl to expect to enjoy and to want to have sex with older men by the enthusiasm of his manner. Ironically, Old Man was one of the three homosexuals in the tribe, and the one of the three who was not able to have erections with women, so assistants had explained in one of our group meetings. Hand's Blossom Girl must have known this too, but she accepted the admonishment anyway in the usual joking spirit.

At the log racing site of the Red versus Black ceremony during my second year, Kô-?kaprôô (water-blood) carried off a young female non-virgin toward the woods to the amusement of all present, as if she were a racing log held over his left shoulder. At first she was struggling and screaming loudly in delight, but when her screams turned from joy to fear, Water's Blood released her. Then the two returned slowly together to the group. Although she had not agreed to go with Red Boar, she had not objected at first. However, since no observers were in the woods to limit the sex game, she began to become fearful and objected seriously. A number of virginal girls present on this occasion, helping their mothers prepare food, witnessed the joking abduction. They were thus exposed to the appeal of single, non-sequential sex, but also witnessed the limitations provided by consensus.

During the Facsimile Warriors' festival of my second year, Amkro-?khwèy (sun-light girl), 11, who was thought still to be a virgin, enjoyed the protection of her "virginity." She was the younger female associate of this ceremonial men's troop and was treated as a virgin because she had had sex only with her husband and not yet with a number of her "other husbands." In contrast, Tsêp-khwèy (bat-girl), 13, the older non-virginal female associate of this men's society, gave herself on traditional occasions to her other husbands in the group.

At the time of the great ceremonial Wild Boar day log race near the end of the Facsimile Warriors' festival of my 10th stay, four young women went off into the woods from the place where the 30 to 40 male log racers and the 40 to 50 observers had lunched and rested. Some of the latter were still virginal girls around 10 years old, who were helping their female relatives prepare food for the racers. About 20 racers ambled off into the woods after the young women in an irregular manner and returned with them about 45 minutes later. The women and men were covered with patches of black charcoal recently slapped on the latex that had been carelessly hand-applied to their bodies. This style of body paint conveyed one principal message to the virgins, who by this age were keenly anticipating sex, including sequential sex.

Steps into full marriage   While Sun Light Girl did not have to have sexual relations with her other husbands in the Facsimile Warriors' troop, she was nevertheless married, though this fact was not yet generally known. She had given her virginity to Khrúwa-tsè (arrow-bitter) a few weeks earlier when he had enticed her into the woods. In this case, the act of sex constituted the first step into marriage, though there are other possible preceding acts.

Marriage (*mē hikhwa:* they lie-down-together) may be arranged ahead of time by the mothers of the couple. The couple may be brought before their kin for a marital meeting (*mē aypēn pa:* they to-each-other listen) during which their uncles lecture them on the responsibilities of marriage. Then the couple are engaged (*mē aypēn tê:* they for-each-other reserved) and are left alone together much of the time so they may have sex, as their mothers hope they will.

One Canela assistant reported that after his marriage had been arranged, his mother took him and his future wife on an extended visit to a backland community. Eventually, after two weeks of living close together and some *cachaça* (cane alcohol) on the final night, he and his fiancée finally became joined sexually. Thus, they had become married, according to the Canela definition. In contrast, a girl may give her virginity to an adolescent of her choice, without being engaged, which is referred to by the parents as the youth "having stolen" (*to hà?khíya*) the girl. In either case, they are married by the act of sexual intercourse, and the marriage continues unless the boy's extended family pays a fine for his release, the amount being set in an open interfamily trial.

Virginity loss is only the first step into full marriage for a woman. Other important steps are: (1) the ceremonial purchase of the son-in-law by the bride's extended family; (2) the bride's winning her ceremonial belt through her service in a festival men's society, which includes sequential sex; (3) the painting of the bride's ceremonial belt by her female in-laws; (4) the mother-in-law's receipt of meat earned by the bride through extramarital sex on the Red and Black great racing day; (5) the birth of her first baby and its survival; and (6) the celebration of the postpartum rite about 40 days later by the extended kin of the couple. After the birth of a baby, unless the baby dies, the marriage is unbreakable until the children of the marriage are mid- to late adolescents. Divorce is traditionally not allowed until then, although in the '80s "divorce from children" began to occur.

Teaching a "stingy" girl to be generous   After a girl has been married for several months, her other husbands begin to ask her for private trysts. If she refuses them too often over a period of several weeks, the rejected other husbands develop a plan to "teach her to be generous," as they say, or to "tame her." They usually seek the cooperation of certain of her female kin, aunts or sisters who have been warning her about what could happen if she did not comply with the ancestors' custom of sexual generosity.

Hill Climber reported dramatically on herself in an assistant group session that she was too slow in becoming generous with men after she was first married. One day when she was gathering buriti palm fruits with several members of her female kin, all except one left her. The remaining woman tried even by holding her to keep her from leaving the spot where they were gathering fruit. Soon about six of her other husbands appeared, and she knew immediately that she was in trouble. She did not struggle, because she recognized the inevitable. Besides, her aunts had warned her that if she were physically hurt under such circumstances, her uncles would not be able to bring her case to trial. This was because she had already broken the traditional law of sexual generosity, or these men would not be forcing sequential sex on her.

Some ethnologists call such an action "rape," but I prefer not to use such a negative word when the individual involved could have avoided the forced sequential sex experience by obeying the mores of the tribe. Hill Climber's other husbands were not forcing sequential sex on her to humiliate her or to express any hate or disrespect for women. They were bringing her a step closer to accepting sequential sex as a female associate of a men's society. Being such an associate is a prerequisite step to further steps into marriage, such as earning her ceremonial belt and having it painted red by her female in-laws.

The Canela believe that husbands have to be taught not to be jealous of their wives, keeping them at home. Canela assistants reported that during a sing-dancing Great Day celebration one morning, a young husband, Three Forests, saw his wife of a few months in a dancing line consisting of men of his opposing age class moiety. He knew this meant that by the afternoon most of her other husbands in that line would have had sex with her. When the dancing line had snaked along the boulevard close to his house, he dashed out, consumed by jealousy, and grabbed his wife by the wrist, dragging her into their house to keep her for himself. Then he stood by the door and waved his machete in defiance at the men of the other moiety.

He succeeded in indulging his personal jealousy that day, rather than the demands of his society. However, several days later when he was away at his family's garden, members of his opposing age class moiety entered his house, abducted his partially compliant wife, and ran with her far into the woods, passing her from shoulder to shoulder like a racing log. Once in the woods they enjoyed her sexually in turn. Her mother followed them, running with a machete in hand, but could not keep up.

Women who cooperate in group sequential sex on tribal work days or even "daily" work situations receive small gifts, that are not considered payments, from each of the men. But the jealous husband's wife receives no gifts at all to take home to help her support her female kin. We may feel that she is being unfairly punished for her husband's error, but Canela men know that wives and mothers-in-law have much to do with whether a husband or son-in-law can get away with being sexually selfish. Surely the machete-wielding mother-in-law in this case was violating custom and supporting her son-in-law's wishes in order to keep him for her daughter. She had not been telling her daughter, and especially her sons, to advise her son-in-law well.

Stinginess by men with their own sexual assets rarely occurs. When they are somewhat sick or undergoing food and sex restrictions, they can say no, with appropriate and acceptable justifications, to desiring women (*mẽ khraakhrak to mõ:* they itching/desiring with go-along). Otherwise, men are required by the culture to be generous in all respects, far more so than women. This is the case with their material possessions (bows and arrows), the game they just killed and happen to be carrying (venison), their special skills (sing-dance leading or curing), or their sexual abilities. Granting sexual favors is really more a matter of obligation for men than a matter of generosity. It is also an expression of empathy with the strongly expressed needs of a demanding and desirous woman.

Socialization of non-virginal girls for sequential sex   Amyi-kaarã (self-clarifier), 13, was appointed during my fourth year by the Council of Elders as the older and therefore the non-virginal female associate to the men's festival Society of Masks. The younger female associate she was paired with in this society, Te-tsêê (leg's-decoration), 10, was still virginal, and so could not be drawn into performing in the society's several sequential sex occasions. She could only observe them, and most likely was developing expectations for the time when she could enjoy them also. In contrast, Self Clarifier, on prescribed occasions, gave herself to most of her other husbands among the membership of the Masks' society.

Self Clarifier was well prepared for these occasions. She had grown up hearing that sex was fun and joyous. She had been sent as a messenger between lovers many times, and she had witnessed an older female associate to a men's society enjoy group sequential sex. Most important of all, Self Clarifier had been generous with her other husbands several months after first marriage, so she had already had sex with many different men, but only one at a time in private trysts. Nevertheless, Self Clarifier was surely fearful of what would happen if she had to receive as many as 15 to 20 men in turn. Female assistants said that young girls about to have their first sequential sex were afraid that some penises would be too big for their still small and tight vaginas. They were afraid they would dislike some of the men who would approach them so that their feelings would be inhibited. But Self Clarifier could re-assure herself because she knew that all of the men coming to her well-prepared nests in the woods would be other husbands to her, and that she would have had re-lations with most of them in private trysts already and would continue to do so for the rest of her life. Moreover, most of them had joked sexually with her since she was about 3 years old.

Self Clarifier had been brought up to be generous, but if she refused any of the men, she could develop a reputation for being stingy. Then she would have few or no lovers, and eventually a witch might "throw" some disease into her which could lead to her death. Besides, her aunts had made it clear to her that she simply had to go through with this generosity to men, even if it were unpleasant. However, the aunts had said it was fun to please men sexually, and that after several men had come in her, her sexual feelings would get better and better so that she might even begin to "cry" (*nkwèl/amra*) with pleasure and delight.

Sequential sex was something you had to get used to doing before you could re-ally like it, the aunts had said. It was a way of becoming really popular and sought after by your other husbands for private trysts. Then several of your other husbands might become special lovers, and this was really enjoying life at its best. Moreover, the aunts emphasized that if she did not submit herself to sequential sex, she could not win her ceremonial belt. And if she had not won such a belt, her mother-in-law and sisters-in-law could not paint it red, thus securing her husband for eventual ba-bies and a family of her own. After securing her husband and before having babies, she would have a good time sexually as a "free" young woman.

It encouraged Self Clarifier further that the older Endures Water, the head of the Masks, was kind to her, as were the other male members of the Masks' society. They always had a lot of fun and jokes with their two female associates for most of the morning before a sequential sex occasion, building enthusiasm well before involv-ing the non-virginal one in the group bonding activity. Referring to the activities leading to sequential sex, one of my female assistant's explained, *Ampoo kwèlyapê kahãy koo, kuupên kwèlyapê* (what from woman wet, caressing from: Why does a woman get aroused, it is from [male] caressing). After all, they were all members of the same tribe, and she had known them all since childhood. Often, the virginal girl associate to a men's society in such a three-month-long festival gave her virginity to a young man privately and then, married to him, became available sexually to her other husbands in the men's same society.

I still had trouble believing young girls could get involved voluntarily in sequential sex until a female assistant gave our research assistant group her story. Hô-?khrã (palm-straw balled) was married to a chief and was a classificatory wife to me. Thus, she was not worried about losing prestige, nor was she even slightly embarrassed by my presence. We had to throw sex-flavored jokes at each other every time we met, as classificatory spouses do. Balled Straw's account about how she first experienced sequential sex was a moment in field research I will never forget. She had been one of the two girls of highest honor in the tribe, a Wè?tè girl, and so was related to her male society—half of the men of the entire tribe—as a classificatory sister instead of as a classificatory wife, that is, as an "other" wife. Therefore, having sex with the men of her group was forbidden; it was ceremonial incest. These men called her "sister" and her parents "father" and "mother," and they rested and drank water in their "parents'" (her parents') house before every log race and were often served by her. Nevertheless, on a Ceremonial Chief sing-dance day, Balled Straw was overcome by desire for her "brothers." When her brothers had danced around the boulevard with the young wives of the men of the other half of the tribe, they brought these young women, dancing, into their (her) parents' house and placed them in prepared cubicles for sequential sex. Balled Straw, hearing what was going on in her house, was overcome with sexual desire and joined the other women. She could have said after this occasion, Mẽ hakhrã ?te i-nin pal (plural society did me-fuck all: All the society's members had sex with me.)

Female orgasm?   The verb *nkwèl/amra* refers to certain sounds made by dogs and cats, but also by people when they are crying. Certain women are said to make these sounds occasionally when they are enjoying sex. One assistant said in our group session, *Puyê hàn te ?khwè amra, san-re pùràk* (Women's desire because-of, some cry, cat-little like: In sexual desire, some women cry like little cats). Another assistant said, *Hitsôt tsen te apu amra* (penis liking because-of, continuously crying: Because of enjoying penises, they keep crying). This much I knew, but it was quite a challenge for a male nonparticipant observer to find some reliable way of discovering whether Canela women really had orgasms, and if so, to what extent and in what way they had them.

In keeping with the method of much of my research, I decided during my 10th stay to ask my trained research assistants to give me expressions in their language that were descriptive of orgasms. Writing down such expressions, and eliciting them again from a group of informants days or years later, lends considerable reliability to the findings. To start with, I knew that *hatswèl-tsà* (pouring-out moment) was the expression for the male orgasm, but this term obviously could not be applied to women. Unfortunately, neither female nor male assistants could furnish terms that did apply to women, except for *nkwèl/amra*. Consequently, I turned to the subject of the male orgasm to identify additional descriptive terms. My regular male informants denied the occurrence of anything like mild convulsions, but a female helper, Hill Climber, said that *?khrã khãm way* (head in dizziness), *hĩĩ kuniá teltet* (flesh all quivering),

?khrã piktol (head lost), and *nto ankhrê* (eyes stilled) applied to a very few men some of the time. This physical state and its responses occurred especially when a man took his time having sex with his wife, or with one of his other wives with whom he was having a long-term relationship. Hill Climber's statements were eventually supported by one male assistant I brought into the research especially for this purpose. This kind and imaginative middle-aged man was not part of my usual group. Other assistants had reported, pejoratively, that this particular man was quite slow in completing the sex act, but this "weakness" was precisely why I sought his help.

Then I asked my usual group if these terms, which describe the type of male orgasm that results in mild tremors, could ever be applied to women, but the answer was never, except in one case. Men reported that a certain Canela woman, who liked to have sex with backlanders, sometimes "lost her head" as she "became dizzy" and her "body quivered," just as some men occasionally did. They also said that she was the only woman who would raise her hips and rotate them (*?khat to api nẽ ayrõ:* hips with raise and rotate) to help the older Sticky Urucu (age 80-plus) achieve orgasm, and that she was the only woman who would want to sit or lie on top of a man. These were all unusual and therefore shameful activities. The Canela especially disapproved of having sex with backlanders. My assistants said this deviant woman, who was in fact the prophetess of the messianic movement of 1963, Maria Castello, had learned the unfamiliar practices from backlanders.

I collected an interesting story during my first trip to the Canela, but did not appreciate its significance at the time. Before the arrival of the Indian Service, a man from a large city lived with the Canela, and was liked sufficiently well so that they gave him a woman to sleep with, as was their custom in earlier times. He used to take her out into the savannahs alone late at night, contrary to custom, to have sex with her. But she complained to her aunt, giving details, and the practice was stopped. Assistants reported that, whatever he did to her, he caused her to "die" while having sex, but that he was able to bring her back to life again. In any case, extreme female reactions during sex are not expected.

After studying all the information on this topic from research assistant sessions of several different years, I have come to believe that Canela women do not have orgasms. This is understandable if we consider that the Canela customary practices do not include direct manual access to the clitoris, and that little or no attention is paid to it verbally. Even though the Canela joking system is extensive and open, I have never heard the clitoris joked about, while the penis and the vagina are brought into much of the daily pleasantry. For instance, a female expression for your husband is "your pestle" (*a-khô-?khrã:* your-stick's-head), and the vagina is referred to as a mortar (*kahúwa*).

Additionally supporting the point that the clitoris is largely ignored is the usual position for trysts and sequential sex—the woman lying on her back with her legs spread wide and the man squatting low between them swinging his buttocks. This position does not stimulate the clitoris to the same extent as is possible in most other positions. For instance, the contact is not as direct as in the so-called missionary position. Moreover, the hands must not be used. The emphasis in the extramarital sex system is on the quick tryst—6 to 12 male thrusts—so that the couple will not be discovered and talked about. The emphasis is also on the male's pleasing himself.

In the late 1950s and earlier, the position described above was the only one for quick trysts. In long-term extramarital relationships and in marriage, the couple might lie down together, though the man was always on top. By the 1970s, new ideas from the outside brought some variety in positions, but only for married couples and long-time lovers. Even then, there was no kissing, no labial-genital contact, no circular movement of hips by the woman, and no entrance from behind.

Even if, as my research indicates, Canela women do not have orgasms,[64] it is obvious from statements of female and male assistants that they enjoy sex immensely, especially with their long-term other husbands. One female assistant described good sex to be like entwined snakes struggling with each other, as she twisted her body, writhing before us: *Hĩ teltet pê kagãã pùràk, hàn te* (flesh quivering is snake similar, desire because-of: When in sexual desire, we writhe like snakes). In addition, there are statements that some women like the mounting stimulation of sequential sex, exhibiting few if any visible physical responses but emitting little groans and grunts of pleasure (*hàn te apu amra:* pleasure because-of [it, they] continuously cry: Sexual arousal keep them crying). The most revealing sentence I was able to elicit from the group, and reconfirm with them on a later day, was the following: *Mẽ ha?khrã pi nin tsà yipôk ri, mẽ kahãy mã hàn ipikamen to mõ* (they grouped past sex occasion middle-of there, they woman for pleasure grows with going-along: During group sequential sex, women's sexual pleasure kept increasing). On the other hand, assistants made it clear that some women merely put up with sequential sex because it was expected of them, though they gain much through this cooperation.

We may wonder how women can be happy with sexuality which does not include full orgasm. However, anthropologists know that there are many cultures whose sexual practices do not include female orgasm. Women of these cultures seem not to have demanded or even to have known of the possibility of this type of sexual satisfaction. People generally want no more than their expectations and can gain happiness within the limitations of their cultures, knowing nothing else. We conclude that the sexuality of the human being is highly variable and molded by culture.

Winning her maturity belt   Just after the termination of a great summer festival in which a girl has performed as a female associate to a men's society, including involvement in group sequential sex, she is secluded in her maternal house to facilitate the "growth" and "coming into maturity" of her newly won belt. (See Chapter 2 for a description of the belt.) She is considered the "mother" of the belt and therefore has to undergo food and sex restrictions to enhance the growth of her "daughter." To achieve this purpose, the "mother" and "daughter" are placed in an enclosure of mats in a corner of the house of the belt's "mother" and "grandmother," where the consumption of food and the abstention from sex can be enforced, as in the much longer postpartum seclusion for the health and growth of the newly arrived baby. After about four days of seclusion, but really when her "uncles" have managed to kill a deer and have deposited it with her mother, the girl's kin send her out alone toward the plaza carrying the deer on her shoulders, holding its legs around her neck.

As the bride emerges from her maternal house, walking down her radial pathway toward the plaza and carrying the deer on her shoulders, her husband's sisters and "sisters" sprint from their arc of houses, each woman competing to reach her first. They race directly to her, running in the disorderly manner (*mẽ ?prōt:* they scrounge) symbolic of extramarital sex. They dash joyously across the radial pathways through the grass. These competing sisters-in-law take the deer from the bride's shoulders and escort her slowly back to her husband's maternal house, where her mother-in-law receives her. The bride delivers her still green belt to her mother-in-law, an act which is symbolic of the passing of considerable responsibility from her kin to her affines. Under the direction of her mother-in-law, her many "mothers-" and "sisters-in-law" from several houses pass the entire length of the belt, which may be 50 meters, through hands covered with greasy red urucu paint. In this way the belt is turned from the original green color of fresh tucum fibers to the processed red color of familial care, attention, and concern. Then her in-laws hold the cord in turn as she rotates her body to wind the cord back into a belt around her hips. The bride has just been more completely accepted in her husband's house by her female "in" in-laws, and she is their "out" daughter- or "out" sister-in-law.

On the next Red versus Black day, the bride chooses a man (other than her husband) from the other Regeneration season moiety to go hunting with for game animals. She may give him sex if the game is sufficient and if she likes him enough. The bride gives this earned meat to her mother-in-law, who prepares a bowl of food for her daughter-in-law to give publicly in the evening to the men of her lover's

Her sisters-in-law take the deer from the shoulders of the bride. She is wearing her still-green belt with leaf apron, which she will deliver to her mother-in-law.

moiety, necessarily the opposite moiety from her husband's. In this way the mother-in-law has connived with her daughter-in-law against her own son's selfish sexual desire to keep his wife to himself. The mother-in-law has not only accepted her daughter-in-law's extramarital sex activity by receiving the meat of the animal killed by her lover, but she has also paid off her daughter-in-law's lover's moiety for the lover's meat. That is, the mother-in-law has paid her daughter-in-law's debt, especially if the latter did not give the hunter sex, which she does not necessarily have to do. This act is like buying the daughter-in-law, but the purchase is from her other husbands rather than from her maternal kin.

The bride's female in-laws have now accepted her as an in-law to the extent that they will forgo complaining when she participates in the public extramarital sex activities, not just in individual trysts. Thus, the mother-in-law, if she finds her daughter-in-law having sex in the bushes with a man other than her son, will pass them by and not mention the occurrence to anyone, especially not to her son.

At this point the bride has become an adolescent woman and is recognized as an *nkrekrel-re* (slippery), "free" person, who should participate in most of the festival and other extramarital occasions to keep the morale of the men high, especially during their morning work activities when they work in moiety groups for the good of the tribe as a whole. However, she is not completely married, nor a fully responsible adult, until she has produced a baby.

Her free adolescent years   The bride, now a "free" adolescent, is usually from 12 to 17 years old, though women who cannot bear children remain in this stage of life much longer. The bride is free in this "slippery" period (from belt painting to childbirth) to go on all the traditional extramarital sex occasions described earlier, without her husband or his kin having the right to complain. She is said to be slippery because she is hard to catch, like the greased pig in a game backlanders play for fun. They mean that she is hard to catch for sex trysts, that she is relatively free but very busy sexually.

Some of the extramarital sex occasions allow the free adolescent woman to accept or reject sexual participation. The Red versus Black hunting ceremony, which occurs once a year, involves her with only one hunter of her choice, but having sex then is not compulsory. The Wild Boar days, which take place about six times a decade, allow her to choose whether she wants to have sex or not, but if she goes into the woods at all with several women, the female–male ratio on these occasions almost requires her to be generous with several men. On the sing-dancing Great Days, occurring three times a year at most, men of the opposing age class moiety to her husband's entice her from her house into their dancing line going around the boulevard, while her husband is in another dancing line. She can simply refuse such invitations; but if she joins the dancing line, she is likely to be one of half a dozen women who satisfy 40 to 50 men. If she chooses to go on the week-to-10-days long Festival of Oranges trip, which occurs once a year, she can involve herself in sex to the extent she wishes. She is among 40 to 50 women who have brought along about half a dozen men.

There are three occasions which present the adolescent bride with more of a challenge, because she has been appointed to be a female associate in each one; she has not volunteered her sexual services. Usually, she has been appointed by one of the principal chiefs of the tribe, who will designate only women with belts but without children at the morning meeting of the elders. She can always refuse, but it is difficult to refuse the sitting elders when summoned to appear before them in the center of the plaza. Moreover, if she refuses too often without sufficient reason, she will be considered stingy and could be subject to the discipline described earlier. Canela assistants tell me that the "stingy girl" situation occurs every now and then, maybe every other year, after a few months of a first marriage, and they cited a number of examples.

The first of these occasions, which occurs once a year, is when the two age class moieties take about six women each for two weeks to cook the game caught for the terminal phase of the summer's great festival. The second occasion, taking place several times a year, is when the two age class moieties go out in work groups to clear roads or boundaries. Each moiety takes along two to four "free" women for the day. The third occasion happens whenever there are enough men working on their gardens to assemble for a log race. The two age class moiety leaders, themselves tribal chiefs, try to convince several "free" women to come along with each working group of men to encourage them and have sex with them while they are resting before the log race.

Though technically married, a bride in her "free" state may move from man to man, according to her inclinations. Each new man she settles with becomes her new husband. While these men have to pay a fine set in a public trial to take the initiative in leaving her, she pays nothing to initiate leaving one of them. She follows her feelings, trying and testing each man she likes. This marital musical chairs is stopped by the conception of a child. Then, the man she happens to be living with is her husband until all their children are grown, unless she has a miscarriage or the baby that is born to them dies. If they have no baby to cement their marriage, the husband's family can pay a fine, set in a trial, for him to leave her. A female assistant in her mid-70s, Striped Earth, said that in earlier times this adolescent marital partner changing was far more extensive than currently.

The jealousy of a young husband after his mother has painted his wife's belt can be well understood and sympathized with. Nevertheless, he can only wait patiently and hope that his wife does not turn to some other man as a husband before she becomes pregnant. If she continues to consider him her husband, he remains such. But she may have to name certain of the other men "contributing fathers" if she has had sex often enough with them. She must declare them for the sake of her baby, because any man who has contributed semen significantly during her pregnancy must hold postpartum food and sex restrictions for the health and survival of the baby, just as the social father and mother must do.

Canela research assistants insist that a young woman must have all the sexual fun and experience she can get at this free stage in her life, because later as a mother she will be heavily burdened by the responsibilities of a household from which she will find it difficult to get away even to have private trysts. Moreover, assistants say that women age faster than men through bearing many children, so that they must have their fun while they are young and physically beautiful. Women who become pregnant just after winning their belts are pitied. It is said that such a woman will not be as contented in domestic life as the one who had several years of sexual freedom, because she may want to have too many extramarital trysts to make up for the fun she missed, possibly embarrassing her husbands' family.

Childbirth and its limitations   Childbirth comes as a shock to both sexes. The free young "slippery" adolescent is confined with her infant and husband to an enclosure made of mats within her mother's house for about 40 days, though she is allowed to make some excursions. This confinement, or couvade, is enforced on the couple partly to prevent their eating foods that would pollute their blood (*kaprôô*) systems, as explained in the preceding chapter.

This first postpartum confinement contrasts sharply with a woman's recent adolescent phase of life. During her free adolescent period, she is not allowed to hold babies because the smell of the secretions of her recent sex act would be about her. This smell could harm the baby, making it cry and eventually become sick. Moreover, residues under her finger nails could harm the baby if she scratched it even slightly. Older women could be trusted to wash well and wait a sufficient time before holding a baby, but an adolescent in her free stage is believed to be spontaneous, thoughtless, and irresponsible, so she cannot be trusted to prepare herself to hold a baby or refrain from holding it because of her condition. Thus, the free adolescent is left to her own devices and activities, relieved of many of the household activities she had carried out while still a virgin.

Quite obviously, a sharp social discontinuity exists for both sexes between adolescence and parenthood. The "slippery" and free adolescent female has become an adult woman through childbirth. She must look after her baby first of all. Later she must join her sisters and mother of the household, and often her "sisters" and "mothers" next door on either side, in carrying out the chores necessary for the maintenance of the group of households of her extended family, her longhouse. In compensation, the new adult can find many baby-sitters among her several sisters in her house and her numerous "sisters" in the neighboring houses of her longhouse. Consequently, with their cooperation in tending her baby, she can still slip off for a private tryst with her husband, or a lover, when she is no longer breast-feeding her baby after a year or two. Of the various festival extramarital sex occasions, the Wild Boar day is the only one which is constructed so that she can still participate. While her sisters and "sisters" are preparing the food for the whole group at a garden's hut, she can slip off into the woods with women to join one of several of her other husbands.

Socialization of boys for sequential sex   One morning in the house of the western Ceremonial Girl (Wè?tè), I observed the middle-aged Standing Water teasing a young boy, his "nephew" or "grandchild." Standing Water was sitting on the platform bed on which the boy was lying. He was repeatedly grabbing at the boy's testicles, penis, and nose, while the boy protested loudly, though not desperately. The 7-year-old boy was trying unsuccessfully to fend off his uncle's thrusts and was somewhat distressed, but he was liking the attention; he was not running away. He could have easily escaped his tormentor. As Standing Water asserted his traditional authority over his nephew, he was softening it with sexual teasing and fun. Moreover, many others were present to limit the game in case it went too far for the boy.

During the terminal phase of an initiation festival on the Wild Boar day, the commandant of the troop of male initiates requires all the youths who have already had sex to have sex in the sequential style with one of the several postmenopausal women who volunteer for the occasion. These older women's strength, through their having survived so many years, is transmitted through sex to the boys. In the first of the four or five initiation festivals,[65] which take place one or two years apart over a period of about 10 years, none of the boys is old enough to have had sex. However, at the time of the subsequent festivals more of them will have had sex, and so are *required* to have sequential sex once on each Wild Boar occasion. The younger boys become used to the expectation of sequential sex by being near the scene of the action. By the time of the last performance of an initiation festival, all of the adolescent youths are somewhat experienced at paired sex, so they must have sequential sex on this occasion. Thus, male youths must perform in the ceremonial sequential sex situation under the command of their quasi-military leader. They have no choice; their performance is compulsory.

Some of the youths may be relatively inexperienced even in private paired sex and may be having semipublic sequential sex for the first time. When there is some doubt about whether a youth will carry out such orders, the troop's commandant sends one of the troop's two messenger boys to watch the act closely, so the commandant can be sure whether it really took place and in what way. How any female or male in the tribe performs sexually is public knowledge and talked about generally, though not in the presence of the subject or to embarrass her or him directly. However, age classmates do joke with each other about their abilities, especially if they are Informal Friends.

In contrast with the socialization of adolescent girls into sequential sex, the socialization of boys into the act is compulsory. In Canela life, women generally are allowed more individual variations than men. For instance, men have to pay a fine to get out of a childless marriage, while women do not. Men are supposed to be prompt and complete with their generosity; they are supposed to give up certain possessions, instantly, upon demand. Women are allowed to take their time in deciding whether to comply with a demand, whether to modify it, or, occasionally, whether to refuse it.

Summary and further thoughts   Children up to 6 or 7 grow up watching and hearing adults being open about extramarital trysts and sequential sex and learn how their role models enjoy these activities. Extramarital sex thus becomes a valued expectation of these young people. Experiences continue to enhance this expectation for both sexes into adolescence, when young people become thoroughly involved in extramarital sex themselves. The general atmosphere of joy and fun surrounding extramarital sex may be the principal factor which influences young people to accept and enjoy sequential sex.

Girls of 6 up to about 11 to 13, the age at which they privately give away their virginities to their young husbands, are carefully protected from packs of little boys who may want to experiment with them sexually, though full intercourse is not usually their objective. Occurrences of untraditional sex with adults are minimal. Child abuse, as the Canela would define it, hardly exists. Thus, young girls growing up are not likely to be traumatized by acts which violate the prevailing sexual code. Our concept of child abuse includes the destruction of the child's trust in kin and others who are supposed to be her or his protectors. We also think of such abuse as involving pain and physical damage to the sexually immature child. The clear and public definition of kinship roles in Canela society makes incest, as we would define it, very infrequent. The experience of pain in first sex is not a part of Canela sexual lore. Although girls had some anxiety before their first sequential sex, I never heard any discussion of painful experiences. Here again, cultural expectations heavily influence the physical experience.

Masturbation for both sexes is strictly forbidden. A girl is warned by her aunts that she might lose her virginity payment if she were to stretch or break her hymen (*kuror:* thin skin, paper). Such a loss would make a preferable marriage more difficult. (If presented by her family as a virgin, an adolescent youth could leave his bride without a payment if she were found through a trial to have been non-virginal.) If the girl had even the faintest odors of sexual secretions on her hands, they would cause babies to cry, foods to become tasteless, and crops to wilt. Young girls are seldom left alone and are continuously kept involved in domestic activities, so that the time and place for self-fondling would be difficult to find.

Uncles warn their nephews that handling themselves may loosen their foreskins and thereby cause the loss of their virginity payments, which would become generally known and an embarrassment to their families. Any slight male sexual odors on hands cause arrows to fly off their courses and axes to miss their marks, as well as leg muscles to become cramped during running. Much of the time boys are kept in age class groups to which older men tell myths on various topics, some exemplifying the traditional parameters of sex. They also tell stories about their sexual experiences as youths or about their current ones. It is feared that letting boys be alone for too much time will allow them to develop antisocial attitudes. Activities requiring long periods of time alone, such as hunting and fishing, are generally for adolescents and older men.

Because of the precautions described above, sexual use of the genitals for both sexes is largely reserved for heterosexual intercourse at the age when this first becomes possible. Though some masturbation and boys' handling of each other's genitals surely occur occasionally, such activities are not frequent enough to influence the course of maturation. This channeling of the sexual drive is what we might expect for such an action- and group-oriented society.

Canela socialization also seems to suppress homosexuality. A relatively permissive atmosphere during the maturing of the age class of older Thunder allowed two homosexuals to express their orientation. A third emerged in the age class of younger Thunder 20 years later. The older two wore wraparound skirts to just above their knees, while women wear their skirts to just below the knees. Research assistants said that one of the older homosexuals was used as a passive sex partner by members of his age class several times when they were all in their twenties. This individual was said to be an ineffective worker, and his wife told him to leave even though their children were still young. Evidently his wife had conceived children with him. The other older homosexual was a very effective worker in the household of his female kin. Both males worked on their farms, but neither joined the log races or met often in the plaza with the elders.

The homosexual from the younger age class was one of the men who emigrated from the tribe after the messianic movement and worked for several years as a cook's assistant. Before he left the tribe, he had worked at the Indian Service post, where he excelled at sewing. He enjoyed helping visitors to the tribe, almost as a servant.

Although the one homosexual played the passive sex role with his age class members when they were in their twenties, the practice did not continue. The other two males did not have sex with other men. Their homosexuality expressed itself in the assumption of female roles and the rejection of male activities.

Returning to our summary, still-virginal girls nearing puberty become female associates of men's ceremonial societies. In these social settings, they learn more about the group sequential sex experienced by the older, non-virginal female associate of the same men's society by being near the site of its occurrence. Their introduction to sequential sex is gradual and experienced in an atmosphere of fun, flirtation, and sharing.

Still-virginal boys become more aware of the aspects of sequential sex during several initiation festival Wild Boar days, since nearby on this day their older non-virginal age classmates are having compulsory sequential sex with far older women organized by the commandant of their initiation troop. The introduction of males to sequential sex is gradual. They have heard about it for most of their lives, they are positioned near the site where it occurs, and eventually they carry out the act with other members of their age class. For initiation festival novices, this act is compulsory as part of their intense socialization into an age class and as part of their maturation toward becoming relatively selfless men who are willing to surrender many of their individual "rights" and preferences for the welfare of other individuals in their tribe. Male group sequential sex is an act of lifelong age class bonding.

A girl gives her virginity to a young, unattached man who thereby becomes her husband. "Unattached" means he has fathered no children except, maybe, as a contributing father. After several months alone with her new husband, the young married girl begins to accept secret trysts with her numerous other husbands. When next assigned to a men's society as a female associate, she is expected to become involved in sequential sex on several traditional occasions with her other husbands in the society. As a result of her various sorts of performances in this society over a period of several months, she wins her maturity belt. She has cooked for, flirted and joked with, and generally helped to raise the morale of the male members of her society, and occasionally has had sequential sex with them. Next, in the course of her socialization sequence, her mother-in-law and sisters-in-law paint her newly won belt, accepting her more completely and giving her license to go on the extramarital sex occasions. This is the "free" period of her life which is terminated only by childbirth. Then the responsibilities of motherhood and household maintenance keep her occupied. She is no longer allowed to become involved in group extramarital sex activities, except voluntarily on a Wild Boar day. Nevertheless, she can still manage to have occasional secret trysts with her other husbands.

It is clear that a girl's having sequential sex in a men's society is a prerequisite for securing her husband, for having a "free" period of fun, and for establishing a family. Thus, her motivation to become involved in sequential sex is strong. However, she is not absolutely required to become involved in sequential sex, as a boy is. She can refuse to cooperate on any one of several occasions. Nevertheless, traditional social forces make it almost impossible for her not to cooperate eventually at a time more favorable to her feelings. Later, women who are not responsive on sequential sex occasions are seldom designated by a chief to appear.

An adolescent male gives his virginity to an older woman in his other wife category who is particularly fond of him and who has taken the initiative to bring him to or to find him in their tryst's location. She probably has been joking with him since he was very small. The older woman makes a small payment to the youth's principal disciplinary aunt. Subsequently, on Wild Boar days, along with his age classmates, he is required to have sequential sex with one of the older women, one of his other wives, assigned to his age class by its commandant.

A male adolescent goes through a period of severe food and sex restrictions for one to three years, during which period he is supposed to have sex rarely with adolescent girls and only occasionally with postmenopausal women. In this way he avoids the formers' weaknesses and gains the latters' strengths. After completing sufficient food and sex restrictions to build his own strengths and abilities in hunting, running, perhaps shamanism, and formerly in warfare, he experiences a relatively free period of running with his age classmates and having sex as often as he desires wherever he can obtain it. Sooner or later the restrictions and responsibilities of fatherhood begin to take over his time; nevertheless, he is still considerably freer than his wife to experience secret trysts, and he is totally free to participate in any of the sequential sex occasions.

The data presented above make it clear that Canela men are required, under considerable pressure, to undergo their initial experience in sequential sex. After their age class processing has graduated them into male maturity, men are never again compelled to become involved in sequential sex. However, most men frequently engage in sequential sex on a voluntary basis. During the yearly Festival of Oranges, women draw on a much larger pool of men to get six voluntary male associates (*mẽ kuytswè*) than the pool of childless young women men draw upon to get three or four appointed female associates (*mẽ kuytswè*) for group workday sequential sex. Thus, the social pressure on men to practice sequential sex is less than on the much smaller number of childless women.

A man of elite standing who is also good at sex finds it easy to "catch" (*to pro*) an abundant variety of women for private trysts. In contrast, a man of poor standing with limited sexual abilities finds it harder to arrange personal trysts. Sequential sex on workdays give the less gifted man a chance for frequent sexual outlets, and it also motivates him to work on tribal projects. Like so many other Canela institutions, group sequential sex tends to equalize relative advantages, in this case disparities among men, and thus contributes to male bonding and tribal morale.

Men appear to be exploiting women through group sequential sex, and to a certain extent this may be true. Why do women continue to let themselves be used in this way? A girl is drawn into the experience of sequential sex by the expectations of gaining a belt, a husband, and a family. Moreover, she knows that this is the favored route to a plentiful source of private extramarital trysts and general social popularity and respect. Women in their twenties and thirties continue to cooperate with this practice, because lacking children, they can, nevertheless, contribute in this other way to societal morale. Moreover, some women have come to enjoy the sexual side of a sequential sex day as well as its festive side. Finally, it is clear that full intromission is the only permissible sexual outlet; masturbation is not an alternative. This lack of an alternative sexual outlet helps explain the value of sequential sex for both sexes, especially for those who find private trysts difficult to obtain.

If we keep in mind the deepest values of Canela life, the practices of extensive extramarital sex and group sequential sex seem less bizarre and repellent than they might seem at first glance. In Canela society, which no longer experiences economic riches or the male opportunities for military activities, sex is a paramount pleasure and gratification. It is immensely important for the ease and assurance with which the Canela carry out both extramarital trysts and sequential sex that these acts are legitimized in a number of traditional ceremonies.

It is difficult for members of our modern individualistic society to imagine the extent to which the Canela see the group and the tribe as more important than the individual. Generosity and sharing are the ideal, while withholding is a social evil. Generosity with possessions brings esteem. Generosity with one's person, including one's body, is a direct corollary. Desiring control over one's goods and self is a form of stinginess. In this context, it is easy to understand why women choose to please men and why men choose to please women who express strong sexual needs. *No one is so self-important that satisfying a fellow tribesman is not more gratifying than most personal gains.* Another great Canela value, besides being generous and not being bigger than others, is having empathy and compassion for a person in need. Thus, a self-respecting, generous, and caring Canela woman or man finds it extremely difficult to turn away from the strongly expressed sexual need of another.

The intricate pattern of socialization for extensive extramarital trysts and group sequential sex, which we have traced in this chapter, may seem to the outsider to amount to severe coercion. However, we are all coerced in our own cultures while undergoing the pressures of various stages of socialization. In most societies, there are penalties for not conforming to custom. In the Canela case, the stingy person receives few favors from others and may find it difficult to borrow foods when hungry, especially pieces of meat. Obtaining partners for extramarital trysts becomes extremely difficult. The ultimate penalty is extreme. Some rejected shaman throws a spell of illness which may eventually result in death. On the other hand, the Canela social coercion is ameliorated for children by good fun and sexual joking with aunts and uncles. For adolescents, the compulsory aspect of the social escalator is ameliorated by long flirtations and sexual activities with familiar and friendly other spouses.

In the final analysis, if we consider the extent to which Canela society provides the support for a strong ethic of caring and generosity, partly through extramarital trysts and sequential sex, we may find these customs more understandable.

NOTES

56. See Nimuendajú (1946:169) and Crocker (1990:280–281) for a description of the Wild Boar day, when the Canela kill a tame peccary and have arranged extramarital sex. This ceremony is part of the Pepyê festival, which I call here the Warriors' festival.

57. See Nimuendajú (1946:129) for his views on Canela infidelity, adultery, and divorce, which differ considerably from those reported by my Canela research assistants.

58. My field trips to the Canela are numbered 1 through 10, as described in Crocker (1990, Appendix 1). My first, second, third, and fourth years among the Canela were 1957, 1958, 1959, and 1960. This information is supplied so that professionals can associate the years of these materials with the years of the materials in my other publications.

59. Canela research assistants associate *?-hê* (vulva) with the vertical lines of house posts and honeycombs, and with the single, thin straight line of a pressed stalk of sugar cane—thus a vertical "cleft."

60. Nimuendajú (1946:168–170) and Crocker (1990:281–282) describe the rainy season (or the Regeneration season) moieties, consisting of the Red (Kàà) and Black (Atùk) log racing teams.

61. See Crocker (1990:283–284) for a description of Ceremonial Chief days and their Mē Aykhē style of dancing.

62. In Crocker (1990:270–271, 278–279) and Nimuendajú (1946:92–93) the activities of the two Ceremonial Girls, the Wè?tè girls, are described in detail.

63. See Nimuendajú (1946:102) for his account of this mock-erotic behavior.

64. See Gregor (1985:3) for comparative purposes.

65. For accounts of these Khêêtúwayê and Pepyê initiation festivals, see Crocker (1990:272–274) and Nimuendajú (1946:171–201).

5/The Balance
Between the Sexes

How a society divides up power and responsibility between men and women is always a vital cultural question, and one of special interest to us today. The Northern Gê tribes are known for their relatively high status for women, and Canela women are especially confident and influential. This chapter is devoted to evaluating the balance between Canela men and women. The topic is not part of the main argument of our case study, but it does contribute to an understanding of social control in the tribe. It is important to recognize that the strong bonding in Canela culture is not all spontaneous and joyful. Penalties of various kinds enforce social conformity. Although some of these negative pressures have already been mentioned, this chapter brings them together and adds more detail, as well as new material on agriculture, the distribution of food, and the status of single women. As I examine the balance of the sexes in various social sectors, I will summarize the basic facts about that sector. Thus, there will be some repetition, but also, I hope, a useful review and new insights.

The chapter will take up the balance between the sexes in the following social sectors: (1) the intertribal world of warfare, (2) the political life of the chiefs and the Council of Elders, (3) the ceremonial arena of three-to-four-month-long festivals, (4) the judicial trials for resolving conflicts between extended families, (5) the supernatural dimension consisting of shamans and ghosts, (6) the domestic scene of supplying food and raising children, (7) the rituals for celebrating the life passages of individuals, (8) the life on Canela farms as it differs from life in their village, and (8) the extensive extramarital sex life with its social expression and social controls.

As our discussion moves through these sectors, we will be moving from those governed by men to those which are controlled by women. I will also consider how the balance of the sexes has changed over time.

Visiting protection chiefs In pre-contact times, the Timbira nations which formed alliances instead of fighting each other exchanged visiting protection chiefs.[66] These individuals tried to keep the peace in their nation for the visitors they represented. Nation A picked a male member of nation B to be its visiting protection chief, its *tàmhàk,* in order to guarantee the safety of a member of nation A who was visiting nation B. Reciprocally, nation B picked a male member of nation A to be its visiting protection chief. Women were never chosen to be visiting protection chiefs in earlier times. However, this practice has survived into modern times with the difference that married couples, since 1964, are selected to be visiting protection chiefs instead of just men. Of course, the role of such chiefs has changed, since intertribal dangers have become minimal. Nevertheless, this inclusion of wives is one measure of the extent to which the aboriginal sex balance has shifted from being more male-oriented in the war-dominated era of the 1700s to being more evenly balanced in modern times.

Political power   In the political life of the tribe, males seem clearly to dominate. The number one chief of the tribe is always a male, and the potential chiefs, who are contending to be the principal chief, are always men. For many decades, the women have had their own nominal chief of the women. This has been the woman who has taken the responsibility for organizing the Festival of Oranges, the annual female-ascendancy festival in which the sex roles are reversed. This female leader of the Festival of Oranges was not appointed by the men and had no authority over men. The position was not permanent and could change from one year to the next. However, for the first time, in October 1991, a woman, Hill Climber, was appointed chief of all the women by the male principal chief of the tribe, Burnt Path. This development indicates increased male recognition of the significance of female political power, even though the political realm is still clearly governed and dominated by men.

In the political arena, again, the elders, who meet twice a day, are only men. I have heard it said a number of times that women contribute significantly to the elders' deliberations and decisions by influencing their husbands when they are at home. No one would argue, of course, that such indirect influence is as powerful as direct participation. Clearly, the balance among older Canela individuals of both sexes, as manifested most prominently among the elders and among their smaller Council of Elders, is heavily in favor of men. Older women have no such group to represent them.

Ceremonial models for behavior   The ceremonial sector of life among the Canela includes tribe-oriented ceremonies and extended family-oriented rites. These are two different and very distinct categories. I will discuss the family-oriented ceremonies later because they are governed by women. The tribe-oriented ceremonies or festivals take as long as four months to carry out and involve *all* tribal members. Festivals are run by the male Council of Elders. The members of this council appoint most of the significant festival performers, both males and females, to their traditional positions. Thus, the most prestigious festival roles that women ever carry out are assigned to them by men.

The composition of almost all festival groups is the following: Two girls, or two young women, are assigned as female associates to almost every festival group, each of which consists of 30 to 40 men. Six of these paired female roles identify to the tribe that the incumbents are high ceremonial honor persons for the rest of their lives, a significant advantage for these women. Other roles assigned to these pairs of women serving in large male groups are middle level or low level in prestige. Any female roles assigned by the Council of Elders can be refused by the women in the role-holder's extended family, aided by their uncles or brothers, but appointment to festival roles cannot be initiated at the extended family level. Thus, at the tribe-oriented festival level, the male-female balance is strikingly in the favor of men. The girls or young women appointed to the most prestigious festival positions are chosen to reward their "good" social behavior, as judged by the male councilors.

The two female associates of each large male festival group are considered ceremonial "wives" to the men of the group, except for one pair of females who are considered "sisters," the Wè?tè girls. The ceremonial wives engage in sex with the members of the ceremonial male groups. We have seen how certain days of these three-to-four-month-long festivals involve a pair of women performing sex sequentially with a number of men. This facet of ceremonial life may seem overwhelmingly to favor men, but the women enjoy it too and acquire considerable influence over men through their participation. Sequential sex bonds the festival group together with pleasurable memories.

Judicial system   The Canela judicial system is another sector of tribal life which men control. Problems between extended families, such as a wife's complaint about her husband's too public affairs, first surface as rumors in the meetings of the elders. The elders meet twice a day, in the morning between about 7 and 8 and in the evening between about 5 and 6:30. At first, much of their talk amounts to male chatter, which fosters camaraderie. Later the first chief arrives and calls the meeting to order. Then the session becomes formal, and only well-evolved topics are brought up for debate. If a matter disturbs the peace of the community sufficiently, or if the family of the offended person or persons is sufficiently angry and upset, a grandfather or uncle of each side schedule a trial. The offended and the offender are heard at the trial and witnesses are called. Usually the case is resolved in this way, and if the offender is found guilty, his extended kin have to make a payment to the extended kin of the offended person. If the case is not resolved through reaching a consensus, the chief of the tribe accepts the case for binding arbitration in which the chief sets the fine if he finds the offender guilty.

The judicial system is thus totally dominated by men, but during a trial a woman may be the plaintiff and women are called as witnesses. A female plaintiff is strongly supported by her principal male relative. As in the case described in Chapter 3, women speak out freely and at great length. They are listened to carefully and are treated as fairly as men. The trial is between extended families, not just between individuals, so men on each side champion their female kin, and men have to pay the fines. These facts tend to bring about a more even balance between the sexes even though the cases are managed totally by men. In marital cases, since husbands are seen as being more intransigent than wives, fines are imposed on husbands if they want a divorce, while fines are not imposed on wives who want a divorce, unless children are involved.

Supernatural world   Shamanism is the last cultural sector we will consider in which males have the greater power. Before the influence of folk Catholicism entered Canela life, the Canela did not have a concept of God, but they did have culture heroes as models for behavior and they had ghosts, who are representations of the recently departed dead. Only Canela shamans can communicate with ghosts. Ordinary Canela die or become very ill if ghosts appear to them. When ghosts appear to shamans, however, ghosts impart psychic powers to them, enabling them both to cure illnesses and to cast evil spells.

Ghosts also supply shamans with considerable information, such as why a certain person is ill or has died. Thus, a shaman's declaration about a social problem amounts to an indictment or even a conviction of the wrongdoer. Since shamans have access to supernatural information, their decrees are definitive, even today.

Most shamans were and are male, but at least two women were shamans in the Canela ancient war stories and myths. One female shaman was able to "see" enemy warriors at a distance and tell that they would arrive at dawn. Consequently, she had time to flee with her family from the village to their farm, where they were not found by the enemy. However, many tribal members were killed during the dawn attack, because they had not believed her revelation, made before the all-male meeting of the elders the evening before.

Nevertheless, shamans who have developed evil powers (i.e., antisocial ones) may "throw" illnesses into a man who has offended a woman, thus supporting the status of women. In 1960, for example, in a trial between two extended families, the uncles on both sides ordered a youth to return to his wife, but the youth refused to do so. He also ignored the decision of the first chief of the tribe, who held a second trial. Two years later, the youth died of what I thought was pneumonia. However, a "good" shaman revealed that a certain "bad" shaman had cast a disease into the antisocial youth for disobeying the orders of the uncles and those of the chief.

One of my best and closest Canela research helpers was a female shaman. Shamanism, however, with its powerful institutional defining of social fact, is largely in the hands of men, a power which constitutes an unquestionable and highly significant advantage for men.

Domestic scene   We now turn to the domestic unit of the extended family, the cultural sector of family life and kinship governed by women. The Canela are matrilocal, but not matrilineal. They are bilateral, reckoning kinship through mothers and fathers, with a strong emphasis on the matrilateral side, the mothers' side.

The principal significance of the term "matrilocal" is that every young man upon marriage goes to live in the house of his wife, where her sisters, her mother, and her mother's sisters dominate the domestic scene. In the Canela case, a man lives in his wife's house even after he has become a grandfather in it, and until he dies. Nevertheless, he continues to maintain contacts with the house of his birth, where he is made to feel most at home and where formerly he administered discipline to the young of the domestic unit, along with the rest of his male kin. These older males still manage festival roles for their young male and female kin, but seldom administer discipline these days.

A characteristic Canela domestic unit is composed of from three to six closely related women living in one house with their children and their husbands, who were born in other houses. Domestic unit size ranges from 2 to 40 individuals, all of whom live in one house. Stated differently, these closely related women's adult sons, brothers, and mother's brothers (their uncles) live away in other houses with their wives and children. The closely related women of the domestic unit seldom allow men who are closely related to each other, brothers or cousins, to join their domestic unit in marriage. Consequently, the husbands of the domestic unit—these unrelated men—are, in effect, easily divided and conquered by the closely related women, who are mothers, sisters, daughters, or cousins to each other.

In theory, the sons, brothers, and mother's brothers of these closely related women come home to where they were born and grew up to govern these women, their children, their grandchildren, and their husbands. In modern times, however, they seldom do so, and consequently the control of the household is left to the older and more dominant females of the domestic group. This modern lessening of visits and influences from the male kin constitutes a very important change in the balance between the sexes, a change which conveys more power and responsibility to women.

This domestic group is also the effective economic unit, because all meat, cereals, and root crops procured by any member of the unit are shared by the unit. Only one location exists for the hearth with its fire, though several cast-iron pots may be balanced on the three to six large rocks, which form the hearth, for boiling different foods at the same time. Not by coincidence, the Canela call the domestic unit the hearth unit (the *hàwmrõ*).

Within this hearth or domestic unit, nuclear families, a husband and wife with their children, eat and sleep separately from the rest of the nuclear families in the house. Consequently, while each mother is basically oriented to taking care of her own children, she can get help from her sisters, her female cousins, and her mother should she need to absent herself for whatever purpose, including an extramarital tryst. Because female kin like to help one another have a good time in this way, the domestic unit has a number of willing baby-sitters built into its social structure. The older unmarried daughters, girls of 9 to 12, also carry out these baby-sitting roles.

The baby, and later the child, are brought up in a network of closely related women, most of whom are bearing children themselves, so the characteristic domestic unit includes from 10 to 20 children of all ages. They call each other brother and sister, though some may be first or even second cousins. The domestic group provides a healthy assortment of children, with many parents looking on, and the neighboring houses can provide even more children. The matrilocal domestic unit thus provides extensive female support to both mothers and children. There are many hands for tasks, and no woman finds herself isolated at any stage of life.

While the women of a domestic unit care for children, fetch water from streams in gourds, gather firewood from the savannahs, and bring root crops from their individual farms, the men go hunting or fishing, or they may go to backland Brazilian communities to trade for or buy food and equipment. The men also cut down the stream-edge woods to prepare their wives' farms, and then fence them. Each man married-in to the domestic unit—that is, each husband—is obligated to support economically his particular wife and children. His networking within the domestic unit is limited to them. He is not associated with the domestic unit as a whole, unless he is married to the dominant woman of the unit. Then, as senior father-in-law, he may lead the other males in work on the various farms of the women of the domestic unit.

In contrast, women of the domestic unit associate easily with *all* the other women of the unit, their close kin. A wife takes the meat and foods her husband supplies, and after keeping some small items for her family, gives the rest of these provisions to the leading woman of the domestic unit, who redistributes these goods to any of the nuclear families of the unit according to their needs of the day and depending on their records of cooperation.

The return on male activities such as hunting is uncertain, unlike the steady provision of field crops by females. Most hunters do not bring in meat every day. If some of the husbands of a domestic unit are able to hunt, the unit may eat some fresh meat every third day. However, meat is relatively scarce, so it is important for the status of women that *it is they who distribute meat* within the domestic unit, not the men. Moreover, the women reward cooperative behavior through their distributive preferences.

Thus, in the Canela domestic unit, designed for everyday living and raising children, the women clearly have an advantage over the men, gained through their distributive powers and through their greater solidarity from kinship bonding.

The epitome of female ascendancy in the domestic unit occurs during childbirth. No men are allowed in a house where childbirth is about to occur. A prospective mother receives all the help she needs from her sisters and her mother, while her mother-in-law waits to "catch" the baby as it "falls," the expression for birth. The father may be anywhere else in the village, waiting anxiously.

Rites for individuals   Because women dominate the extended family, usually composed of several neighboring domestic units (i.e., several houses), they control most rites for individuals of the family. These ceremonies take place within the extended family and are not celebrated by the tribe as a whole. One rite of the nine steps into secure marriage among the Canela is called "the purchase of the son-in-law." Here, the female relatives of the bride carry two or three large meat pies, each about a yard in diameter, over to the house of the groom, where his female relatives receive the meat pies. Neither the bride nor the groom, nor any men, are involved in this rite. It serves to secure the groom to the bride's kin so that if the young man tries to leave, his kin must pay back the meat pies in kind.

The structure of the domestic unit made possible in earlier times a special option for women who preferred to remain single, to decline remarriage once widowed, or to have status and independence even if barren. This special option was provided by the institution called the *mpíyapit,* which has all but ceased to exist today. The *mpíyapit* constituted a respected alternative way of life. There was no dishonor in this state of singleness, though wives were often jealous of an *mpíyapit* woman who attracted their husbands too often. An *mpíyapit* enjoyed several lovers, who hunted for her, cleared her farm, and fathered her children. An *mpíyapit* lived with her mother and sisters, who helped raise her children, and she usually contributed more meat to her domestic unit's economic support than most of its married women did through their husbands. This freedom for women to choose how they want to lead their lives contrasts sharply with conditions in some other tribes, where women are beaten if caught in an infidelity[67] or are gang raped if they happen to see a man blowing a sacred flute.[68] In some Amazonian tribes, the Mundurucu, for example, women found walking alone in the woods are considered fair game by men.[69] Such a concept would be totally foreign to Canela men.

Life on farms away from the village   The Canela work on their farms, living in their farm settlement huts intermittently, about half the year. All women above the age of about 18—whether married, single, with children, or childless—must maintain their own farms, producing bitter and sweet manioc, rice, corn, beans, lima beans, yams, sweet potatoes, peanuts, squash, and other garden crops. Like houses, farm gardens belong to women only. The women's gardens are generally clustered geographically according to the same grouping of nuclear families which composes the domestic hearth units back in the village. Thus, the same nuclear families which live together in the village according to female kinship usually farm together in the same region of the tribal reservation. Many exceptions occur, however, because husbands can exert their preferences more effectively when on their wives' farms. Husbands are politically stronger on the farming scene because the ecology of the region usually requires the farms to be scattered. They are located sufficiently far apart so that sisters of a village domestic unit are often parted by distance when living on their farms, having to spend their nights in nuclear family huts by their separate farm gardens. Consequently, a village unit with one hearth is often split into several farm hearths. Since husbands carry out the heavy work to prepare farms and like to work in male groups, a firm husband may sometimes convince his wife to go with their children to farm a garden near his male relative's wife's farm, or near his male friend's wife's farm. His justification to his wife might be that the male friend is a hard worker, that the soil is better there, or that the political alliance there could be advantageous.

Thus, in the farm setting, the male–female balance is more even, though still favorable to women. In modern times, this balance increasingly shifts to men because of growth in the extensiveness and importance of slash-and-burn agriculture, in contrast to the earlier reliance on hunting, gathering, and fishing. These days, extended families must rely more than they did earlier on their daughters' husbands to do most of the heavy work on their many farms. Consequently, the status of young husbands has risen, as has their influence in the domestic unit.

Canela social control in general   All societies have a number of forms of social control. Large societies, in which any individual knows only a small percentage of the national members, must have formal institutions empowered to enforce the laws. In small societies, such as the Canela, most individuals know each other well. Consequently, institutions enforcing traditions can be informal and interpersonal, so they may be obscure and difficult to identify. Nevertheless, institutions of social control must exist for the effective functioning of all societies, though it might take a social scientist to identify them and clarify how they operate. I find that the extramarital sex system of the Canela may be their most immediate and therefore their most effective institution of social control, and this system is enforced mainly by young women during their almost daily extramarital contacts with men.

Many other forms of social control exist among the Canela. To give some examples: First, the principal chief issues orders to determine which groups of men work on which family fields during the occasional tribal work days; second, the Council of Elders gives good youthful performers in festivals highly prestigious awards—artifacts such as special gourds for girls and feathered lances for boys—to reward and maintain positive behavior among these adolescents; third, the uncles or grandfathers of extended families, as the result of trials, levy fines on uncooperative individuals, who in this case are almost always young males; fourth, shamans, backed by ghosts, decree who has broken certain traditions, explaining illnesses and mishaps at the expense of socially uncooperative individuals, males or females; fifth, strong middle-aged women impose order on their domestic households and on their farms, providing more advantages and food, including preferred cuts of meat, to cooperative individuals. In addition, we must consider a sixth form of social control: uncooperative individuals of either sex experience far greater difficulty in acquiring partners for extramarital sex, the great recreation of the Canela.

While the first four examples of social control are applied *occasionally* and by men, the last two examples, the domestic and extramarital ones, are likely to be applied *every day* and by women, especially to young people. Thus, the domestic and extramarital rewards and disappointments, which are directly interpersonal—that is, they occur largely between two individuals—may be among the most effective forms of Canela social control, and they are enforced by women. Again, such direct person-to-person checks and balances are what we should expect to find among a people who know almost all the members of their group very well and who will be living with each other for the rest of their lives.

Social context of the extramarital sex system   The Canela individual sees him- or herself in relation to the whole tribe, as being a very small part of the whole. This small part—the individual—does almost anything to please the rest of the members, partly because living for the whole society, and its happiness and welfare, is a principal Canela purpose of being alive. This is why these people are characterized by generosity, if automatic giving *is* generosity, and why they give their sexual assets so easily: These assets are not theirs to control fully, but their society's. This is also partly why the Canela extramarital system can be so extensive. And since it is so all-pervasive, it is a principal mechanism of social control.

Furthermore, a crucial aspect of the system is the following: Every time a person has extramarital sex, any different or unusual activities of the tryst are likely to be topics of conversation among the women down by the stream washing clothes, or among the men in the plaza waiting for a meeting to start. Most certainly, a person's awareness that what he or she is doing during a tryst may soon become public knowledge restrains and restricts this person's behavior. Moreover, this person would not want to have a tryst at all with an individual well known for his or her antisocial behavior, because most of the tribe might soon know about the tryst and surely would disapprove of this person's comforting and abetting an individual who, in the tribe's terms, is a "criminal." Thus, the setting of the tryst holds great rewards and effective punishments, especially for young men.

Young men are more completely controlled than young women in the context of the extramarital tryst, because Canela women use the double-edged sword of sexual negatives far more often than men. The culture allows women to say no, or to be evasive, while men must be immediately generous and serving or be branded as stingy, which is equivalent to being evil. While I often heard and saw young men singing all day around the boulevard with ceremonial lances to help forget a woman's scorn, I never heard of women turned down by men. The culture allows strong female initiatives, so the pining-while-waiting type of woman is not the model. Women go out and get what they want.

Thus, the male–female balance on the day-to-day extramarital playing field, out in the savannahs far away from the village, is tipped very much in favor of women. Additional evidence for this advantage is that men have to give women small presents, often meat, to please them into cooperation to keep the system operating.

Female socialization for extramarital sex   Turning to another side of the extramarital system, to when it is part of the adolescent growing-up process, our view of the male–female balance favoring women may be different. Adolescent girls, even if married already, have to win their maturity belts to secure their husbands.

They do this by serving a men's festival society group. As said before, service as female associates to a men's society involves young women giving themselves on certain traditional days during a three-to-four-month-long festival to most of the men in the group, sequentially, maybe to between 15 and 25 men. Such days are filled with great festivity and are highly complementary and flattering to the pair of females associated with their male group. These young women are familiar with all the men involved and will know them for the rest of their lives. In theory, a woman can turn down any one of these men—a difficult and rare occurrence, because, if continued, this antisocial behavior could lead to illness or even death through witchcraft. Most important of all for our assessing the situation, however, is the fact that these young women know they must cooperate to secure their husbands' families' full acceptance as daughters-in-law. Thus, they are "forced" to comply not only because of their society's tradition for generosity but also because of their hope for a good and full future life in a large extended family with many children of their own.

The purpose of these sequential sex occasions, the Canela say, is to bring out these adolescent women from their shyness, from their fears, or from other selfish tendencies into the joyous world of tribal sharing, where the whole society is greater than any one individual. When brought out they will become truly generous and loving people, it is believed, and they will come to enjoy and enter voluntarily into many of the other extramarital tribal-bonding occasions.

Male–female balance in the extramarital sex system   Considering again the male–female balance in the all-important extramarital sex system of the Canela, the Council of Elders—men—governs the festivals and appoints two young female associates to each of the large male festival groups. In effect, older men select young women to occupy the higher or the lower ceremonial positions. Thus, older men stratify young women at the ceremonial levels they occupy for the rest of their lives. Women, however, on formal sequential sex days and in day-to-day informal extramarital situations, tend to control men through varying degrees of favors or rejections. My assessment of the balance is that older men enforce the cooperative behavior of younger men and women, while women overwhelmingly control the younger men on the interpersonal level, as in the domestic scene.

Male–female balance viewed in general   Social control throughout the rest of the Canela society is similar to the pattern of social control found in the extramarital sex system. Older men control the society on the macro level—the higher, more general, and more occasionally applied level. Older men put in place most of the long-term, socio-ceremonial arrangements for individuals, especially for young men and women. In this way, older men maintain a balance of power and responsibility throughout the tribe that basically favors men. In contrast, women control much of the daily life on the micro level—the immediately interpersonal level—causing men and women of all ages, but especially young men, to conform. Clearly, as in most tribal societies, Canela men hold more basic power than Canela women, though Canela women are powerful too, but in quite a different way. Canela women are certainly not oppressed.

Changes over 180 years   Considering changes through time, it is clear that warfare during the 1700s favored male over female power and that peace and stability since 1840 have favored women, redressing the balance between the sexes to some extent. Closer contacts with backlanders and with personnel of the Brazilian Indian Service since 1940 have favored men, since the Brazilian backlander is distinctly male-oriented. Especially the young men who carry out the recently introduced and far more extensive practice of slash-and-burn agriculture are more valued now as young sons-in-law in their domestic units than they were formerly. Thus, young husbands are no longer as completely subjected to the whims of females of the domestic unit they married into as they were even in the 1930s, during the time of Nimuendajú. Currently, young husbands are more likely to succeed in taking their wives' farms to join farms of male allies, thus separating sisters and reducing their power. The new high value of young husbands in agriculture also has led to their being able to act upon their jealousy, aroused by their wives' customary extramarital affairs. Thus, the jealousy of the young husbands limited the group practices of the extramarital sex system in the 1970s and all but terminated them by the end of the 1980s. Ironically, this attrition in the extramarital sex system constitutes a great loss to women.

Young husbands are also able to express jealousy against their wives more effectively because of the growing weakness of males of the older generations, due again to the proximity of Brazilian custom. Thus, in the 1990s, uncles can no longer suppress the sexual jealousy of their nephews or keep them from divorcing, even when they are raising children. The Canela are experiencing a serious generation gap, because of which the older males are becoming less powerful and the younger males more influential, thus limiting female power in both the domestic unit and as applied through the extramarital sex system. An easy prediction to make is that, as the Canela become more Brazilianized by the surrounding backlanders, they will become even more male-oriented.

Eventually, young male power, and its consequent nuclear family orientation, might break up the village circle and the female domestic unit of power which is based on the circle. Already, two Canela families have left the village circle and have placed their houses along the street of the Indian Service post buildings. Without tribal bonding through the group aspects of extramarital sex, nuclear family individualism could undermine the social cohesion of the tribe.

NOTES

66. Nimuendajú (1946:98–100) described the institution of the *tàmhàk*, the visiting chief, more completely than my Canela research assistants were able to do during the late 1950s.
67. See Kracke (1978:28).
68. See Gregor (1985:100).
69. See Yolanda & Robert Murphy (1974:134).

Epilogue: 1991

When I returned to the Canela for a three-week visit in 1991 to prepare for a final year of field work in 1993, it had been 12 years since my last visit. A regular flow of audio tapes from the younger Thunder sent on by Jack Popjes had kept me informed about the tribe. Only a visit in person, however, could allow me to assess the most recent changes and analyze them with confidence.

In my time and earlier, chiefs had stayed in office for life. Since 1979, however, six different chiefs had been deposed by the elders. The Council of Elders of the late 1970s had been replaced by the age class 20 years younger, and the current chief was Burnt Path, my brother and the brother of Waterfall. In order to remain in office these days, chiefs had to go out and bring benefits such as trucks back to the tribe and attend pan-Indian meetings to bring the Canela prestige. The most successful chief, the younger Thunder, had obtained funds to sharecrop fields—more extensively than ever before—with an outside company, the Vale do Rio Doce. This chief had to buy Canela lunches for them to work in the gardens; the elders no longer had the authority to enforce work by the age classes. When he could no longer get funds after two years, Thunder was deposed. The failure of the Canela to sustain this enterprise on their own suggested that they were not yet ready to adopt the agricultural solution to self-reliance.

The opposite solution to developing self-sufficiency through agriculture is the current Canela tendency to look to the supernatural for aid. The Canela, who were earlier this-worldly in outlook, could understandably be influenced by the surrounding folk Catholicism of the backlanders. Since 1979, three minor messianic movements had claimed some followers. One prophet had a trunk full of dollars; another promised salvation only to those who would fabricate squares of ornamental cloth, and another was again receiving power from the culture hero Awkhêê. All of these movements failed to develop any momentum, even though the decline in support by the Indian Service during the time of my absence might have made the Canela especially vulnerable.

The worsening economic conditions in Brazil were reflected in the inability of the Indian Service to maintain services to the Canela on the same level as in the past. The Service had been unable for some time to recruit any teacher for the post school, and only three youths continued their education by going to school in Barra do Corda. These youths needed funds to support them while they lived in the Indian shelter in the town, so only the sons or grandsons of Canela who had Indian Service salaries could attend school. The younger children coming along were receiving no formal education. Jean tried to help some of the youths read and write in Portuguese in their school workbooks, which they proudly retrieved from places of safekeeping in their houses, but they were not motivated to sustain the effort. Low funding by the government had resulted in the disrepair and lack of equipment. We paid for the repair of the post radio before we moved to the village. The position of post nurse was being filled temporarily by an Italian nun, but she was short of supplies. Upon her request we brought in numerous medicines, including serum for snake bites donated by Public Health in Brasília. Some of the bottled gas we had brought for lamps had to be used to run the refrigeration for the serum. Perhaps some of the inefficiency was due to the fact that the Indian Service in Barra do Corda was now headed by an acculturated Guajajara Indian. The Canela still felt their tribal antipathy toward him and would not cooperate with the agency.

The educational and practical contributions of the SIL/Wycliffe missionaries, the Popjeses, had of course come to an end in 1990 when they left. Their spiritual influence was impossible to assess in three weeks, though some Canela did show us the translated Bible. The Popjeses plan to come back every two years to Brazil to keep their passport status renewed and to drop by to visit the Canela. Missionaries of another Protestant group, who have been with the Krahó, intend to come and work with the Canela to keep up the Popjeses' work. Whatever the extent of Christian conversion in the tribe, the Canela must have missed the devotion of the Popjeses.

A German anthropologist, Jakob Mehringer, had been doing extensive filming in the Canela village for the last three years. The Canela had begun to look to him for extensive aid such as purchases of cattle to slaughter. Promises by Mehringer to bring in experts in agriculture and health were raising their expectations. And of course they were filled with anticipation of my return. Even though the Canela had had news from me through Jack Popjes, and more recently through Júlio Tavares, the Canela must have wondered if I really had been true to my promise to tell their story through the book (1990) I had labored over for so long. Fortunately, we had prepared picture versions of the monograph by copying all the photographs and stapling them into booklets. Some of the introductory sections had been translated into Portuguese and were also available for distribution. The photo booklets were such a success that equitable distribution by families became a touchy enterprise. Perusing these booklets became a favorite occupation of the Canela during the more leisurely late afternoons. Individuals eagerly looked for pictures of their relatives. Since these photographs represented the accumulation of my many years of work with the Canela, some of them showed brothers, sisters, and other kin as they were as long as 34 years ago. Often a Canela would spot the photo of a loved one who had died. The early pictures of artifacts were also of great interest. Younger Canela brought out newer artifacts and compared them with the earlier versions in the photographs. We could expect with some confidence that this honoring of their culture would provide a boost in morale.

Of the three great areas of cultural strength which we have discussed in this book, the system of kinship was the best preserved. Kinship is widely recognized to be an aspect of culture which is extremely resistant to change. Kinship was still the great conveyor of meaning in human relationships for the Canela. A prime consideration in bringing Jean was fitting her into a network of kinship through her adoptive family. The Canela spent many hours of entertaining conversation exploring her relationship to all her resulting kin. Younger Canela found it highly amusing to accost me in my walks around the village and ask, "Who am I?" I had to try to remember some child's face behind the young adult's face before me and then identify his or her family connections. One sign of weakening of the kinship system did become evident to me,

Canela examine a picture version of Bill's 1990 monograph.

however. The number of cousins addressed as "father" had declined. The bonding created by calling certain categories of kin "father" obviously would suffer along with the loss of terminology.

The festival system was still largely intact, though some attrition had taken place. One worrisome development was the staging of a festival at the "wrong" or untraditional time of the year. The Warriors' festival, which is normally begun in March, was begun during our stay in October. I suspected that since the Canela anticipated the arrival of Mehringer and his filming crew soon, they were beginning the festival for his convenience. On the other hand, they might have been doing it because of our presence, in the hope that I would support the festival by purchasing cattle. I refused to do so because of the lack of authenticity of the festival at this time of year. Canela elders agreed that the timing was inappropriate, but they proceeded with the festival anyway. The cycle of increasing Canela demands for goods and their partial satisfaction by visiting anthropologists thus seemed for the first time to be a potential threat to the traditional festival system.

More gradual but perhaps more permanent was attrition through forgetfulness or lack of effort. It was easy to forget details of festivals which took place only once in every 10 years. The Mask festival, for instance, has not been carried out since 1960. The festival was begun a couple of times in the 1970s but was aborted because of supposedly inauspicious signs. The making of the full-length masks is traditionally the task of the older people in the Masks' society, and they seem no longer willing to make the effort, or they are no longer sure of the technique. The primary activity of the masked figures in the festival is to go from door to door begging. The festival thus sanctions the tradition of the practice which is in turn justified by the myth of Awkhêê. In spite of the persistence of the rationalizing myth, the Canela feel ambivalent about begging these days. They are somewhat embarrassed by the practice, even though still driven to it. Thus, the Mask festival may be omitted because of an underlying, perhaps even unconscious, sense of shame. Unless it is performed again in the near future, there will be no Canela living who can pass on the exact techniques of mask-making and other details of the festival.

The extramarital sex system was the area most significantly changed in my 12-year absence. With the decline in hunting and growing dependence on the distasteful task of gardening, parents were increasingly dependent on their sons-in-law for support. As we have seen in Chapter 1, the aunts and uncles had gradually lost much authority over the young adults. It now fell to the parents to curtail the sexual jealousy of the young husbands, which they were loathe to do. Not only were the parents more economically dependent on the sons-in-law, but they were reluctant to promote extramarital sex. Discussion of sex between parents and children was always embarrassing; the aunts and uncles had been responsible for explaining and maintaining extramarital sex customs. The increased power of young husbands could also be seen in the increased acceptability of divorce before the children were grown. Disgruntled sons-in-law might divorce and leave the household, effectively removing their economic support. This development could be the most disruptive of all. Without the gratifications of extramarital sex in ceremonial situations, the festivals could have less appeal and seem less worth all the trouble and expense. The many facets of Canela culture which the festivals traditionally honored and sanctioned could be weakened. The bonding produced by the extensive sexual familiarity in the extramarital system would diminish. Nevertheless, Canela culture had survived the removal of warfare as one of the prime reasons for so many of their traditional practices. Perhaps it would also survive the loss of the extramarital sex system.

In 1991 the tribe evidently had not been exposed to AIDS, which obviously would be devastating even with reduced extramarital sex. The Indian Service had thoroughly warned the Canela on the dangers of this epidemic.

Two developments since 1979 showed how adaptable Canela culture could be. Both provided new roles for women, perhaps as a response to the changing balance between the sexes. For the first time ever there was a chief of the women, Hill Climber, appointed by Chief Burnt Path while we were there. Women had also begun racing with Pàlrà logs as a follow-up to the Pàlrà festival which had taken place just before we returned. The growth in population meant that there were many young women who had not yet had children, the only group of women who could participate in this activity. It was a good sign that the Canela could adapt their customs to new circumstances.

Indeed, my first impression of the Canela village upon my return was one of vigor and high morale. As we approached the welcoming group of my brother and the elders, the plaza opened out before us. Instead of the single circle of houses around the circular boulevard, as when the village was founded in 1969, the houses were now two and sometimes even three deep. Rather than split the village and suffer another schism, the Canela were building new houses for their growing families behind the original house on the circle. The numbers of Canela lined up across the plaza to greet us were huge. The tribe had increased to almost 1,000 from 600 or so in 1979. As we finished greeting the elders and my family members, others pressed forward to shake our hands. Then, as the initial ceremonial solemnity gave way to more spontaneous delight, dozens of small children crowded in front to mimic their parents, laughing and offering their hands. The children we observed in the following days were so numerous that Jean would describe the village as a giant sand box. Medical care had obviously reaped benefits. But the Canela's own decisions to forgo emigration and schisms had brought them to this point as well. Instead of the bare plaza, circle of houses, and then the low brush of the savannah, tall coconut palms and luxuriant mango trees, which had grown up during their long stay in this location, rose among the houses. During our three-week visit, we saw the sing-dance line of girls and young women form many times in the plaza. The enthusiasm for singing brought out so many participants that the line had to bend forward at both ends to fit across the plaza. Likewise, the male activity of log racing took place regularly in the afternoons, producing another of the most memorable of Canela sounds—the thundering of bare feet in the sand. The spontaneous joy evident in these two most characteristic Canela activities convinced me once again that the Canela culture would survive awhile longer.

Orthography

The orthography used follows Crocker 1990:9–10 for consistency, except for /ą/ and /ų/. Each letter in italics represents a phoneme in Canela, or its equivalent or approximation in another language.[70]

Vowels

Since there are no nasalized vowel phonemes in English, examples in Portuguese are used.

Unnasalized	English	Nasalized	Portuguese
i	beet	ĩ	pinto
ê	bit		
e	bet	ẽ	pente
a	hurrah	ą	maracanã
u	boot	ũ	junto
ô	boat		
o	bought	õ	ponto

The following vowel phonemes have no equivalents in English, Portuguese, Spanish, or French, but approximations are included. For the linguist, these five phonemes are "back" and "unrounded" and the varying placements are indicated.

Unnasalized			Nasalized	Placements
ù	tu	French	ų	high and closed
è	peu	French		mid and closed
à	puddle	English	ã	mid and open

Semivowels

w west, pew

y yes, coy

189

Consonants

Stops

Unlike in English, the phonemes *p*, *t*, and *k* are unaspirated; they are found as both unvoiced [p, t, k] and voiced [b, d, g] allophones. The phoneme *kh* is aspirated and unvoiced.

English approximates

p	[p varies with b]	*p*ill and *b*ill
t	[t varies with d]	*t*ick and *D*ick
k	[k varies with g]	*k*ill and *g*ill
kh		*k*iss
?	[glottal]	bo'le (as sometimes in "bottle")

Affricative

ts	cen*ts*

Fricative

h	*h*ome

Lateral

r [r varies with 1]	o*r*ar, Isabe*l* (Spanish)

Nasals

m	*m*et
n	*n*et
g	*g*aunt

Vowel Length

Vowel length can be phonemic: *ka*tswa: night
                                 *kaa*tswa: salt

Stress

Word stress almost always falls on the last syllable, though it is ultimately determined by the phrase and sentence.

NOTES

[70] While I worked out all the phonemes except for *a* and *u* before the linguist/missionary Jack Popjes arrived, I am much indebted to him for teaching me all the Canela grammar beyond the elementary level I had learned. I am also grateful for the vast dictionary of phrases he provided me.

References

Basso, Ellen B.
1973.   The Kalapalo Indians of Central Brazil. *In* George and Louise Spindler, editors, *Case Studies in Cultural Anthropology.* 157 pages. New York: Holt, Rinehart and Winston, Inc.

Chagnon, Napoleon A.
1968.   Yanomamö: The Fierce People. *In* George and Louise Spinder, editors, *Case Studies in Cultural Anthropology.* 142 pages. New York: Holt, Rinehart and Winston, Inc.

Crocker, William H.
1961.   The Canela since Nimuendajú: A Preliminary Report on Cultural Change. *Anthropological Quarterly,* 34(2):69–84. Washington, D.C.: The Catholic University of America Press.
1973.   Xikrĩn-Brazil. *In* P. Riviere, editor, Amazonia, Orinoco and Pampas. In *Peoples of the World,* 6:22–31. Danbury, Connecticut: The Danbury Press.
1974.   Extramarital Sexual Practices of the Ramkokamekra-Canela Indians: An Analysis of Sociocultural Factors. *In* P.J. Lyon, editor, *Native South Americans: Ethnology of the Least Known Continent,* pages 184–194. Prospect Heights, Illinois: Waveland Press.
1982.   Canela Initiation Festivals: "Helping Hands" through Life. *In* V. Turner, editor, *Celebration: Studies in Festivity and Ritual,* pages 147–158. Washington, D.C.: Smithsonian Institution Press.
1984.   Canela Marriage: Factors in Change. *In* K. Kensinger, editor, Marriage Practices in Lowland South America. *Illinois Studies in Anthropology,* 14:63–98. Urbana and Chicago: University of Illinois Press.
1990.   The Canela (Eastern Timbira), I: An Ethnographic Introduction. *Smithsonian Contributions to Anthropology, No. 33.* Washington, D.C. Smithsonian Institution Press. 487 pages.

Da Matta, Roberto
1982.   A Divided World: Apinayé Social Structure. *Harvard Studies in Cultural Anthropology,* 6: 186 pages. Cambridge, Massachusetts: Harvard University Press.

Dole, Gertrude E.
1973.   Shamanism and Political Control among the Kuikúru. *In* D. Gross, editor, *Peoples and Cultures of Native South America: An Anthropological Reader,* pages 294–307. New York: Doubleday, Natural History Press.

Gregor, Thomas
1985.   *Anxious Pleasures: The Sexual Lives of an Amazonian People.* 223 pages. Chicago: University of Chicago Press.

Hemming, John
1987.   *Amazon Frontier: The Defeat of the Brazilian Indians.* 647 pages. Cambridge, Massachusetts: Harvard University Press.

Kracke, Waud H.
1978.   *Force and Persuasion: Leadership in an Amazonian Society.* 322 pages. Chicago: University of Chicago Press.

Lizot, Jacques
1986.   Tales of the Yanomami: Daily Life in the Venezuelan Forest. *Cambridge Studies in Social Anthropology,* 55: 201 pages. Cambridge, Massachusetts; Cambridge University Press.

Lounsbury, F.G.
1964.   The Formal Analysis of Crow- and Omaha-Type Kinship Terminologies. *In* W.H. Goodenough, editor, *Explorations in Cultural Anthropology,* pages 351–393. New York: McGraw Hill.

Maybury-Lewis, David
1965.   *The Savage and the Innocent: Life with the Primitive Tribes of Brazil.* 270 pages. Cleveland: World Publishing Co.
1979.   Conclusion: Kinship, Ideology and Culture. *In* D. Maybury-Lewis, editor, *Dialectical Societies: The Gê and Bororo of Central Brazil. Harvard Studies in Cultural Anthropology,* 1:301–312. Cambridge, Massachusetts: Harvard University Press.

Meggers, Betty J.
1971.   Amazonia: Man and Culture in a Counterfeit Paradise. *In* W. Goldschmidt, editor, *Worlds of Man: Studies in Cultural Ecology.* 182 pages. Chicago: Aldine.

Melatti, Júlio C.
1967.   Índios e Criadores: A Situação dos Krahó na Área Pastoril do Tocantins. *Monografías do Instituto Ciências Sociais,* 3: 166 pages. Rio de Janeiro.
1972.   *O Messianismo Krahó.* 140 pages. São Paulo: Editora Herder.

Mooney, James
1896 [1897].   The Ghost-dance Religion and the Sioux Outbreak of 1890. *Fourteenth Annual Report of the Bureau of Ethnology,* 2:641–1110, plates 85–122, figures 56–104. Washington, D.C.: Smithsonian Institution.

Morse, Richard M., editor
1965.   *The Bandeirantes: The Historical Role of the Brazilian Pathfinders.* 211 pages. New York: Alfred A. Knopf.

Murphy, Yolanda, and Robert F. Murphy
1985.   *Women of the Forest.* Second edition, 236 pages. New York: Columbia University Press.

Nimuendajú, Curt [Nimuendajú Ukel, Curt]
1946.   The Eastern Timbira. *In* Robert Lowie, translator and editor, *University of California Publications in American Archaeology and Ethnology,* 41: 357 pages, 42 plates, 16 figures, 3 maps. Berkeley: University of California Press.

Popjes, Jack
1990.   Pahpãm Jarkwa Cupahti Jõ Kàhhoc. Liga Biblica do Brasil. Brasília: Summer Institute of Linguistics [Subtitle: Seleçoes da Bíblia Sagrada, Traducão no dialeto ramkokamekra—canela].

Ribeiro, Francisco de Paula
1815 [1870].   Roteiro da Viagem que Fez o Capitão . . . Às Fronteiras da Capitania do Maranhão e da de Goyaz. *Revista de Instituto Histórico,* 10:5–80.
1819a [1841].   Memória sobre as Nações Gentias que Presentemente Habitam o Continente do Maranhão. *Revista de Instituto Histórica,* 3:184–197, 297–322, 442–456.
1819b [1874].   Descripção do Território de Pastos Bons, nos Sertões do Maranhão. *Revista de Instituto Histórica,* 12:6–86.

Rumsey, Alan
   1971.   A Comparative Lexicon and Glottochronology of Some Gê Languages. [Manuscript in the files of W.H. Crocker, National Museum of Natural History, Smithsonian Institution.]

Seeger, Anthony
   1975.   The Meaning of Body Ornaments: A Suya Example. *Ethnology,* 14(3):211–224.
   1981.   Nature and Society in Central Brazil: The Suya Indians of Mato Grosso. In *Harvard Studies in Cultural Anthropology* 4: 278 pages. Cambridge, Massachusetts: Harvard University Press.

Steward, Julian, and Louis C. Faron
   1959.   *Native Peoples of South America.* 481 pages. New York: McGraw-Hill.

Turner, Terence
   1969.   Tchikrin: A Central Brazilian Tribe and Its Symbolic Language of Bodily Adornment. *Natural History,* 78(8):50–59, 70.

Werner, Dennis
   1984.   *Amazon Journey: An Anthropologist's Year among Brazil's Mekranoti Indians.* 296 pages. New York: Simon and Schuster.

Wilbert, Johannes, and Karin Simoneau, editors
   1984.   Folk Literature of the Gê Indians, Volume Two. *UCLA Latin American Studies,* 58: 684 pages. Los Angèles: UCLA Latin American Center Publications.

Index

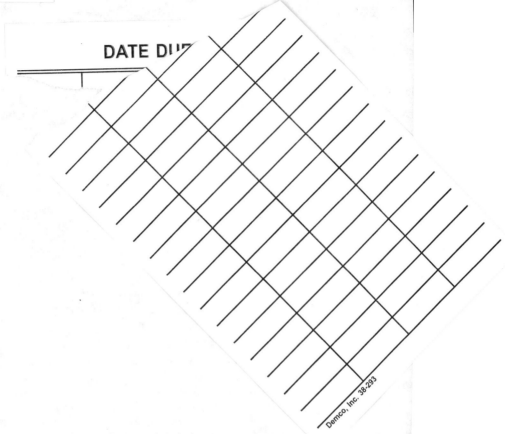

DATE DUE

Demco, Inc. 38-293